PARENTING WITHOUT GUILT

The Predictable and Situational Misbehaviors of Childhood

By

G. KENNETH WEST, Ph.D.

Associate Professor, Lynchburg College
Director of the Parent Study Program
Lynchburg College and Virginia Baptist Hospital
Part-Time Private Practice in
Marriage and Family Counseling

CHARLES C THOMAS • PUBLISHER
Springfield • Illinois • U.S.A.

Published and Distributed Throughout the World by

CHARLES C THOMAS • PUBLISHER
2600 South First Street
Springfield, Illinois 62708-4709

This book is protected by copyright. No part of it may be reproduced in any manner without written permission from the publisher.

© *1986 by* CHARLES C THOMAS • PUBLISHER
ISBN 0-398-05267-0
Library of Congress Catalog Card Number: 85-5948

With THOMAS BOOKS *careful attention is given to all details of manufacturing and design. It is the Publisher's desire to present books that are satisfactory as to their physical qualities and artistic possibilities and appropriate for their particular use.* THOMAS BOOKS *will be true to those laws of quality that assure a good name and good will.*

Printed in the United States of America
Q-R-3

Library of Congress Cataloging in Publication Data
West, G. Kenneth
    Parenting without guilt.

    Includes bibliographies and index.
    1. Discipline of children. 2. Child psychology. 3. Child rearing. I. Title. [DNLM: 1. Child Behavior Disorders--prevention & control. 2. Child Psychology. 3. Child Rearing. 4. Parent-Child Relations. WS 350.6 W517p]
HQ770.4.W47 1986   649'.64   85-5948
ISBN 0-398-05267-0

*To my wife, Patty, and our children,
Patrick, Emily, and Dustin.
They have given me more than I can ever return.*

FOREWORD

I RECOMMEND this book without reservation. **Parenting Without Guilt** is an example of old wines in a new bottle, a mixture that is an improvement on the separate elements. Essentially, it is an integration of a number of theoretical views on developmental psychology, but so well has the combination been made that what emerges is a sound, practical, easy-to-read position, with strong ethical elements that can readily serve as a primary text for academic courses and as a practical guide for perplexed parents. All should read it; all parents should have it.

But why still another book on parenting? The answer lies in the telling. What counts is not **what** is said, but rather **how** it is said. An analogy should suffice.

Say that you have heard Beethoven's Ninth Symphony many times and that once again you go hear it. Say that an inspired conductor and a superb orchestra play the familiar music so well that you are transported to the heights of musical ecstacy. The familiar is new.

This is one of the unique values of G. Kenneth West's book. It is told engagingly, indeed pleasantly, almost in a narrative fashion and in persuasive terms. There is an art in the telling. I found myself reading the material in this book with the same fascinations that I experienced as a child when my mother would retell me a familiar story.

The fundamental base of Dr. West's **Parenting Without Guilt** is that of Alfred Adler's Individual Psychology. The concepts were originally presented by Dr. Rudolph Dreikurs, who was a student and colleague of Dr. Adler, just as I was a student and colleague of Dr. Dreikurs. This is the oldest theoretical/operational position in child psychology and family counseling, going back to Adler's pioneering work with families and schools in 1922.

Importantly, Dr. West has also incorporated in this work the theories of Erik Erikson, Jean Piaget, and Lawrence Kohlberg to take into consideration various stages of growth and development of children relating to their total personality (Erikson), their cognitive development (Piaget), and their moral development (Kohlberg).

Ideas of several family therapists are explored, including Salvador Minuchin and Ray Bardill. Parents will be challenged to investigate the effects that their marriage and home atmosphere have on children's behavior. Special concerns of large segments of the population, including single parents, parents using daycare, and stepfamilies are discussed in a sensitive, pragmatic manner.

Parenting, as this book suggests, is a neglected art: and the most important of all occupations. How often it is said that parents should be educated. But, unfortunately, no one gets training for this demanding task. Parenting can be the single most delightful and meaningful experience in one's life — and it can be a nightmare! The difference can simply be knowing the right and the wrong way of "dancing" with children.

If the child calls the time, or if parents beat the drums, the result is an unhappy family. But if the total family works together like a good orchestra, family harmony is a result.

The tenets of this book offer a good solution. It is an easy-to-read, sound book explaining a number of values, with the accent on making children more responsible, more respectful, more resourceful, and more responsive to the needs of others. This book gives step-by-step instructions on how to start parenting and how to change parenting strategies.

I strongly endorse this book as being sound in its theory and philosophy, practical in its suggestions, and perhaps most of all, easy to read. It is an excellent text for a variety of courses in child development and child and family counseling, a book to give to new parents who want to make their task of parenting at the same time enjoyable and effective.

Raymond Corsini, Ph.D.
Honolulu, Hawaii

PREFACE

PARENTS in our present day culture are often burdened by guilt because their children do not behave or think like miniature adults. Some experts promote this kind of guilt by naively suggesting that children are capable of perfect behavior. Other theorists make parents feel inadequate by implying that any properly nurtured child can become a Mozart or Picasso. The attempt to steal childhood away from life is a contemporary tragedy; the result is that children may feel like failures or gods. Parents blame themselves in either case.

Children must be allowed to be children. Parents must be relieved of the guilt inevitably collected when attempting to be perfect parents of perfect children. **Parenting Without Guilt** is a book about real children, the ones parents live with daily. Parents will see the misbehaviors of their children in each chapter. Of equal importance, parents will find assurance in discovering that children from families worldwide share identical challenges in raising children of similar age and circumstance. That children are alike is the basis for Part One, entitled "The Predictable Behaviors of Childhood."

Part One explores misbehaviors that are predictable due to age, family ordination, moral development, and special goals. Parents who mistakenly believe children are controlled young adults who should never misbehave will be left hurt, humiliated, and guilty by the misbehaviors discussed. But parents who understand the place of misbehavior in a child's growth will remain confident and optimistic. Such parents will be free to enjoy, rather than resist, childhood.

The second part, entitled "Working With Misbehaviors," suggests the most positive methods of handling misbehavior and of helping children become cooperative and responsible.

Special family situations promote behaviors in children that often appear to be unique. Yet, despite the fact that all children do not share these behaviors, many or most children from similar situations do. For example, single parent families and stepfamilies experience many common challenges in raising children. Unfortunately, because parents are often overworked and isolated, they may be unaware that their children's misbehaviors are not uncommon. Fearing that the misbehaviors are a certain sign of a child's and parent's failure, parents often feel incompetent, unsuccessful, and guilty.

In Part Three, situational misbehaviors and challenges within stepfamilies and single parent homes are discussed. In addition, two chapters from the discipline of marriage and family therapy will help parents understand the influence on children of unsatisfactory marriages and undesirable family dynamics. Alternatives are presented that will allow parents to create changes potentially beneficial to all family members.

Guilt is not always a negative emotion. At best, guilt warns us that we are not living up to our well-considered standards. But many parents live with unrealistic guilt. By accepting the myths of our culture—those that imply children should and can be perfect in behavior, morals, and thoughts—parents will inevitably fail. Adults cannot make their children into miniature adults: instead, they can learn to enjoy the world of childhood. Parents who understand children's misbehavior and can respond positively to it need not feel inadequate, or like failures. Instead, they can take a long, enjoyable stride toward **Parenting Without Guilt.**

ACKNOWLEDGEMENTS

MY FAMILY'S extraordinary excitement over the writing of **Parenting Without Guilt** has been a constant inspiration. My wife provided many insights and painstakingly proofread each chapter many times. Our three children, Patrick, Emily, and Dustin played a role in each page, because their lives gave confirmation of and enthusiasm for each idea presented. This book is a creation of our family.

Mrs. Betty Leighton served tirelessly as the editor of and enthusiast for this book. Her positive spirit never swayed. As the editor of the *Jackpine Press* in Winston-Salem, North Carolina, Betty has spent years encouraging young writers. Indeed, I am one of her many products. Betty has read and reread this manuscript so often that I consider it to be our book. Deep thanks also are extended to her husband, Jim, who was my mentor during undergraduate days at Wake Forest University and has remained a close friend ever since. The Leightons' gifts to me made this book a possibility, then a reality.

Several colleagues at Lynchburg College have given essential assistance in the production of this book. A special thanks goes to Ms. Betty Johnson who typed many versions of each chapter. Betty worked diligently and without reservation. Her positive spirit made the difficult work of revision a more enjoyable undertaking.

Two special friends, Dr. Ed Polloway and Dr. David Smith, have encouraged me, both by work and by professional example. Both are prolific writers in the field of special education. Their devotion to their field indeed may have been the original inspiration for my writing this book. As importantly, they have remained encouraging friends throughout our years together. Dr. Pete Warren brought me to Lynchburg College in 1976. As chairman of my department, Pete has always supported my pursuits, both inside and outside of the classroom. I have grown as a person and as a professional, due to his warm acceptance, support, and love. A broad thanks is extended to Lynchburg College for providing financial assistance in writing and preparing the manuscript. My sister, Ms. Mary Margaret Russ, deserves a special thanks for her help in developing the chapter on single parent families. As a single parent, she has overcome many obstacles in raising two wonderful sons, Kenneth and David. Heartfelt appreciation also is extended to Dr. Raymond Corsini, who read the completed manuscript, provided encouragement, and wrote the Foreword.

One organization deserves a special note of thanks, The North American Society of Adlerian Psychology. NASAP and its members have spread parenting information throughout the world. It was through two of their members at Florida State University, Dr. Don Kelly and Dr. Tom Fisher, that I became acquainted with many of the ideas of Alfred Adler and Rudolf Dreikurs. NASAP and its members are a major force in providing parent education throughout the world.

My parents, the late Dr. R. Frederick West and Mrs. Mary L. West, are, in a true sense, a part of everything I do. Their contributions to me have been endless, and my thanks to them is equally immeasurable. Also, a special thanks for the support of my sister, Becky McKeown, her husband, Dwight, and their two marvelous children, Steve and Karen.

Most importantly, a special thanks to Mr. Payne E. L. Thomas, of Charles C Thomas, Publisher, for believing in and publishing this book.

CONTENTS

Page

Foreword by Raymond Corsini vii

PART ONE: THE PREDICTABLE MISBEHAVIORS OF CHILDHOOD

CHAPTER 1. THE PREDICTABLE MISBEHAVIORS:
            DAILY STRUGGLES 5
CHAPTER 2. THE PREDICTABLE MISBEHAVIORS: BY
            BIRTH ORDER 23
CHAPTER 3. THE PREDICTABLE MISBEHAVIORS: BY AGE 43
CHAPTER 4. THE PREDICTABLE MISBEHAVIORS:
            COGNITIVE DEVELOPMENT 67
CHAPTER 5. THE PREDICTABLE MISBEHAVIORS:
            MORAL DEVELOPMENT 93

PART TWO: WORKING WITH MISBEHAVIORS

CHAPTER 6. ACTIVE APPROACHES TO MISBEHAVIORS 117
CHAPTER 7. DARING TO BE CLOSE: ENCOURAGING
            AND COMMUNICATING WITH CHILDREN 147

**PART THREE: THE SITUATIONAL MISBEHAVIORS
OF CHILDHOOD**

CHAPTER 8. WHEN THE MARRIAGE IS WEAK 169
CHAPTER 9. WHEN THE FAMILY IS EXTREME 189
CHAPTER 10. SINGLE PARENT HOMES 211
CHAPTER 11. NEW CARETAKERS: DAYCARE AND
            STEPFAMILIES 231
CHAPTER 12. PARENTS AND REVOLUTION 253

CONCLUSION — PARENTING WITHOUT GUILT 269

Index 271

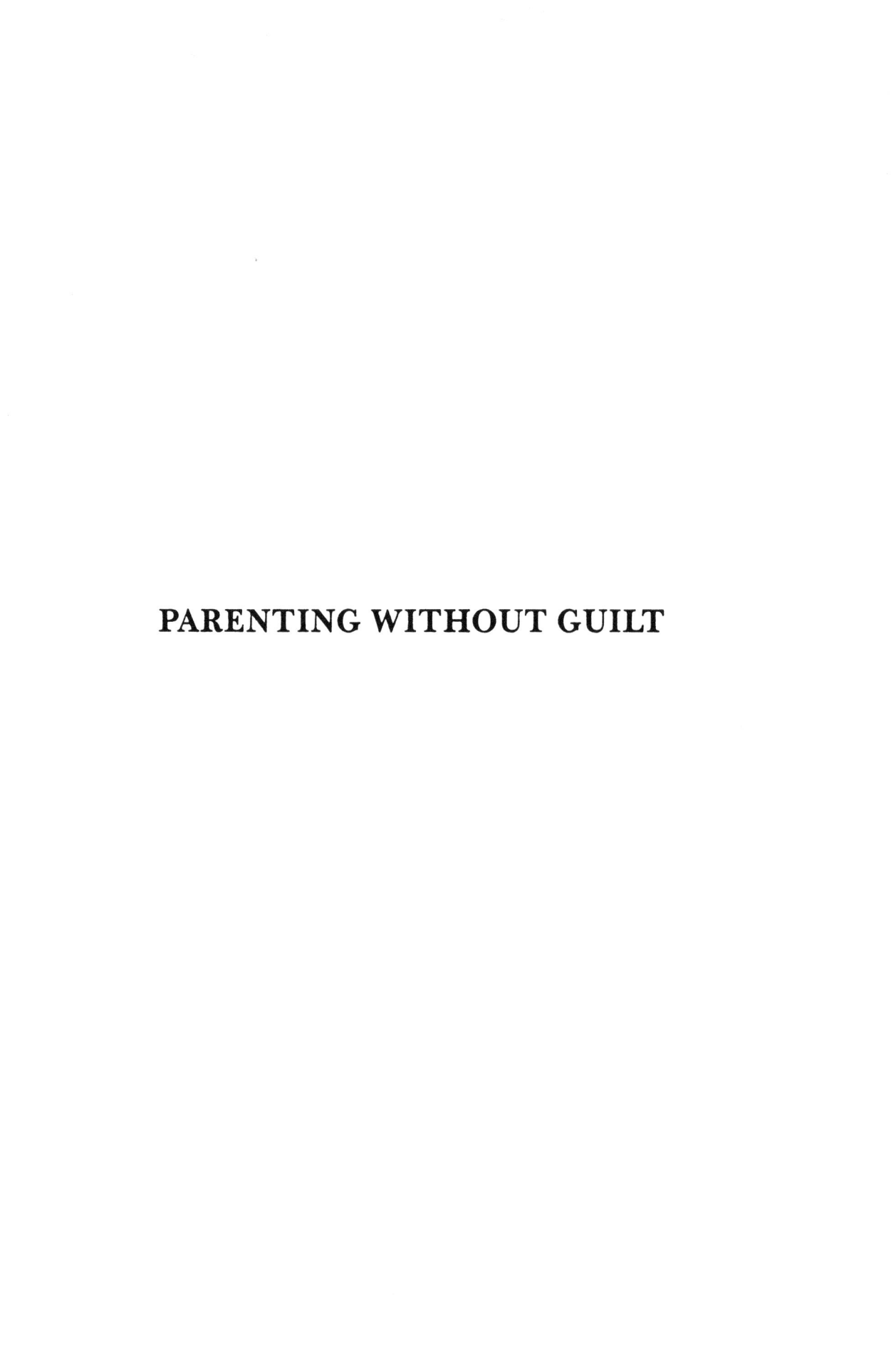

PARENTING WITHOUT GUILT

PART ONE

THE PREDICTABLE MISBEHAVIORS OF CHILDHOOD

CHAPTER ONE

THE PREDICTABLE MISBEHAVIORS: DAILY STRUGGLES

HOW OFTEN have you witnessed scenes like the following? "Johnny, we are in a restaurant, you must sit still and be quiet!"... "Johnny, don't play with your food!"..."Johnny, come back and sit in your seat—right now!"..."Johnny, put the catsup bottle down!"... Mother grabs the catsup bottle. Johnny pulls away, and the catsup goes flying out of the bottle and splatters an innocent party at the next table. At that point, Mom reaches out and slaps Johnny's hand. Johnny howls with pain and yells at Mom: "I hate you!! You are the worst mother in the world!"...Embarrassed, Mom tries to shove candy into Johnny's mouth. He refuses it and continues to humiliate her publicly. Mother picks him up and storms out of the restaurant, squeezing his arm tighter and tighter. The entire outing is a complete disaster.

Untrained parents go through such frustrating battles with children daily. The struggles are the same everywhere. The locations may be grocery markets, department stores, or classrooms. Participants and situations may vary also, yet the basic themes of misbehavior remain constant.

Misbehavior is so predictable and consistent in children under ten that Rudolph Dreikurs was able to divide misbehavior into four specific goals. He believed these four were sufficient to describe and promote understanding of why children misbehave. For years, Dreikurs's disciples have helped parents understand how to react to a child's misbehavior by properly identifying the child's goal and reacting appropriately.

It appears to me that goals of misbehavior are better understood as "dances of misbehavior." Each of the four dances requires that a child select an unwilling partner. Once selected, the dance partner is trained to sway and rock to the sounds of the child's favorite tunes. Although the child's music, her partners, and the dance floors may change, the beat of the music and the essential dance steps remain constant. To work successfully with misbehavior, parents must learn to identify quickly the movements and rhythm of the four dances. Then they must refuse to be led on to the dance floor.

Unfortunately, adults are easily programmed to become unwilling partners in misbehavior's dances. Before the age of two, most children have learned to control unsuspecting parents. The child needs only to select the preferred dance and push the correct button to engage the parent in the desired routine.

In my travels, while speaking to groups of concerned parents, I always enjoy showing how each child has trained adults to enter into the ritual of the unwanted dance. One simple question to ask children is: "What do you do to drive your parents 'up the wall'?" Immediately smiles appear on the faces of children. One by one, each exposes her particular invitations: "I play with my food." Or, "I won't go to bed on time." Or, "I tell my stepfather that he can never take the place of my real father." Although parents generally sense that they are being controlled, they are rarely trained in the art of discipline. Having no alternatives, they cooperate with the child's intentions by joining her on the dance floor.

The experience of becoming unwittingly entangled in a child's goal is depressing. As one parent said to me, "It is as if I am a puppet and she is the puppet master. I am never in control. She is. I'm forever reacting to some manipulation on her part. She stays a step ahead of me."

To be effective with daily misbehavior, parents must liberate themselves from the child's manipulation. They must, in a sense, free themselves of the child's program and reprogram themselves to act independently and effectively. When a child cannot control a parent, misbehavior decreases. Not having a partner, children generally will find little pleasure in dancing alone.

However, it should be remembered that dancing is enjoyable. The four dances of misbehavior are so rewarding to children that they will consistently attempt to reprogram parents by using new techniques and themes. Nevertheless, although the child may change the tune, the basic rhythms stay the same. One need only listen to the beat of the music or look at the steps of the child to know how to be free of the dance.

DREIKURS'S FIRST IDENTIFIED DANCE: THE ATTENTION ADDICTION SHUFFLE

All children need attention. The need for attention is not a misbehavior. Certainly, children should receive encouragement for positive behavior and contributions. Indeed, children deserve attention simply because they are marvelous humans whom we love and cherish. Hugs, kisses, and compliments should be plentiful in any home.

However, some children suffer Attention Addiction. They demand attention in great quantities and without regard for the needs of adults or the situation at hand. For such children, demands for attention are constant, whether in a shopping center, in church, in public, in private, in social situations, or at home during dinner.

When children are successful in programming caretakers to become inappropriately responsive, an addiction for attention builds. This addiction is one which cannot be satisfied by normal love, affection, and encouragement. Then, like an addict, the Attention Addicted child suffers violently when not receiving the demanded dose of time and concentration.

The sad problem with an Attention Addicted child is that he (or she) is handicapped in becoming autonomous. They often become dependent on the approval or disapproval of others. They may have little ability to feel confident in personal evaluations of their goals, behaviors, or feelings. Dependency may be continued throughout adulthood. Sources of the needed attention and approval may change from mother to father, to teacher, to grades, to spouses, to success, to in-laws, and ironically, to one's own children. Yet the dance steps carry the same music: "I am nothing unless attended to or affirmed."

Seeing adults still addicted to attention-getting schemes can be a sobering experience. At a large state university, I counseled a freshman who was accustomed to receiving attention for her accomplishments in a small-town high school. There she had excelled in sports and was at the top of her class academically. Her feats and achievement drew raves from her parents and teachers, but it was not the achievements she treasured, but the recognition.

In the large university, she blended in without distinction. In sports, she did not make the teams and she was earning mediocre grades. All extra attention stopped. She felt totally lost. She had no self-direction. Soon she started drinking excessively and driving recklessly to gain the approval of the students with whom she lived. Receiving attention for negative antics seemed preferable to receiving none at all. Only after a severe accident did she enter counseling. It was then she began to realize how dependent she was on the approval of others.

All children will seek attention. Fortunately, few will become addicted as severely as the coed described above. Actually, the demand for attention at inappropriate times is the most minor of misbehavior's goals. Some attention-getting acts are not inappropriate and may be expected as a natural part of childhood. For example, children will show off new skills, new stunts, and new language in order to produce a reaction in parents. But inappropriate attention-seeking is equally common. Even children developing beautifully will demand attention at inappropriate times. For example, most parents have experienced phone calls or visits from friends which were disrupted by an overdemanding child. Attention-getting becomes a problem if the child's needs to keep parents involved are interfering with family goals or causing consistent frustration.

One of the mothers in a recent parenting class woefully recounted her past weekend, when a long awaited family reunion was spoiled by her overdemanding child. The mother tried to talk with family members, many of whom she had not seen for over five years. But each time she tried, her four-year-old would tug at her skirt or invent an emergency to keep the mother in her service. Other children seemed to play well with each other, but not hers. Only Mom could satisfy the child. Frustrations such as these can ruin family outings and make life unpleasant. Children need to learn how and when to be self-sufficient. Even toddlers can learn to enjoy playing independently.

Children quickly learn two methods of gaining attention from parents. One is through positive actions, and the other is through negative actions. Initially, most children will try to gain attention through positive contributions. They may be helpful around the house or successful in school, sports, or outside activities. Such behaviors generally carry internal satisfaction. Parental acknowledgement is encouraging but not demanded. However, even positive behavior can move into the negative sphere. Some children foster a belief that unless they accomplish something approved of by the parents, they will not receive the recognition they need. In such cases, children may become addicted to accomplishments in school, in sports, or other areas. These behaviors become the primary methods for gaining parental recognition.

Ironically, the most important occupation in our society — being a parent — is one which receives little positive recognition. After the end of a long day of changing diapers, cleaning house, and preparing meals, a parent does not receive an A from a professor or a pay raise from an employer. In fact, rarely are children appreciative of such contributions, and often such work is taken for granted by spouses. Adults accustomed to receiving praise for accomplishments may find it difficult to adjust to the rigors of being a parent. Never is the work so hard and the recognition so low. Woe to those entering parenthood who are dependent upon external rewards.

To prevent "positive" addiction, one must be careful to encourage the process with children and not accent the outcome. For example, one might say, "I am glad you enjoy history," rather than the addictive statement, "I am glad you made an A." Likewise, one might say to a younger child, "I am glad you enjoy helping to keep our house clean," rather than: "You did such a fantastic job cleaning the living room." Positive attention addiction often goes unnoticed in a family. These children usually are supported by our competitive society. But while positive addiction may contribute to achievement and family harmony, it may be destructive to autonomy. Children may give up creating their own music in order to dance to the tunes of others.

Most parents are concerned more with Negative Attention Addicts. A Negative Attention Addict knows that it is far easier and faster to demand a parent's attention by misbehaving than by behaving positively. These children have trained their parents to accept predictable invitations to dance. A few of the best known include starting fights with siblings, cursing, interrupting, playing with food, dressing slowly, sucking thumbs, or not waking for school. The goal of the child is to involve the parent in the waltz. Variations of attention-getting steps are often creative and always changing. Yet, the basic steps revolve around the repeated theme: "How can I force Mom or Dad to concentrate on me?"

Parents need to reprogram themselves not to give attention to a child upon demand—at least not in the way the child expects. Two responses have been particularly successful for parents. Some parents are good at training themselves to ignore the child. Thus, they refuse to respond to the child's demands. Others avoid the invitation of a child by continuing adult pursuits while giving the child a quiet hug. This second method suggested by the Kvols-Riedlers requires that the parent avoid eye contact with the child but recognize the child's need by giving attention on the parent's own terms. In either method, the parent frees himself of the child's unreasonable demands.

Often, when parents try new reactions, misbehavior becomes worse before it becomes better. Attention Addicts go through withdrawal pains in the same way those physically addicted to a drug do. Upon not being able to control the parent's behavior, a desperate child will redouble efforts to gain attention inappropriately.

Many parents cannot tolerate seeing the child in such need. These parents give in to the escalated demands of the child and resume the dance. Being back in control of the relationship, the child is once more satisfied. But in avoiding a period of training, which may last two weeks, parents have reinforced a negative dependency which may endure for years. It takes great courage for parents to free their children of attention-getting behaviors. Yet through the courage to respond appropriately to a child, a parent gives the child a lifetime of self-satisfaction and self-evaluation.

Training a child is usually frustrating and difficult. I vividly recall training Emily when she was four to be more patient. For a week or so, she had decided that Patty and I should stop upon demand and read or play with her. Of course, she picked times when we were busiest, like right before meals. I recorded in my journal: "When we finally admitted that Emily was in the habit of demanding that we drop everything to attend to her, we knew our sanity depended on change. We explained to her that we would no longer read or play before supper or at other busy times. We set times with her when we would play or read. This act of freedom on our part intensified her efforts to have her way. When we refused her demands, she swirled like a tornado through the house, uprooting everything in her path. It took three days for her to realize our will would not be broken by her storms. At times during those periods, I was sure calmer days would not come. But they soon did." It should be noted that I recorded this after the training period ended. During her testing of our will, I considered the question that most parents secretly ask: "Why didn't I become a priest or a nun?"

The first movement is always the parent's initial declaration of freedom from a child's misbehavior: the refusal to dance with her. For the dance of the Attention Addict, this means refusing to give attention on demand and on the child's terms. As suggested above, it is never easy. Chapter Six's discussion on logical and natural consequences will help parents set up conditions which will further reduce inappropriate demands for attention.

THE SECOND DANCE: POWER MOVEMENTS-THE WAR DANCE

When I was a child, we drew lines in the dirt and told a temporary enemy: "If you cross this line, you're in for it!" Immediately the challenged child would jump across the line, and the fight was in full throttle. Both children and parents are skilled at drawing lines and asking for fights. Neither parents nor children seem naturally skilled in avoiding the challenge. Power dances are easily spotted and understood. Simply said, two parties "at war" insist on their own way and are determined to win.

Anyone who has witnessed a two-year-old defiantly look her parents in the eyes and yell, "NO! I DO IT MYSELF!" has seen a parent frustrated by a power struggle. This theme occurs throughout childhood.

Unfortunately, as Dreikurs often said, an adult can never win a fight with a child. Children in battle simply do not follow the same rules as adults. Even when parents do appear to have defeated a child, the child will then enter the more serious dance of revenge and eventually will punish the parent. This punishment only adds to the discouragement that most parents already feel for getting down on the child's level and fighting on the child's terms.

Power struggles all have the same steps. The following example will display the common movements of the war dance:

While at the supper table, Johnny begins to play with his food. Dad sternly demands: "Stop playing with your food and eat! Right now!" Knowing that Dad has drawn the line, Johnny confidently says nothing and refuses to eat. He has accepted the challenge. Feeling his authority threatened, Dad mistakenly decides to escalate: "Johnny, eat it now or spend the evening in your room!" Johnny is now firmly in control of the fight and refuses to eat. Predictably, Dad grabs Johnny and drags him back to his room. Johnny cries and screams as Dad slams the door. A deathly silence greets Dad as he returns to the table. Everyone's meal is ruined. Dad cooperated by entering a battle he could never win.

These are the common movements of the dance. There are no winners in power struggles. Unfortunately, many parents take years to find this out. Continuing to believe that victory is possible, they draw lines or cross over the child's well-drawn lines and hope to be victorious. Yet, the conclusion is always the same: the adult never wins.

The preferences for types of power struggles are different for children at different ages. For instance, in early childhood, children will engage parents during meals, bathtime, bedtime, naps, and dressing times. Special techniques are often employed like biting, hitting, and kicking. Now that pediatricians often recommend not fighting over toilet training, mandatory use of seat belts has replaced toilet training as a frequent challenge.

Older preschool children enjoy many of these same tunes. But others are added, such as new demands for changing bedtimes, buying toys in stores, trying dangerous stunts, doing what older children do, violating long established rules, and generally crossing established family boundaries. Despite the changing challenges and locations, the steps of the war dance remain the same.

School-age children recognize that new territory is available for the battle. Routines and values become a new field for combat. Studying is challenged, as is waking for school, getting dressed quickly, or watching television. New curse words learned at school can be brought home and tried as attention-getting invitations. But they are elevated to power plays if parents draw a line and challenge the child to cross it. Lying and stealing become new possibilities for parental-child conflict. The child learns quickly to declare unliked activities to be boring and to stop playing games when losing seems inevitable, or even when it appears to be a possibility. There are so many opportunities for warfare that children could forever engage an uncompromising parent.

Mr. Roberts was a policeman who rather unwillingly accompanied his wife to our parent study program. He was a man who demanded adherence to rules. Accustomed to arresting adults who defied him, he was shocked to find his children resisted his commands. Mr. Roberts loved absolute order, so he made rules for everything. When dad was home his two children (8 and 6) were required to eat everything on their plates, help wash dishes, spend thirty minutes on homework, be in the bathtub at 8 o'clock, and have lights out at 8:30. Additionally, each child was forced to say prayers and kiss both parents goodnight whether he (or she) wanted to or not. Needless to say, the Roberts's home was the proverbial china shop waiting for a bullish child. Finally, the Roberts's eight-year-old son decided he would no longer follow these rules. Dad was astounded. Mr. Roberts yelled, scolded, threatened, and spanked. Nothing worked. The rigid rules set by Mr. Roberts turned into a predictable routine of fights and tears that started at the supper table and ended with the child's withheld nightly kiss. Mr. Roberts was humiliated. How could a successful policeman not be able to force his children to obey his will in his own home?

Families with a parent who is both controlling and competitive rarely survive power struggles well. If the basic, mistaken notion of a parent is, "I am going to win and she is going to lose," then the home will face unhappy days. Such parents often act like a two-year-old in the middle of autonomy formation. Not having their own way seems to be a primary threat to their status in life. For secure parents not threatened by a child's autonomy, the guiding notion needs to become: "How can we both end up winning and continue good relations in our home?"

As children grow, they naturally become thrilled with their power and control. But often the energy is misdirected. Think of the joy of a forty-pound child in being able to turn a respectable adult into a fighting, screaming, uncontrolled giant. In just a few seconds, a child can drag a parent down to his level and defeat him. Fortunately, most parents sense that they are being pulled into a no-win situation; yet most do not know how to avoid entering the losing battles.

The first movement toward peace is always the same; parents must declare a personal freedom from the child's control. Instead of responding to a child's invitation to fight, parents must refuse to be manipulated. As Dreikurs suggested, the most effective movement for a parent is to "sidestep the struggles for power." Such an initial response will free the parent from a child's usual control. Signs of anger should be a warning to parents that a fight is in progress. Knowing that as an adult one can only lose, parents should refuse to fight and should allow natural consequences (See Chapter Six) to teach the child. The major point to remember now is that one cannot lose a power struggle in which one does not engage. However, those engaged in will be lost!

Not all professionals take their own advice. I unhappily recall one Sunday morning engaging my four-year-old son, Patrick, in a power struggle. He had been practicing with a preschool choir and was to sing in public. Ten minutes before the event, he angrily announced, "I am not going to sing. I don't like the song and I am not going to do it." Instead of sidestepping the struggle, I met his resistance and escalated it by saying, "Yes, you are going to sing. You practiced, and you have to sing."

My wife was amazed by my lack of technique! Privately she said, "Ken, if you had given him a choice to sit by himself or sing, he would have chosen to sing. You're going to pay, I bet."

As I squirmed uncomfortably in the audience, I heard the choir director say, "OK children, come to the front." Patrick remained seated. My heart stopped beating. The director said, "Everyone come to the front." He remained: silent and defiant before the entire world! Everyone went forward but one child. Why did it have to be mine! As my journal recalls, "There I sat, as humiliated as a naked man in front of an open bathroom door. Here I was, the child development professor and parent study leader with a child who was totally uncooperative. It was a new low in childraising." Needless to say, I have tried to take my own advice since that long morning: "Never enter a power struggle with a child."

Parents should realize that they, like children, utilize negative techniques of fighting, which are destructive to family life. Some parents fight totally with reason. They try to overwhelm the child with speeches and logic, despite the fact that their words are generally ignored by the child. After thirty seconds of reasoning with a child who is not listening, the parent should realize that a power struggle is under way. Many children of parents who fight with speeches and reason fight back with emotions. If a child feels she cannot "out-logic" a parent, she may feel more certain of winning with tantrums, tears, and misbehavior. Some even choose to run away from a home in which they cannot win an argument by traditional "fighting."

The Browner family reported that they had a daughter out of the parents' control. She ran away from home twice and seemed to always end family discussions with hysterical outbursts of anger and crying. Soon after the family entered counseling, I understood the daughter's plight. Mr. Browner was a successful accountant. He was the voice of total reason and never showed emotion. When his daughter tried to explain her ideas, Mr. Browner would respond with a tedious list of facts to support his opposing position.

He was always right. He was always long-winded. He was always boring. His daughter felt trapped by his cold logic. She did not want to adopt his values and will, but how could she fight? She brilliantly fought ice with fire. She fought with the weapons her father had never developed. Unfortunately, the entire family suffered because of their lack of cooperation and skills. The need to always be right or to always win is not conducive to family harmony.

Not all parents fight with logic. A larger number use emotions and force when they attempt to break the will of the child through fear and punishment; these parents find themselves in a dilemma. If they lose, they will create in the child a will that knows no boundaries. Such a child becomes a power-hungry "monster" who will disregard the rights and feelings of others.

Although power struggles with children should be avoided, realistically, no parent can avoid them all. Occasionally, the law, so to speak, must be laid down. In a crisis, a parent must demand obedience "or else." But these occasions should be rare enough that the child immediately understands that the situation is unusual. If a good relationship exists between parent and child, a child will more often than not go along with a parent's demand for obedience in an emergency. But if parents consistently try to overpower children, daily warfare will soon evolve. Once a child is engaged in the dances of war, no request is met easily.

I am intrigued with a story told by a colleague of mine about an eight-year-old boy at war with his father. The father was an authoritarian who consistently gave commands to his son. As the son began to stand up for himself, he openly defied his dad at every opportunity. The young boy refused to go to school, fought with his younger siblings, came late to dinner, and resisted going to bed. The father met the child's defiance with increased physical force. As the story goes, the family was visiting their lakeside cabin one summer. After a particularly difficult evening of family arguments, the father was awakened by smoke. He investigated and found that fire was spreading quickly through the house. He ran into his children's bedroom to wake them. He quickly awakened his son and said: "Hurry, run to the front door. The house is burning down." Defiantly the son looked up at his dad and responded, "Make me!"

Remember, the first step to peace in the home is the refusal of a parent to be engaged in the war dance. Do not enter self-destructive fights. Replace the tendency to fight back with a tendency to sidestep the struggle. Battles will always lead to loss.

The second step of the parent's new dance will be learned later, in Chapter Six, with the use of natural and logical consequences. Consequences will allow a child to fully learn from their mistakes and poor judgment. Cooperation will be the reward for withdrawing from power struggles and using consequences. Destruction of both a positive family atmosphere and of relationships within the family results from engaging in the dances of war.

DANCE THREE: REVENGE THE DANCE OF DESTRUCTION AND HURT

"Gee, I wish you could be nice like Tommy's mother. I would rather have her for a Mom."

Revenge is the first serious goal of misbehavior. All children will occasionally be angry at losing a power struggle with a parent and may attempt to "get back" by hurting them. These occasions should be rare. But if parents find the child hurting them often, then it becomes a signal that something is seriously wrong with the relationship.

What is wrong is that the child is feeling defeated and hurt. Feeling overwhelmed and unable to win against the parents, or others, on any terms, causes the child to feel unloved. Still having some spirit, the child attempts to return the hurt. It is a clear case of revenge: "I am hurt, and I will hurt you in return."

When a child hurts a parent, the immediate reaction of a parent may be to hurt back. This is the worst of all mistakes, because it causes a chain of pain and discouragement. A revengeful response by the parent mistakenly proves to the child that she is indeed unloved. Often, I have heard parents in counseling respond to a revengeful child by saying such things as: "Maybe you should be placed in a home where you would fit;" or "Well, if you had half the brains you sister had, then. . ." As in all misbehavior's themes, it is up to the parent to act like an adult. Remember, an adult can hurt a developing child far more than the child can hurt an adult. Parents must realize what the child is trying to say through her misbehavior. The message is: "You do not love me. You hurt me; therefore, I will hurt you in return."

As in other dances, the parent's first response to a vengeful child must be the refusal to dance. The parent must avoid the impulse to retaliate. Second, the parent must look at the relationship itself and ask, "How can I show my child that she is truly loved?" Instead, many parents mistakenly put the child in a position where the young person must "earn" love and trust. Such parents are refusing to be adults.

I worked with a nine-year-old girl and her mother who were involved in a destructive battle of revenge. During the midst of their angry interactions, I asked the mother to consider using more positive approaches. She responded: "My daughter is acting like a child, and I am going to treat her like one. I refuse to talk with her, cook her meals, or wash her clothes until she comes to me and apologizes for her childish behaviors." This battle was between two children. The dance of revenge can hook the most mature adult into childish and irresponsible behavior.

Adults need to be responsible enough to place themselves in the position of initiating overtures of love. Many techniques may help parents express love. Time spent alone with the revengeful child seems essential. Doing things the child enjoys is helpful. For example, letting the child choose a movie, or sporting event, or joint project, or a weekend alone camping with the child can be constructive. Staying out of power struggles and opening communications are essential.

If parents find it difficult to objectively answer questions about the family system, a family counselor could serve as a neutral observer and advisor. Sometimes, in families where revenge is often experienced, family counselors can teach new skills and give advice that allows a much quicker, positive reorientation in the family to occur.

Whether a family seeks the advice of a professional in the area or tries to reconstruct the family alone, "more of the same" is never the answer to family problems. A new approach needs to be instituted. Anger and hostility will go away only after the behaviors within a family change in a way that allows cooperation and feelings of appreciation and love to be experienced by all its members.

THE FOURTH DANCE: ASSUMED DISABILITY THE DANCE OF SORROW

When life becomes too difficult to believe there is any hope of success, a child will often give up. There is little spirit left in such a child. The last dance is a mournful one. The child wishes to dance alone. No partner is sought. In fact, the child wishes not to be engaged by adults. Many children may give up across-the-board in almost every phase of life. They emotionally surrender to the world and retreat to their individual rooms or their safe worlds. Others may be discouraged only in one area. In this area, they refuse to take risks because they have found no success. Outside of the single area, some children still maintain enthusiasm.

Parents and teachers often throw up their hands in despair over the surrendering child. Adults will try everything to influence the child to work in school, or to make friends, or to engage in a physical activity, or whatever seems beneficial. But all attempts meet with failure. At this point, adults usually bring specialists in to discover whether the child suffers from an organic problem or dietary complication. It is wise to seek out a specialist's help. In some cases, there is a physiological problem underlying the cause of the difficulty, but in many cases the source of the problem is the child's perception of her lack of ability. When a person is certain (even mistakenly) that success is impossible, then attempting success makes no sense. Not only is it a waste of effort, but it continues to foster the feelings of humiliation and failing. For a child who assumes a disability, the logic of a confident person makes no sense. The maxim, "You can do better if you try" becomes another discouraging indication that adults do not understand the problem. The child's logic is simple: I cannot succeed, so let me alone. Don't make me humiliate myself by exposing my weaknesses.

Interestingly enough, a few children who are called "gifted" by the schools are soon forced to assume a disability. Once, the parent of a marvelous nine-year-old joined my class for parents of learning disabled children. Apparently, the child was doing well in school until she was tested and awarded the label "gifted." At that point, her parents escalated their expectations. Outstanding work became the required norm. Work which once pleased the child no longer pleased the parents.

The child's teachers joined the parents in telling her, "You can do better." But she believed she could only do what she had always done. The pressure mounted. The parents began to search for an explanation for why she failed to reach their expectations. A well-meaning school psychologist told the parents that the child might have some type of learning disability, but it was more likely that she was just not trying hard enough. The parents immediately declared her learning disabled and also pushed her into the shadowy children's world of no return — the kingdom of the unmotivated. The truth is, the overambition of the parents and the misuse of labels at times by the school system stole the child's confidence and initiative. She was discouraged.

There are simple techniques or solutions for helping a child who has given up. The adult must realize that the discouragement felt by such a child is profound. Giving up on the child is a common reaction of adults in this situation. But that is what the child wants — to be left alone in his private dance of failure.

As in other goals, the parent needs to create a new program, one that is not controlled by the child. The parent must discover ways to encourage the child. The smallest success may seem inconsequential to an encouraged adult; yet to a discouraged child, it may be the first step toward success. If a child can say hello to one friend or try to solve one easy math problem, then brighter days may come.

Education majors in college sometimes claim not to understand why a child won't at least try to do something she fears. To help them understand, I often ask these future teachers to stand on the seat of their chairs. All can do that. Then I ask them to put one foot on the top of the chair's back. Each can do that. Then I ask each person to put both feet on the back of the chair and balance on the edge. No one tries. At that point, I urge them on as insensitive adults do. "But how do you know you can't do it, if you have never tried? I'm sure you can do it; it's just a matter of balance. Try it. Come on. What's wrong with you?" Usually, no one tries. They are certain they will fail. No one wants to fail in front of others. When failures seems certain, there is safety in not trying at all.

Several family dynamics should be investigated when a child is totally discouraged. When one child has an assumed disability, it is not unusual to have another child in the family who is excellent in the area of the disability or in all phases of life. The "perfect angel" is a curse to other children in the family. If one child is functioning extremely well, then parents need to follow the guidelines for dealing with an intense sibling rivalry (suggested in the next chapter).

A second area worthy of personal investigation is parental expectations and pressure. All parents want their children to be successful. But some want more from the child than the child feels capable of giving. If the parents want the child to do more, this is usually discouraging to the child. The reaction of a child then may be: "Since I will never be what my parents want me to be, I will not try."

A father I know has a master's and doctorate from an Ivy League university. His academic accomplishments are known to everyone, particularly his son. His degrees are prominently placed in his home, and his stationery is adorned with both his degrees and the granting institution's name. For years, the father talked to the son about going to his university and the pride this would bring him. However, the son was of only average ability. At first, he tried extremely hard to live up to his father's dreams. But his grades never rose far above a B average.

Finally, the son grew discouraged and stopped working. The father continued to push him, until the son finally quit school. Although he was a fine student, he was not as good as his father needed for him to be. The gap between the son's ability and the father's dreams for him handicapped the child's life. A child who was destined for success under normal conditions finally gave up because he was overwhelmed by his parents' expectations.

The formula "More of the Same" again will fail to work. If a child has developed an assumed disability, then new skills and interactions are needed. As in the third dance, a family counselor can often guide a family back to positive interactions. When a child reaches this point, specialists should always be consulted. Parents often are too discouraged to be resourceful; thus new resources must be found outside. School specialists, child guidance clinics, family counselors, and other professionals are trained to help parents work through this challenging situation. But remember: Never give up!

CONCLUDING THOUGHTS

Dreikurs describes four goals of misbehavior that I believe are daily predictable dances of childhood. In the first three goals, children wish to have a partner. The invitations to the parent to join in the movements of misbehavior are obvious. It is up to the parent to recognize the themes of the dance and to decline the invitation. Once the parent refuses to respond as the child wishes, the parent is free to create healthy responses guided by encouragement and cooperation. Most of this chapter concentrated on the parents' ability NOT TO ACT in predictable ways. But certainly, there are times when parents must act in order to discipline children. Chapters Six and Seven will help parents add to their existing skills for helping children develop responsibility.

RUDOLF DREIKURS

Dr. Rudolf Dreikurs was one of the most influential teachers in the history of psychology and counseling. With his peers, he could be overwhelming, challenging, and demanding. With his clients, especially children and parents, he was strikingly gentle, warm, and successful.

Born in Vienna in 1897, he completed his medical training at the Vienna Medical School in 1923. There he became greatly influenced by the practical psychology of Alfred Adler. Dreikurs embraced the optimistic philosophy that "anyone can change." All of his work was grounded in this belief. In Vienna, he became a pioneer in the fields of social psychiatry and group psychotherapy.

After coming to the United States in 1937, Dreikurs fought against difficult odds to place psychology in the hands of parents and teachers. He opposed any psychology which considered misbehaving children as sick or disturbed; instead, he was convinced that children misbehaved when they were discouraged. In the 1930's, he devised his brilliant theory that allowed adults to understand the four goals of their children's misbehavior. This, along with other common sense advice to parents, has enriched the lives of parents throughout the world. Dr. Dreikurs was a professor of psychiatry at the Chicago Medical School from 1942 to 1967. He died in 1972. Through the works of his students and followers, his ideas are becoming increasingly more influential with parents and in the school system.

RELATED READINGS

Dinkmeyer, D. & McKay, G. D. (1973). *Raising a responsible child.* New York: Simon & Schuster.
Dreikurs, R. (1968). *Psychology in the classroom.* New York: Harper and Row.
Dreikurs, R. (1972). *The challenge of child training: A parent's guide.* New York: Hawthorn Books.
Dreikurs, R. (1978). *The challenge of marriage.* New York: Hawthorn.
Dreikurs, R. (1979). *The challenge of parenthood.* New York: Duell, Sloan and Pearce.
Dreikurs, R. & Dinkmeyer, D. (1963). *Encouraging children to learn.* New York: Prentice-Hall.
Dreikurs, R., et al. (1964). *Children: The challenge.* New York: Hawthorn.
Dreikurs, R., et al. (1968). *Logical consequences: A new approach to discipline.* New York: Hawthorn Press.
Dreikurs, R., et al. (1971). *Maintaining sanity in the classroom.* New York: Harper and Row.
Dreikurs, R., et al. (1974). *Discipline without tears.* New York: Hawthorn.
Kvols-Riedler, B. & Kvols-Riedler, K. (1979). *Redirecting children's misbehavior.* Boulder, CO: R.D.I.C. Pub.

CHAPTER TWO

THE PREDICTABLE MISBEHAVIORS: BY BIRTH ORDER

"MOMMY, MOMMY, he's killing me! Help me!," squeals the youngest child as her older brother pushes her to the floor. Immediately, Dad comes thundering into the room, yelling at the older child. The eldest stands red-faced with a fist clenched above the cringing body of an apparently defeated sibling. The oldest is given a tough sentence: "Go to your room for an hour and don't even think of coming out!" A defense is attempted, although without hope: "But she started it." Provoked, Dad replies: "Get to your room. Right now! While you can still walk!" The youngest whimpers safely in the arms of her savior. At the corners of her lips, a hint of a smile appears. Once again, injustice is done, and the sibling rivalry grows stronger. What the parent did not see makes all the difference!

Characteristically, the youngest child orchestrates such fights; then, at the strategic moment, the cavalry is called forth. Each child seeks a unique place within the family by manipulating others and life in a way that insures significance. Alfred Adler and Walter Toman have been giants in the field of predicting traditional patterns that children develop to find a secure identity. Recognizing the advantages and disadvantages of being an oldest, second, youngest, or only child can be of crucial importance to parents. Each child develops a unique pattern of positive behavior and misbehavior, based largely on her ordinal world. Understanding these ordinal worlds will allow you to handle misbehavior in each of your children with added tolerance and a greater degree of success.

RULES OF FAMILY ORDINATION

Many people misunderstand ordinal theory because they are not familiar with the basic rules. For example, to be in the same constellation of children, each sibling must be within four years of the sibling on either side. Although some authors mention six years on either side as a guideline, my practice with families suggests that four years is a more helpful estimate.

For examples, let's look at a few model families.

1) Tom   8
   Mark   6
   Emily 3

In the constellation above, each child is within four years of the child both immediately above and immediately below. Therefore, this is a family with one constellation of children: an eldest, a second, and a youngest.

2) Marcia 10
   Sally   8
   Mark   2
   Mary   6 months

In the family above, there are two constellations of children. Marcia is an oldest, and Sally a second and youngest. Mark is separated from Sally by more than four years; therefore, he begins a new constellation. He will be considered an oldest. Mary will be the youngest and second child in this constellation of influence.

3) Tom   14
   Jane 12
   Paul   5

In this example, there are again two sets of children. Tom is the oldest. Jane is the combined second and youngest of the two. Paul is separated by more than four years and is most like an only child. But his is a special position. I call him the "Whoops Child" or "Jehovah's Gift" child. Traditionally, Paul is called "Super Baby."

Often a child like Paul is an unexpected addition. After seven years, many parents have given away their baby furniture and supplies. The surprise is like beginning parenthood again. Only now, the child is born into a family where older siblings may act more like parents than brothers and sisters. Because the arrival comes later in the lives of parents, many consider her to be a special gift of God or fate. With adoring siblings and older parents treasuring her, the Gift Child has an automatic position of prominence. Woe to any person who finds fault with this child!

How often parents are heard saying: "You won't believe how different all of my children are!" The opposite is true. Ordinal experts would be surprised to hear "how similar" personalities in a family might be. In fact, the primary rule of first and second children is that they will be "opposite" in personality. Since each wishes to be unique, an area where one is successful will be an area the other will avoid.

Occasionally, the eldest child will view the second as so powerful that the traditional place of first child is surrendered. Thus, the first child will become like a traditional second child and the second like a traditional first. Although the switch occurs, the major ordinal rule remains: first and second children within four years of age will be opposite in personality. The only exceptions occur where "family values" insist that "all children" share a similar characteristic.

A "family value" is defined as a belief shared by both parents. For example, both parents (even if separated) may join forces in stressing the importance of education. Thus, each child in the family may be successful in school; still, each will generally pick a unique area of study or interest where competition is not as brisk. I have noted, however, that family values must be practiced by parents for all children to share them. For example, both parents may stress academics, but if at night one routinely settles down for an evening of television, rather than reading, the family value may be seen by the children to be false.

Mr. and Mrs. McDonald were thrilled with their son's progress in Suzuki® violin lessons. At age eight, he completed the introductory books and seemed well on his way to becoming an accomplished young violinist. But making John practice was worse than pulling weeds. Mrs. McDonald begged, bribed, and even punished John for not practicing. Soon John declared he hated violin lessons and would never play again. Neither parent could understand why John was so unmotivated.

Knowing the home life of the parents was the key. Neither parent played a musical instrument and neither listened to classical or, for that matter, any music. Neither parent attended or took John to concerts. Dad openly said concerts were too boring for him to endure. John was not a child who lacked motivation. He was motivated to be just like his parents. Clearly the value they modeled was that violin music was not worth listening to. Therefore, John believed that it must not be worth playing either.

Other factors are influential in determining how a child finds an identity within the family. Walter Toman is particularly helpful in studying the variation of sex on the constellation's influence. For example, females living with all brothers tend to have good rapport with males. Particularly, they are successful with males who are similar in age to their brothers. Below, Jill should be on good terms with older males. She will interact with them in ways that are characteristic of a youngest child.

Paul   8
Sam   6
Jill   3

Below, one might expect Harold to be at his best with males. He has experienced relationships with males daily for years. On the other hand, Harold may have more trouble understanding females. As an adult, an evening with the boys around may be more attractive to him than a night alone with his wife.

Harold 8
Jack   6
Jimmy   3

The most helpful hint concerning sexual influence is that females usually develop much more quickly than males. With such quick growth comes the possibility of discouragement to slower males close in age. If females quickly take the socially acceptable identities in the family, a male may abandon such roles for less enhancing but "acceptable" behaviors. These behaviors fall under the mistaken rubric "boys will be boys."

The Anthonys had two children. Their nine-year-old daughter, Rebecca, excelled in everything from school work to helping around the house. She exhibited impeccable manners and was, as her parents said, "a perfect little lady." With so many positive spots reserved by his sister, five-year-old Tommy had little chance to find a successful place for himself.

Instead, Tommy became a loud, domineering child. He pushed, hit, and yelled at other children. After demanding his own way, he would fight whenever his will was denied. But Mrs. Anthony refused to see his behavior as a problem. Instead she simply said on each occasion, "Tommy is all boy." Although the Anthonys chose to believe that Tommy was all boy, those who put up with his behavior thought he was "all jerk." Neither was right. In truth, Tommy was a discouraged young boy who thought there was no other way for him to feel significant. His sister was too good at everything.

Unfortunately, there are no "best" guidelines for the spacing of children, although most psychologists have a preference. Each position has advantages and disadvantages. For example, to space children over four years apart may reduce sibling rivalry. But in exchange for less sibling rivalry, each child grows up with the same challenges as an only child.

One warning about ordinal theory needs to be kept in mind. Ordinal theory should be used only as a tool to help understand the very different worlds of children in the same family. Because children find significance by dividing many possible roles, it is unlikely any child will fit traditional descriptions perfectly. Thus, the theory should never be used to pigeonhole or mark children with labels. Still, from each position, patterns do emerge which are common enough to help parents understand the disadvantages and advantages of family positions. When one can see the world from the eyes of an eldest or a youngest child, then traditional pitfalls of family positions may be largely avoided.

THE TRADITIONAL OLDEST CHILD

An eldest child was an only child for a period of time. No matter how one prepares her for the coming of another sibling, it is a shock. Adler called the shock "dethronement." The eldest's response is to try to secure a significant position once again. This should not seem unusual to adults. What if your spouse came home with another lover and said: "This person will be living with us from now on. But don't worry. I have so much love I can spread it equally between the two of you." An adult's reaction might be to pack the suitcases and go to court, but since an eldest child cannot divorce the family, she will try to regain the most favorable position.

If encouraged, most oldest children search for a new role by becoming the "helper" in the house. By doing this, they join the parents as part of the family's power structure. The eldest can stress being superior to the infant by helping him. As the infant grows, the eldest child may continue to emphasize what she can do better than the second. And what can an older child do better? Just about everything she chooses. She can dress correctly, learn to read well, and "enforce" rules better.

Sometimes the movements of an eldest are subtle. Our oldest son at age four loved "to read" to his two-year-old sister. He would say warmly, "Sit down and I will read this story to you." Little sister didn't realize he could not read either! But the message in this case was clear: "I can do something you cannot." At this same critical point in their lives, he developed a method of warmly evaluating all of her efforts in a manner which kept her in "place." For example, he would look at her coloring and say: "That's pretty good for a two-year-old."

Because oldest children may choose to excel in socially approved ways, parents often give them reinforcement for both achieving and giving of themselves. The danger is that eldest children may suffer from the continuous demands of self-imposed "shoulds." Such demands often increase the feeling of tension, both in regard to performance and in the desire to be "all things" to all organizations and people. Because excellence requires so much time, oldest children may seek accomplishment in exchange for spontaneity and friendships.

At ten, Mark Edmonson was a straight A student. He was placed in the most advanced reading and math groups. His parents and teachers greatly praised him for his accomplishments. His work far outstripped that of his younger brother and sister. Additionally, Mark was showing promise as a student of piano. The more successful he became, the more he worked. He practiced his piano for hours and worked doubly hard on homework. When Mark made errors, he became angry. He would pick up whatever was near and hurl it across the room. Soon Mark began to develop severe headaches. Nothing relieved him of the pain. It was not until his pediatrician recommended that the Edmonsons take a course in parenting that his parents realized Mark had become a victim of over-ambition. His accomplishments took the place of friendships, and his work took the place of playing. The cost of excellence in achievement was his health and childhood.

With a traditional oldest child, a parent must be careful to reduce the self-imposed stress on the child. To share parental values and to be helpful to others are tendencies worth reinforcing, but there must be room for imperfection and even for failing. Childhood is meant to be a period of risk taking. Should children be too conservative in following society's wishes, they may become chained early to society's evaluations and its demands on their lives. Once chained securely, such children become prisoners of achievement and praise rather than its beneficiaries. Such a secure identity may become a heavy price for finding a significant place in the family. Additionally, the more successful the older child is in taking the socially accepted identities in the family, the more difficult it will be for a second child to find a place on the productive side of life.

THE SECOND CHILD

Nothing is fair to a second child. Rules and memories always favor the first. Scrapbooks abound with pictures of the oldest and dwindle with the arrival of the second. The eldest often becomes part of the power force early in life. Thus, the second finds a quick finger wagging in her face at every error: "You know you're not supposed to do that! I'm going to tell Mom." Certain that rules and tradition never favor her, the second often ignores regulations as she steps to "the beat of a different drummer."

If the first child has become established as the "good child," then the second discovers fewer possibilities to be the best. Remember the curse of any family is to have an almost perfect child at any position. Such a prodigy takes most of the productive positions. For example, if one child is the best in school, most helpful in the home, and in total obedience with family rules, then where does another child find a unique "best" position? Since it's not desirable to be second best, the second may not compete with the eldest in areas already taken. New territory will be conquered. For example, by giving up academics, there is more time for friendships. By giving up rules and the "shoulds" of life, there is more opportunity to experiment and relax in life.

The second child is more spirited and more difficult to discipline. She runs faster, climbs higher, and is more emotional than the eldest. There is a tendency for parents to worry more about the eventual success of this child. Yet, due to the "success" of the first, it is difficult to encourage the second in areas of the eldest's strengths.

It is at this point that family values and lack of making comparisons become the parents' best allies in training. Parents, separated or not, should establish "family values" and model such values to the children. If religion or education is a value, then the parents should live by these tenets, and their children are more likely to embrace them in their own ordinal way. If parents differ in values, then children will probably differ even more radically.

Amy and Sid Lister were parents of two bright children, Sally (8) and Jimmy (6). Amy and Sid met in college where Amy was a Dean's List student and Sid was captain of the basketball team. Amy still loved to read and to take occasional classes. Although Sid was an intelligent man, he was not interested in reading or discussing new ideas. In fact, Sid once reflected, "I guess I haven't read an entire book since I graduated from college." Sid was most interested in sports, and generally, he played golf on Saturday afternoons and tennis on Sunday mornings.

Both parents wanted their children to be good students and to attend a prestigious college like their own alma mater. But only Sally was doing well in school. Jimmy spent most of his time playing with the neighborhood children. Both parents already were warning Jimmy, "Unless you take your studies seriously, you'll never go to a good college." But Jimmy had two strikes against him: a sister who was very successful, and a dad who did not display interest in learning. Children will model after parents they love. Sally copied her mother's interest in learning. Sid displayed his father's values, which did not include an appreciation for academics. For children, actions of parents speak far louder than words.

The Great Error parents commit is the making of comparisons. Comparisons never work as parents intend. Early in my counseling career, I said to parents, "Comparisons rarely work." But after years of observing how comparisons discourage children, I am sure they are **always** in error. To be on the short end of a comparison only motivates the successful child, who already believes she is in the "superior" position. For example, the good student with a low grade in one subject may study harder if it is pointed out that another sibling is gaining. Unfortunately, comparisons are generally made to encourage children who are already discouraged. For example, "Johnny, why can't you behave (study, etc.) like your sister?" Johnny's inferior position is well known to him. After all, he probably chose not to compete in this area because he believed he could not win. To point out that he is "losing" only confirms his suspicion of inferiority.

Our culture thrives on comparisons. We are a country in which emphasis is placed on competition. In comparisons and in competition, there are winners and losers. In a business society, competition is understood to bring out the best. Thus, successful business prospers and generally grows to its fullest capacity. However, businesses that do not "win," do not grow. Eventually, they may declare bankruptcy and close. This closing is the cost of failing in competition. Comparisons and competition which make any child seem less successful than a sibling are a mistake that may unfavorably limit the child's life. So many good intentions of parents are lost to poor technique.

I still remember how sad and distraught I was when Dorothy Johnson introduced her two daughters to me. "This is my youngest daughter Ceilia (8). She is the student-athlete in our family. And this is Marcia (10). Marcia has the most ability and the least drive of anyone in the family. If she ever applied herself, she could be the best. But she just doesn't have the ambition and get up and go that her sister has." How cruel! The mother thought she issued a challenge that would encourage Marcia. Instead, she issued a judgement which Marcia accepted as true. Marcia felt condemned to failure—a victim of her mother's words.

Instead of comparison, encouragement should be used. Very early, our eldest began to do well in school. Often teachers would say in front of his brother and sister, "Your son Patrick is such a good student." I was always struck by the stunned look in Emily's and Dustin's eyes. My wife and I agreed upon a response to reflect our family value: "Yes, all of our children are good students." Immediately, the children neglected by the comment lifted their heads with pride. Parents cannot, of course, totally shelter a growing child from comparisons made by others, or by the siblings themselves.

Children naturally make comparisons. When our eldest son, Patrick, was six, I recorded this in my journal: "Patrick loves school and is tremendously industrious. He creates projects and will work for hours. Unfortunately, he likes to be the fastest at everything. He tells Emily, 'I can dress faster, eat faster and run faster than you can.' As much as we discourage comparisons and encourage Emily, the effect can be seen. Emily dresses and eats as slowly as a human can. If he is best at being fast, she is best at being slow."

Adults also will make unsolicited comparisons. Some of my tennis friends were visiting one night while Patrick and Emily were playing. One friend casually noted that Patrick was heavy and strong, while Emily was slight and quick. He observed: "Well, it looks like Patrick will be the football player and Emily the tennis player. He has the physique of a Walter Peyton and she has the body of Chris Everett." To this day, Patrick will have nothing to do with tennis, while Emily remains interested. Did this contribute? I don't know. But I do know that comparisons occur constantly in children's lives, and comparisons are not helpful. Parents cannot prevent comparisons made by others, but they can discipline themselves never to add to their children's difficulties.

A second child can be the delight of a family if properly encouraged. There is no reason a first and second child cannot be different in personality, yet similar in their shared success in school, or athletics, or at home. But the second child is in a unique position. Understanding the challenges she faces can help parents direct her to make positive contributions.

REVERSALS OF FIRST AND SECOND POSITIONS

It is common to see a second child overcome the first child in the sibling rivalry. In such cases, the eldest may surrender the role of traditional first child to the second. When this occurs, the eldest needs additional encouragement from parents.

Often, first and second children can be observed who have "private logic" or beliefs about themselves which appear to be totally incorrect. Nevertheless, they act as if their logic is true. Once I watched two sisters playing during a picnic. The youngest was taking gymnastics lessons and prided herself on her ability. She was obviously slow and awkward. But the younger girl would laugh and tease her older sister, calling her a "clumsy ox." But, as in the case of Cinderella and her stepsisters, the beauty lay hidden in the less dominant girl.

The older sister picked up a badminton racket and immediately showed the natural timing, rhythm, and quickness her sister lacked. But the young, aggressive sister snatched the racket from her hand, saying, "You can't play this. You're too spastic." The more talented sister sat down and watched, totally defeated. She did not enter another sports activity that day. Certainly she felt inadequate. The two girls live out a myth they created about themselves and believed to be true. Like the fairy tale story of Cinderella, it may take a miracle to liberate the beauty in the older child.

Remember, it is the child's perception of her own ability in relation to her siblings' abilities that causes discouragement, or the abandonment of certain identities. This perception may be totally incorrect yet the loss of will to succeed is real. The task of the parent is to provide the courage for the child through encouragement.

THE YOUNGEST

How opposite of the oldest child's is the world of the youngest! While the oldest encountered new parents who were often slightly tense and careful to obey all of the strictest guidelines, the youngest is raised by more confident parents who may now relax demands and restrictions. There is a tendency both to be lenient with and protective of the youngest child. For many parents, there is more enjoyment in watching the youngest go through the early stages of life. After all, it is the last time parents will experience the pleasures of a growing young child.

Our youngest child was three years old this past Christmas. For me, there was both a sadness and excitement in seeing our last child of three looking forward to Christmas. Yes, I loved this stage with each of the other children, but knowing it was the last time, gave the season a unique intensity. I concentrated on each Christmas song with its confused and garbled lines. I even enjoyed seeing the manger scene rearranged. The Wise Men appeared each morning stacked on top of the shepherds' heads. Mary was usually standing on the roof of the stable, and a sheep found a home in the manger. In the past, I would have said, "The manger scene is for looking at and not for touching." But not this year. I held on to the moments, knowing they will never pass my way again. So it is with many youngest children. By virtue of position, they live special lives.

Youngest children grow up in a world of advanced adults. They wish to be equally successful, but often they do not care to take all of the tedious steps necessary to becoming successful. Therefore, the youngest child masters techniques of getting special attention or help. These techniques are usually charm and humor. Because of their skills in charming others, youngest children are usually successful in securing the help needed to be successful. This interpersonal ability is both a strength and a weakness for the child in this position.

The danger, of course, is that too much can be done to help or protect the youngest child. In such cases, the child may never really become autonomous but may always need others to aid them in times of difficulty. Thus, the rule of Dreikurs: "Never do for the child what she can do for herself" becomes essential in raising a youngest child. The rule applies not only to the parents but also to other siblings. Other siblings who find their place by being helpful may intervene when the youngest encounters difficulties. While intervention may temporarily eliminate frustration for the youngest, it will make the child more dependent on others in the long run.

Ben was a three-and-a-half-year-old who could not dress himself, was not toilet trained, and was delayed in language development. An afternoon with his family showed why. Whenever he became frustrated, he let loose a horrifying scream. Angry tears followed. Immediately someone in the family would come to his service. His two older sisters loved to dress and play with him. He was like a big toy. They answered questions directed at him and even enjoyed changing his diapers. When attended, Ben was a marvelous and cheerful child. But Ben never was given the opportunity to solve his own problems. His family solved the natural conflicts of childhood for him: he simply enjoyed a smooth ride. With three mothers, why should he bother to care for himself?

Generally, youngest children are a pleasure to be near. Often they are highly creative. Their temperament, however, can vary greatly. Also, their work may go to extremes. At a task, they may prefer either to do the best job of anyone in the family, or they may prefer not to be burdened with it at all. Thus, they wash the dishes and clean the kitchen until it absolutely sparkles, or they may simply toss the sponge in the sink and consider the task complete. In some cases, they may charm others into completing a task for them, or they may avoid the task by pleading total incompetency in the area.

Parents should be particularly careful to teach youngest children to handle the small challenges and tasks of life. Youngest children often consider small duties to be boring and insignificant. Of course, it is these same duties that may cause difficulty for them as adults. Cleaning gutters, balancing checkbooks, and fixing broken fixtures around the house may be difficult for the adult who was a youngest child and was allowed to avoid such inconveniences while growing up.

Any practice that the youngest child can be given in caring for others may contribute to the child later in adulthood. Since the youngest has no younger siblings to practice caring for, being a parent can present many frustrations. Youngest children are more accustomed to being cared for themselves. Therefore, the drudgery tasks of parenthood, such as staying up with sick children, changing diapers, and washing bottles, may cause irritation. When youngest children become parents, they often prefer to play with children rather than meet other needs. This attitude can work well if the youngest marries someone who enjoys the other tasks. Thus, a marriage between a traditional oldest child and a traditional youngest child is often successful. However, as Toman points out, a marriage between two traditional youngest may be destined for trouble, unless money is available to help in raising their children and performing household chores! (Toman, 1976).

The youngest is a delight, but the delight she inspires in others can stand in the way of her own confidence and autonomy. As much should be expected of the youngest as was expected of the eldest. Competence in small tasks and abilities for taking care of others need to be encouraged. If parents can raise a youngest child who can combine natural charm with a feeling of competence, then one may have the best of both worlds. Youngest children often become either the most successful member of the family or the most dependent member. The eventual success of the youngest may be tied to the courage of parents to enable the child to become independent. It is a difficult challenge for many parents to allow their "baby" to become an autonomous adult.

ONLY CHILDREN

Authors seem to vary significantly in describing only children. The extremes of these evaluations may well be due to the unique characteristics of an only child. People tend to react either positively or negatively to an only child's strong personality.

Because only children grow up with adults, they grow up fast. They tend to learn to read quickly and to be extremely proficient in school. Often, they appear wise in the ways of the world long before their time. Since they are not distracted by sibling rivalry, they concentrate on the adult's world. Parents tend to talk to them in adult terms and expose them to adult ideas quite early.

This quick growth into adulthood provides them with obvious advantages for success in school or, later in life, in business. But as in all of the ordinal positions, one's advantages are also one's disadvantages. If care is not taken to bring playmates into the home or to allow the child to spend time in the home of others, the art of manipulating one's peers and working with others may be delayed. For example, in school, an only child may prefer the company of the teacher to the interaction of peers.

For parents to teach only children the methods of relating to peers is essential. Only children lack the sibling rivalries which teach children how to argue fairly and successfully. For example, in families with more than one child, every time a trip is taken there may be a dispute over the right to sit by the window. Disputes erupt on a trip over where to eat, what to sing, which games to play, or how close one can sit to another. The only child is not accustomed to such interactions. A danger is that the only child will expect to be allowed to do what she wishes. To her, conflicts with peers seem unfair. Instead of working through conflicts with peers, adults may be summoned to make rational judgments. Although reason may be on the side of the only child in such cases, the art of manipulating others and truly sharing may be lost. Trying to stay out of an only child's fights and encouraging her to interact with peers is a challenging task for parents.

Once I observed a four-year-old child and his parents on an Easter egg hunt with about forty children, all under six years of age. While other parents stayed on the sideline talking and watching their children, this child's parents held his basket and ran interference for him. They pointed to the hidden eggs and blocked the path of other children who saw the same eggs. Many of the young children became predictably annoyed. Soon, they began to pick on the only child. No sooner were the first barbs hurled than the mother yelled back at the children. Although this particular child finished the hunt with a basket full of eggs, his opportunity to learn to play and cooperate with others came up empty.

As with a youngest child, it is helpful to allow the only child opportunities to take care of others. With no younger siblings around, the only child may find it difficult as a parent to provide for the constant demands of a small child. Particularly, noise and fighting among an only child's children may create problems, since it was not a daily reality in earlier years.

Only children often develop outgoing personalities. This strength is usually admired. To build on this attribute, parents can teach an only child the subtleties of communication and cooperation which may not come naturally. When an only child learns to be successful with peers, she will have both the security of a unique family position and the confidence to meet life's challenges.

MIDDLE CHILDREN

The middle child of a family of three may have particular difficulty in finding a special place. In some fortunate cases, the middle child may be the only boy or only girl and thus have a special place by birth. But if this is not the case, the middle child may face the challenges of the famous "squeeze child." Such a child simply does not have the privileges of the oldest, nor the attention of the youngest. The middle child, in this case, may tend to be more rebellious and harder to handle unless a more peaceful path is found.

Middle children can usually tell you exactly how they were discriminated against as children. Samuel Givens (7) was a middle child, sandwiched between a ten-year-old sister and a four-year-old brother named Jake. His sister, Hilda, was allowed to do age-appropriate activities which Samuel, of couse, could not do. Samuel did not understand, even though her rights were justified because of her age.

The youngest child was also the youngest grandchild in the family. His grandfather took a great liking to him and spoiled him unmercifully. Granddad would take the youngest son on trips in his truck and to ball games. Samuel was rarely asked to come. Granddad always said, "I can only handle one. Jake is easy." These special privileges were probably not justified, and Samuel knew it. Samuel grew up to be critical and temperamental. Nothing seemed fair to him. He always seemed to be looking for proof to show he was not loved. He never found it, because he was loved. But he had no special place which brought him automatic distinction. His role in life was more difficult than his siblings! And he knew it!

Parents should pay particular attention to the plight of a middle child. As with any second child, it becomes important to eliminate comparisons. When the middle child is successful, parents should be quick to recognize the success and to help the child carve out a position which does not force her to become the "best at being bad." Particular attention needs to be paid to seeing that the middle child feels special. Spending time alone with each parent can help solve this. Frequently, taking a child to lunch or playing a sport individually with this child will be meaningful. With the realization of parents that the middle child is in a difficult position and through the parents' efforts to reinforce success in positive areas, the middle child can avoid the problems associated with the position.

Although there are many theories concerning middle children of families of five or more children, as a whole, such children seem less predictable, yet less extreme in needs. In large families, there is usually more cooperation among siblings. Probably this cooperation is necessary for the survival of the parents! Middle children often appear to pair off into mini-eldest and mini-youngest children. But every large family I have worked with has been different.

Middle children most often do well as parents. They are accustomed to having others around and to caring for others. Rarely are they overly demanding in having others attend to them, so they are more able to give freely of their time and energy. Also, by necessity, they have practiced the arts of compromise and cooperation. All of these abilities yield what appear to be more stable rates of marital success and positive feelings in being a parent.

SIBLING RIVALRY—CHOOSING TERRITORY

Sibling rivalry exists in many forms. As seen above, rivalries include the choosing of territory or roles where one can be unique in the family. Often, the two least alike children in a family are the greatest rivals, since they divided the turf. This is true, even though the two may have rarely fought. The more competitive the parents are, the more extremely different their children will be. Each child will feel she must be the best at some quality or interest in order to be important. The dividing of territory rarely causes parents great distress unless one child becomes extremely discouraged and cannot find a positive place. One of the experiences I have shared with other family counselors is having a family introduce itself in a manner which identifies the problem child. The Morris family was a good example. The mother opened the session by introducing everyone, "This is my husband, Tom, our daughter, Sherry, and our son, Tim. And THIS is Tommy, who is responsible for our being here."

A response common to many counselors is: "And can you tell me which of your other children is almost perfect?" Usually the surprised response of the parent is like Mrs. Morris's: "Well, how did you know? Our daughter is just outstanding. But actually, we have no trouble with either Sherry or Tim." The Morris family represents one that appreciates excellence. They have one child who is perfectly good. But they do not realize that the family value for perfection has been well accepted by Tommy, also. He is perfect—perfectly bad. No one is "awful" by accident. Tommy just took the course less traveled by in the family. No one had chosen the spot of being best at being bad, and Tommy excelled in the role.

A child like Tommy is extremely ambitious, although parents find this difficult to believe. If a child becomes discouraged or turns toward negative behavior, parents should review several trouble spots. Are comparisons being used? If so, the "bad" one is probably being officially identified in the role of "bad" child. Soon, the role will become a place of significance in the family. The first step in preventing this outcome is to eliminate all comparisons.

Make sure that the good child is not receiving so much praise that the "bad" child receives a message that there is no hope of gaining significance in positive ways. Generally, the good child subtlely discourages the child experiencing difficulty. Parents need to acknowledge the effort of good children without praising the outcome. As mentioned in the first chapter, acknowledgement should be expressed in terms of enjoyment, rather than "excellence." For example, "I am glad that you are enjoying math and baseball." This gives the discouraged child a better chance to become interested in positive pursuits without being defeated by the "excellence" of the other child.

Whenever the child who is "lost" to the world of positive behavior or pursuits does have the courage to try a new behavior, it is wise for parents to quickly acknowledge the effort. Again, no evaluation should be made of the performance. Remember, words such as "great," "the best," or "terrific" are mistakes if made evaluatively.

The discouraged child is the loser in sibling rivalry. The cost of lessening the rivalry may be the loss of "perfection" in the "good" child. But the benefit is to have two children who believe in their abilities to be successful in life in positive ways. When the "bad" child gets better, the "good" child may grow worse. The turf is redivided in ways that allow both to be winners.

SIBLING RIVALRY—FIGHTING

Fighting can be a healthy way of learning how to manipulate others and how to secure what one wants in life. Unfortunately, fighting drives parents to the brink of insanity. Parents need to make some rules about fighting that hold for each child. Since fighting will occur in every home, "there will be no fighting in this house" is a bad rule. Fighting cannot be eliminated in healthy children, but the intensity, method, and location of fighting can be controlled by rules.

One rule in our house is that you cannot hurt another child in a fight. No matter who started the fight, the person who hurts another spends an agreed-upon amount of time isolated. Another rule is that fights cannot take place where parents are; so children are encouraged to go to the basement or outside to fight. Rarely do fights continue without an audience.

Another helpful rule is that if a parent must become involved in a fight, than all children fighting will suffer the same consequence. It is important that parents not become judges and juries for fights. Parents who do this will become full-time arbitrators for their children. The irony in such cases is that parents will inevitably pick the wrong child to punish. Children have elaborate schemes, both to involve others in fights and to appear totally innocent. In the example given at the first of the chapter, it was the youngest child who started the fight, yet appears innocent. Rarely can a parent sift through an event to find the guilty person.

In the midst of one of my children's fights, I overheard my daughter say: "Don't do that, Patrick, . . .You know Dad will just send us both back to our rooms." Satisfied that parents could not be called in as judges or managers, the two dropped the fight. If left alone, children can usually settle their own problems. They prefer to have parental help, but intrusions from parents rob the child of the opportunity to practice the solving of personal disputes. The response of parents summoned to become the judge of a personal feud might commonly be: "I am sure you can handle this among yourselves." Given no easy way out, children will learn to settle their own affairs.

Fighting will never be eliminated in a household which encourages the expression of feelings and the establishment of autonomy. While my children were on vacation from school last Thanksgiving, I recorded this note in a moment of despair: "Patrick (7) and Emily (5) have now developed a new reason for fighting: boredom. They do not know what to do with all of the free time on their hands. So when Patrick cannot find anything to do, he pokes around until he finds one of Emily's sore spots. In an instant, excitement prevails. She willingly jumps into the war, unleashing all of her fury. Well, here we go. Back to the drawing board. No sooner is one set of challenges resolved than another appears."

Although fighting will always be present in families, it will be greatly reduced in homes where parents stand firmly behind family rules and refuse to be pulled into children's problems. In such families, children will begin slowly to replace fighting with cooperation.

Sibling rivalry is as natural to childhood as arguing is to senators. It is a part of childhood that allows children to learn how to get along with others. Children sharing ordinal positions often choose predictable ways to attack the world. Understanding these patterns of positive behavior and misbehavior will allow you to handle each child's behavior in ways that will benefit both the child and the family.

ALFRED ADLER

Dr. Alfred Adler was a creative genius whose theories may still contribute more useful advice to parents than those of any psychologist of his day. Born in Vienna in 1870, he received his M.D. from the University of Vienna Medical School.

Adler was always a man of the people. His early association with Sigmund Freud was often stormy and controversial. His psychology, in most ways, opposed the theories of Freud. Adler chose to develop a psychology of use. Purposefully, he kept his terminology simple and his concepts within comfortable grasp of the average person. In fact, it is likely that his was the first psychology used in schools. Also, he appears to be the first psychologist to use family therapy.

In 1932, Adler recognized the Nazi threat to the safety of Europe. He immigrated to the United States where he had previously lectured and taught. His theories were in perfect accord with the democracy he found in the United States. He believed strongly in social equality and freedom of choice. His ideas are so commonly used by people in the United States today that many are unaware of their founder. Adler died in 1937, during a lecture tour in Scotland. But this man of the people left behind a practical psychology which is used in homes throughout the world.

In 1954, Rudolf Dreikurs joined others influenced by Alfred Adler in creating the Alfred Adler Institute. For more information about either Dreikurs or Adler contact the Institute in care of 159 N. Dearborn Street, Chicago, Illinois, 60601-3597.

RELATED READINGS

Adler, A. (1954). *Understanding human nature*. New York: Garden City Publishing Company.

Adler, A. (1958). *Education of the individual*. Westport, CT: Greenwood.

Adler, A. (1958). *What life should mean to you*. New York: Capricorn Books.

Adler, A. (1963). *The problem child; the life style of the difficult child as analyzed in specific areas*. New York: Capricorn Books.

Ansbacher, H. & Ansbacher, R. (1956). *Individual psychology of Alfred Adler: A systematic presentation in selections from his writings*. New York: Harper and Row.

Ansbacher, H. & Ansbacher, R. (1964). *Superiority and social interest: A collection of later writings*. New York: Norton.

Corsini, R. (1973). *Current Psychotherapies*. Itasca, IL: Peacock.

Dinkmeyer, D., et al. (1979) *Adlerian counseling and psychotherapy*. Monterey, CA: Brooks/Cole.

Dreikurs, R. (1953). *Fundamentals of Adlerian psychology*. Chicago, IL: Alfred Adler Institute.

Mosak, H. (1973). *Alfred Adler: His influence on psychology today*. Park Ridge, NJ: Noyes Press.

Shulman, B. (1973). *Contributions to individual psychology*. Chicago, IL: Alfred Adler Institute.

Toman, W. (1976). *Family constellation: It's effects on personality and social behavior*. New York: Springer Publishing Company.

CHAPTER THREE

THE PREDICTABLE MISBEHAVIORS: BY AGE

THERE HE WAS, three and one-half years old, walking on top of a fence, and I was terrified! My wife was enthusiastically cheering him on, and all I wanted to do was go inside and hide. When I was young, anything that hinted of danger scared my mother into a frenzy. And here I was, at 33, with my stomach swelling into my lungs and my heart threatening to attack. Being trained in such areas, I knew the perfect parental response. I hid behind a bush by the driveway and pretended to dig fishing worms out of the concrete.

With every change of age, there is new challenge. And as a child rounds the corner to a new stage, she often enters territory that was difficult for her parents at that same age and now. Since I know of no perfect adults, I am confident that each of us has some soft spots that our child will poke from time to time. To follow one's child through the early years is to revisit our lives, year by year.

Unfortunately, many psychologists stress what can go wrong during the early years of a child's life. Parents looking at the negative possibilities find parenthood frightening and discouraging. One theorist, Erik Erikson, balances this negative approach by explaining the potential positive gains of children during their early years. By dwelling on the positive, parents can be more enthusiastic and less anxious about raising children. During the first ten years, it is possible to help a child develop the major life stances of trust, autonomy, initiative, and industry.

Each stage discussed below provides the opportunity to develop one of these attributes. Universally, children attempt to develop these same strengths at relatively the same age. To develop them, all children will experience needs which lead them to defy parents and often cause them to be angry and "out of sorts." Although these acts of growth are predictable misbehaviors, they are, in a sense, **positive misbehaviors,** which are the building blocks of strong personality formation. Positive misbehaviors provide parents the opportunity to teach children trust, autonomy, initiative, or industry. Because their occurrence is natural, they represent potential for growth. Positive misbehaviors should be distinguished from the negative misbehaviors discussed in Chapter One. Negative misbehaviors consist primarily of daily struggles rather than movement toward health within a certain stage.

Below follows a discussion of those stages which serve as the opportunities to create lifelong strengths in children. By looking at the positive goals of each stage, parents can gain confidence that all of their work has definite purpose. Looking at stage-related positive misbehavior as opportunities for parents to nurture positive attributes in their children removes the sting from the challenges of living with children.

The most important psychological gifts for children are free, unlike those to be found in toy stores. Parents from all backgrounds and from every economic class can give strength to their children. Americans cherish stories about men and women who become great contributors to the world, despite empoverished backgrounds. Usually, there is a parent or caretaker who provided the love and guidance that enabled the child to become successful. Every area of American life has contributed such success stories.

Think, for instance, about the story of Jackie Robinson, the first black baseball player to break the professional baseball color barrier. Although abandoned by her sharecropper husband, Jackie's mother worked at domestic jobs to support her five children. More importantly, she gave Jackie the optimism and courage needed to withstand years of discrimination and, often, hatred. Jackie left poverty to become a national hero. But he brought with him a personal strength instilled by a loving mother.

From the slums of Odense, Denmark, a young boy named Hans Christian Anderson emerged to become one of the world's most beloved authors. Although the father of Hans Christian Anderson lived in a one-room house, believed himself to be a failure for much of his life, and died when his son was eleven, he taught his son to dream. Biographers squabble about his father's contributions to his family, but Hans believed that the man who read stories to him at night and created puppet theaters for him sparked an imagination which has benefitted thousands of children.

In politics, Americans have known many who defeated poverty to win success. Most Americans can visualize a tall, skinny boy named

Abe Lincoln standing outside of a floorless wood cabin. To escape poverty, his family moved many times. Life was rough and often sad for the Lincolns. But, after all was said and done, one of our greatest presidents shared the secret of his success: the love of his stepmother. Sally Bush Lincoln's belief in Abe allowed him to beat the odds. The greatest gifts in life are truly free.

BIRTH TO ONE AND ONE-HALF: TRUST VS. MISTRUST

Strengths which last a lifetime can be given to children during each stage of childhood. The positive gift of the first one and one-half years is one of trust. Throughout those seemingly endless nights of little sleep for mother, and because of her love and care which conquered pyramids of diapers, dirty dishes, and soiled clothes, a positive feeling begins to grow in an infant. This feeling is one of trust — trust that others are loving and can be depended upon. This is a trust that will last a lifetime, a feeling which eventually will guide the infant toward trust in adult relationships and an optimistic view of the meaning of life.

How do babies learn to trust their parents? There is no gene which teaches them to trust. Instead, trust is learned through daily living. Babies know nothing of life. They search their parents' faces for a sign of what it is to be human. Have you ever looked down at a baby in your arms to find her eyes searching yours? She studies you as if you held all of the answers to life's questions. And in these early moments of her infancy, you do! Most parents respond to a child's smile with a loving dedication. A relationship is sealed. Parents willingly meet the child's need for food, sleep, comfort, and love, and an early cooperation grows.

As trust develops, it is as if the caretaker and child form a partnership like an Olympic ice skating pair. They flow together across the days. Each learns to anticipate and depend upon the movements of the other. Certainly, there are bad days, days often filled with exhaustion. Tempers flare; mistakes are made. Perfection is not possible, nor is it the goal. Despite problems, the child and parent are working together, anticipating the enjoyable moves to come. Trust has developed among the partners of infancy.

It was one of those days we all experience as parents. Our three-year-old suffered from croup for the third straight night. When he did sleep quietly, the baby awoke, either hungry or wet. Everyone was exhausted and nerves were strained. As the day ended, I felt somewhat depressed and sorry for myself. Patty was feeding the baby. With red eyes, caused half by tears and half by exhaustion, she looked up and said, "You know these children have given me more than I will ever be able to return." As a father out of rhythm, I realized I had a wife still in rhythm. No words ever meant so much to me. She was right. But only a trusting mother in concert with her children could feel gratitude in those desolate moments.

It is true that some parents are unable to create a sense of positive rhythm with a child. The gift of trust can be lost. But for most of these parents, personal needs and limitations are so extreme that the child becomes secondary in the parent's life. If the child is looked upon not as an addition to life but as an interruption—a handicap—then the infant faces difficult days where needs for love and closeness are rarely met.

Instead of resembling the confidence felt by Olympic pairs skaters, one finds untrusting relationships that resemble anxious beginning skaters who fear the ice. Their dancing is awkward. There is no sense of joy in the daily progress; instead there is an anticipation of failure. Mistrustful people tend to expect the worst from life and from others. When expected, the worst often happens.

In a class for unwed teenage mothers, I found a woman who anticipated nothing but misery in life. Nothing was ever right for her. The baby kept her up at night. Her parents, with whom she lived, were too demanding. She could not spend enough time with her boyfriend because her baby was sick so often. She saw only the negative in life. On one occasion, parents brought their children to class. While other mothers played and loved their infants, this mother sat like a statue. Her baby's cries were responded to with anger, which created more tears. The parent and child worked against each other. Yes, this young mother had tough challenges to meet in life, and she was meeting them poorly. There was no rhythm in this relationship. Both parties suffered from the awkwardness.

Trust and mistrust are seen in the familiar story of the two brothers who awakened on Christmas morning and were told their Christmas present was outside. One ran outside and stepped in some manure. He yelled his complaint to the heavens: "Only I could have something this terrible happen on Christmas day!" His brother stepped in the manure at the same moment, but yelled: "My gosh! Where is the pony?"

The mistrustful parent sees infancy as a procession of headaches that will cause unhappiness for them; but trustful parents view infancy as a parade of rewarding interactions. Within the daily problems, there is a positive and purposeful spirit maintained. There are hundreds of events in a child's first years that are a cause for celebration in the lives of families.

Today, people are not waiting until after the birth of a child to begin establishing the foundations for trust. Thousands of people have now experienced unique attachment to a child during the birth process. Parents are making birth an integral part of family experience through innovative programs.

Today, studies are indicating that when parents engage in prepared childbirth classes or programs based on the ideas of such men as Frederick Leboyer (gentle birth), or Fernand Lamaze (Lamaze classes), or Grantly Dick-Read, the mothers experience less painful deliveries and appear to create closer bonds with their infants. But you do not need studies to confirm this feeling of closeness. Participation in such classes had become commonplace. Almost anyone involved in special childbirth classes will champion their merits. Even fathers who were a bit skeptical about watching the delivery become enthusiasts during and following the experience. Nothing is comparable to seeing the birth of one's own child. Working together before and during the birth of a child appears to give families a head start on cooperation and, perhaps, closeness.

Other small events of the first months of a child's life are potential occasions for closeness. Early cooing, rolling over, watching mobiles, sitting up, crawling after the cat, playing peek-a-boo, laughing at tickles, and identifying animals in books are but a few of the multitude of wonders present during this stage.

During the first eighteen months, a child will usually take her first step and say her first word. During this period, parents may worry whether their child will ever start talking. But as long as the child understands what is said to her, problems are rare. In fact, by the child's third birthday many parents will begin wondering whether the formerly wordless child will ever stop talking. All of these events are key movements in the excitement of the first stages of life.

Often an unusual moment cements the bond between a parent and child. How happily I remember the first time my oldest child looked across the room, recognized me, and smiled just at his Dad. It was not one of those first month baby smiles caused by the passing of gas. Instead, it was a genuine "I-Thou" smile that began a new stage in our father-child relationship.

Not all of the songs of infancy are as friendly to the ear. There are challenges to parents. It is sometimes difficult to keep focused on the major issue of the stage: to develop trust. Exhaustion seems to be a shared characteristic for all young parents. Nights during the early months are filled with feeding, changing, and sometimes doctoring crying infants. Many were the days I lectured, early in the morning, to childless college students about the joys of parenthood while more coffee than blood ran in my veins.

Lost sleep for parents during the early months of a child's life probably cannot be avoided. But after four months or so, parents will face a major decision. Between four and six months after the baby's birth, parents begin to distinguish between those cries which show need — for food, diaper changes, and/or medical attention — and those cries that demand a midnight bingo partner. When babies awake at night, they know no rules. Certainly, a baby will enjoy having mom or dad around to perform light entertainment at 3 a.m. Like an adult whose favorite show is preempted by a presidential speech, babies will often voice strong disapproval with any postponement.

What should parents do? Loss of sleep is often very damaging to the parents' daily life, as well as to the relationship between parents. How can parents help a child help them sleep through the night, without violating the trust built between them? Many forcefully believe that one should never let a child cry at night unattended. Such parents fear that an early trauma may delay the child or fixate the child in early development. I have found no evidence of this. Nevertheless, if a parent is good at sacrificing sleep and can maintain a strong marriage, quality work, and a level head in the daytime after sleep loss, then I see nothing wrong with the Early Trauma Avoidance Approach.

Personally, I prefer the Early Family Survival Method. Here, a parent decides that four things will survive only if sleep is adequate: each parent, the marriage, and the child. A baby can learn to entertain herself at night. In fact, it is important for a child to learn such independence, to realize: "I woke up. No big deal. It's dull in this empty room. I'll play for a while, then go back to sleep." Children need to develop the confidence to handle nighttime waking moments without help.

My experience has been that it takes at least three days to help a child help you sleep through the night. The first night with the first child is often difficult. After checking the child for any problems, she is returned to bed. Awareness of the loss of nocturnal playmates causes screaming to begin. It may last an hour or longer. When we trained our first child, I recall my muscles were tense, and each second made moments in a dentist's chair seem playful. My wife and I dared neither to talk nor breathe.

Our child's crying soon was without tears, but then it burst up and down in giant spurts, like a museum fountain. Finally, sleep came to the child and to us.

The next morning found the adults exhausted and fearful. I remember trying to eat cereal and drink from a glass without injuring myself, when our son awoke as if nothing had happened. I wasn't sure whether to be pleased that there seemed to be no trauma or angry at myself for overestimating the impact of the training. The second night, the crying was reduced to half an hour, the third, to fifteen minutes. On the fourth, he and we slept through the night.

Like all discipline in the home, helping a child help you sleep through the night is a team performance. The parents must sacrifice a few nights' sleep and have the courage to be resolute. If one parent weakens, then the night's work is lost and harder nights loom ahead.

The use of such techniques does become easier in time. When our third child was ready to surrender his nocturnal playtime, we felt like old pros. What a contrast from our experience with the first child! Instead of tensely holding our breath through every second, we were able to make the most of a long evening. We picked a series of days when sleep could be sacrificed. On the first night of training, we played cards by candlelight. Instead of being miserable in bed, we tried to make the evening reasonably enjoyable. Three nights of blackjack did the trick. And we were all the better for it.

Regulating the time of a child's waking and the length of nap times are also important in training a child to sleep. Many caretakers encourage long naps during the day and wonder why the child does not sleep well at night. Like adults who take naps or sleep late into the mornings, the child is simply not tired. There must be some experimentation in juggling naps and waking times with nighttime sleep.

For example, frequently, children who use daycare facilities encounter sleeping difficulties. Marcia was a young working mother whose three-and-one-half year old did not go to sleep until midnight. Although Marcia tried all of the appropriate techniques to encourage good sleeping habits, they failed. When asked how long the child was allowed to nap at the sitter's, she did not know. Marcia investigated the situation and returned the next week to tell the class that the sitter allowed her child to sleep from 10:00 in the morning until 2:30 in the afternoon. Obviously, the sitter found it easier to have the child asleep than to care for her, but the sitter's approach left the parents with a child who was not tired enough to sleep at night. Caretakers need to fit into the parents' strategy for raising a healthy child, rather than parents conforming to a caretaker's preference. Only after the sitter's habits were changed was Marcia's family able to establish a sane schedule.

Of course, need for brief retraining occurs after the child has shared your companionship (through necessity) during illness or because of the complications of traveling to grandparents' or others' homes. Somehow, visits to relatives always seem to throw a child's rhythm into chaos. No matter how everyone tries to keep on schedule, returning from the visit occasions the same feeling one has after dropping a completed 5,000-piece jigsaw puzzle. All order seems lost.

Our first disastrous trip to a relative's house occurred when our oldest child was two, and we visited his grandparents. His schedule was working beautifully. He went to sleep at 7:30 and awoke about 7:30 the next morning. All of the relatives were visiting at the same time. For the first time, Patrick was old enough to enjoy the excitement. Supper was put off until well past eight. With candy and enjoyment flowing, Patrick remained wide-awake until midnight. Nevertheless, as children will, he awoke at his usual time. By noon, he was a two-footed monster. A three-hour nap followed, and he was ready for another late night. This short vacation gave him a new schedule that disoriented all of our personal routines. It took a week to retrain him. Although we declared this chaos would never occur again, it did occur on most long visits. Nothing demands more energy from parents than the week after a "relaxing" trip to relatives or friends.

There is family conversation from time to time about whether a child should be allowed to sleep in bed with parents. Since my children are standard child sleepers, sprawling sideways in a configuration that puts their tiny feet in my ribs, I have never had much conflict over the dilemma. If children are allowed into bed with parents as young children, there may be a grave danger that parents will not share a bed as the child grows older. Children have a large place in parents' lives, but one rather small space in the middle of the parents' bed should be excluded. Nothing is more important to parents than their continued intimate relationship. An observer in a parent's bed detracts from intimacy.

Marcia and Jim Laney shared a beautiful and cooperative relationship before the birth of their first child. As I talked to them about the problems that had developed during the thirteen months after their child's birth, it was obvious that their life together was tense. Sensing a source of their difficulty, I asked directly, "How's sex between you?" Both turned pale.

When their child was three months old, the parents began to allow her to sleep with them. In fact, to protect the child from falling out of bed, she was placed between the parents. The child seemed to awaken with even the slightest disturbance. Attempts to return her to bed ended in tirades. At thirteen months, she could walk to their room and crawl into bed. Sex between the parents soon ended. But both enjoyed sex. Both missed it. Both were somewhat angry at the child for interfering and with each other for not devising a solution. But neither was willing to discuss sexual frustration openly. Sex should be discussed freely. Due to normal exhaustion, parents may experience less sexual interaction, but sexuality should be an outlet, not a source of tension. Marcia and Jim experienced other problems adjusting to a family of three. However, once the child was trained to use her own bed, Marcia and John's sexual life improved. For them, it was a giant step toward increased family happiness.

Soon after a sleeping pattern is established, a second challenge confronts the parents. This is called the "eight-month anxiety," or "stranger anxiety" period. I prefer to call it "Grandmom's Despair." At about eight months, the child begins to prize the major caretaker's face. Only those who raise her are known. It is a marvelous feeling as you hold her in your arms to see her study your face a second or so, recognize it, and smile. But if an unfamiliar person holds her she will, after some scrutiny, burst into tears. The tears occur simply because questions are not possible. At this age she is unable to inquire: "Pardon me, my dearest Dad, I request to know: who belongs to the massive face with the cold hands and beady eyes?"

At this point, grandparents' feelings often are crushed. It seems so unfair! After all, grandparents raised their own children and now may claim to have raised as many as fifty neighborhood children whom you never met. So certainly it would seem that a lovingly raised child should recognize the relatives' bloodline, experience, and love. But the child does not, and many grandparents reach the only available, but incorrect, conclusion: "You're spoiling her! She's just a 'mother's/father's girl' and will never be normal." Parents rarely need, but often get, this type of erroneous criticism from their own parents.

Stranger anxiety is not a misbehavior. Far from it; it is a sign of the healthy mental growth of your child. Stranger anxiety is common to almost all children and will last as long as one year. Time is the best cure for stranger anxiety. Parents need not worry about it. The days will remove these tears. As a child becomes more verbal and develops skills to handle strangers, anxiety will end. But this takes time. Don't push it!

When Grandmother looks angrily at your child for showing her the tears of stranger anxiety, smile and realize all is well because this is positive misbehavior!

Soon after the appearance of stranger anxiety, another challenge confronts the trusting relationship between caretakers and their children. Separation anxiety develops. I prefer to think of it as the Baby Sitter Plague or the Parents' Prison Syndrome. At this time, the child demands the presence of its parents in the home.

Parents need to maintain their own relationship during a child's second year. But when a babysitter arrives, the child may scream, yell, choke, pass out, and dissolve before the parents leave the front door. On the adults' first night out, the child's cries often are responded to by an avalanche of parental feeling—guilt. The guilt blocks the sidewalk to the car as parents freeze and listen to the child's screams. Brave parents continue on their way and are better for it. Fearful parents return to the child and plant the seed of another generation of fear: that to be separated from loved ones is a tragedy from which one cannot recover. To develop trust in her capabilities, a child must develop confidence in her own ability to handle life's difficult challenges. By leaving her, parents show the child their confidence in her ability to handle the situation.

If a doctor's standard recommendation is to take two aspirin and call in the morning, counselors may often suggest to loving and highly involved parents: "Take two babysitters and call me in two weeks." Once parents are out of the house, they should keep walking toward health. Babysitters often can enhance a marriage as quickly as the best of marriage counselors. Most loving parents want to be with their children and will spend hours playing with them. But time for a marriage is equally essential and less plentiful. Be kind to your children, and take time for your marriage.

John and Sally were concerned. Their six-year-old, Jack, hated to go to school and had no close friends. Jack had a three-year-old sister, Paula, whom he alternated loving and hating. In the course of conversation, I asked how James and Paula reacted to babysitters. Sally's response was, "Oh, we don't use babysitters. You see, very early, Jack threw such violent tantrums when we tried to leave that it just wasn't worth the effort. So we decided to stay at home with them until they are older. We will have plenty of time together then." By giving in to Jack's fears, the parents never allowed him to trust in his own ability to handle life. In a sense, his parents were literally present at all times to attend to his problems. The cost of surrendering to Jack's separation anxiety was to sacrifice his basic sense of self-trust in new situations and with new people. Both marriages and children will be stronger when parents spend time away from home. Be reasonable in your time away from children, but also be fair to the family — take time together outside of the home.

The solution for separation anxiety is, once again, the passing of days. At around two years of age, self-confidence usually has overcome this anxiety. But for fearful parents who hover over their children, separation anxiety will continue longer than necessary. Rough days still loom ahead.

For parents who can keep their sights on trust, the days of lost sleep and constant care will be purposeful. The first years may be demanding, but the resulting gift of trust given to a child is one that has no equal.

AUTONOMY VS. SHAME AND DOUBT: NO! (1½-3 YEARS)

The most important word in becoming a unique individual is "NO!" Between eighteen months and twenty-four months of age, a child decides she wants to be her own person, not a part of her parents' will. "NO!" is a marvelous declaration of independence that is shouted by the child up and down the hallways, through restaurants, churches, grocery stores, and other public places.

Of all the exasperating positive misbehaviors, this declaration "NO!" may be the most challenging to parents. For almost two years the children were totally dependent, but now they can literally stand on their own two feet. At the same time, they want to think for themselves, do things for themselves, and become their own person. To become autonomous, the child must rebel. Like a revolutionary, the child will break all rules of fair play and logic. For the parent, a child's striving means being pressured constantly to stay out of power struggles. Many conflicts are avoidable. Some are not.

Recently, my three-year-old and I investigated a waterfall near the college. The path beside the stream was slippery and dangerous for children. My son decided he wanted to walk by himself without help, not understanding the danger. When I reached for his hand, he withdrew it vehemently. Students from the college were present and it was tempting to allow him to have his way to avoid a scene. But to do so would be wrong. I said, "Either hold my hand or I will have to pick you up." He exclaimed knowingly, "No, neither!" I picked him up and the yelling began. Although it would have been nice to sidestep conflict in this situation, it would have been dangerous to do so. Sometimes parents must resist a child's will. But in many other cases, they do not. Alternative techniques can be used. For example, power can be softened through game playing and humor.

Parent: "Mary, it's time for your bath, please jump in!"
Mary: "NO! NO! NO!"
Parent: "Mary, I'm going to cover my eyes and count to ten and when I open my eyes I don't want anyone in the bathtub!"
Child: Splash

Such techniques have worked for years. Not only are these games enjoyable, but everyone comes out a winner. Some parents enjoy fighting more than playing games and will not be attracted to peaceful methods. That is a pity. So many confrontations face parents at this stage of their child's life that it is best not to engage in skirmishes that can be avoided.

A frequent battleground for autonomy that concerns parents is toilet training. Many parents throw themselves headlong into a fight to make the child "go potty" at a very early age. Parents should relax. Allow the child to train herself. All normal adults learned that it is easier to leave one's rejections in the "potty chair." It takes some children longer than others to acknowledge it. Not one of my colleagues — at least that I know of — goes home after a lecture to be changed. Time takes care of many of life's challenges more effectively than all of the arguing, prodding, and bribing by parents. Time is the greatest ally of parents; yet it is one of their strengths that is least often used. Even I hate to write this age-old maxim in regard to toilet training, but: relax parents, for this, too, will pass.

The search for autonomy can bring a child to battle with his caretaker on almost any battleground: bedtimes, seat belts, meals, toilet training, or countless other fronts. Later chapters will give direct suggestions on how to handle such power contests. But the major point for now is never to lose sight of the primary purpose of the child's struggles with you: she wishes to be independent. In the midst of a child's challenges, it is not important to win the confrontations, but it is important to handle them in a manner that will help the child gain or retain the confidence that she herself can accomplish things. If a parent can handle these challenges in a productive way, then the second great gift of childhood is given to the child: a secure and proud feeling of autonomy.

When forming autonomy, a child must separate from the parent. For most adults, this is a difficult and challenging period. Rewards for doing a good job are few. The greatest satisfaction comes after a child has completed a project or solved a task. At that time, the child will often look proudly toward the parent and utter the motto of autonomous children: "Look! I did it myself."

INITIATIVE VS. GUILT: TO CLIMB A TREE OR NOT TO CLIMB A TREE (3-5 YEARS)

Our son Patrick once went up to a rough-looking motorcycle gang member in a bus station and asked, "How did you get that ugly scar across your face?" Patrick was sincerely interested in the answer. I was sincerely interested in wondering whether my body was about to be jammed into one of the station's footlockers.

What Patrick did was not a negative misbehavior. He did not make the inquiry in order to get me murdered. He was simply exploring the world around him. Children will say anything and try everything during this stage. It is their task to test their boundaries. They are like Icarus, the character in mythology, whose new wax wings allowed him to explore the skies, but when he flew too high the sun melted his wings and back to earth he fell.

Our children are like Icarus. They have new wings, and they want to test them. They want to fly. Often, they will come too close to danger and tumble back into our arms in tears, defeat, and even stitches. It is the parent's task to encourage them to fly once again, maybe a little wiser for the fall.

Fearful parents raise fearful children. Fear is like a disease and it is transmitted through waves of potential anxiety. Fearful of the bruises of childhood, parents may hover over a child. Soon this child also begins to imagine all that can go wrong with life. Fearful parents adroitly think of "seventy-three dozen" reasons why it would be better not to take a child to a circus, or movie, or football game, or on vacation. Such adults stay close to home and cling to safety. In doing so, they experience only a limited number of the pleasures that are waiting to be plucked by those who exhibit confidence and initiative.

Marcia Harrison's daughter Victoria knew few victories in life. Marcia was a constant worrier. In the parent study classes, she could always imagine what might go wrong with any strategy devised to lead a child to increased initiative. Her lack of courage was evident in the response made by such people to new ideas or suggestions: "Yes, but what if this or that happens?" Marcia not only "Yes, butted" challenges, but she also "Yes, butted" life.

Often, I had occasion to watch Marcia and her daughter perform their ritual of anxiety. The mother scattered a litany of warnings to the child: "Don't climb that tree; you might fall down." "Don't run on the sidewalk; you might skin a knee." "Don't pat that cat; he might scratch you." "Don't go into the woods; they are filled with poison ivy." "Don't lift that rock; snakes might live there."

Victoria lived a safe and sheltered life. She learned to be error-free by never taking chances. She did excel when faced with low-risk challenges. For example, she read early, dressed well, and was often polite. But she never experienced the wonder of childhood. She adopted her mother's fear of the woods, snakes, animals, and action. She was a child who read about the world but never fully experienced it. Her lack of childhood excitement was a grave price to pay for an anxiety handed down from generation to generation.

It needs to be emphasized that training a child in this stage is extremely difficult. There is always tension created at making choices between what is safe and what is dangerous. Clearly, if the child is endangering herself or others the behavior must be restricted. Climbing a tree has its dangers, but is a worthy risk of childhood. Climbing an electrical tower is obviously dangerous and is to be forbidden. The difficult challenge for both parents and child at this stage is to distinguish between what can be hazardous and what is normally not. Parents must find their own answers to this. There can be no general list of guidelines.

If a family has two caretakers, they may differ in their concern about which activities may harm a child. Such division presents little confusion for a child. She may learn that "When I'm with Mom, I can slide by myself and try to skate on the driveway, but when I'm with Dad, I must swing low and stay close by." Often, couples realize when one parent is less fearful, and at such times, it is easier for the more confident one to take charge.

For example, I am pitifully frightened of some types of dogs. The kind that scare me the most are those with teeth. I've had several losing encounters with the jaws of canines. Dogs either bite me or make love publicly to my kneecaps. Either way, the results have summoned formidable anxiety in me. Fortunately, my wife loves dogs and seems able to calm the most vicious mongrel. Ours is a clear example of when such an agreement on the subject of taking charge benefits the children. If we are taking a family walk and a dog approaches on my side, I immediately walk around my wife. She models positive behavior with the dog and distracts the children from my unproductive fear. I realize my fear is inappropriate, and to pass it to our children would be as criminal as a dog owner yelling to a jogger, "Don't worry, Killer will only bite if he senses fear."

There are cases, however, when parents may disagree and the fearful one proves to be correct. One couple I counseled owned an airplane, and the dad insisted on flying with the four-year-old in his lap. At times, the mother grew particularly frightened when the child was given total "control" of the plane. In this case, there existed a disagreement which resisted resolution. But it might be sensible, if a genuine disagreement exists, for the bolder parent to model the courage to compromise. Continued disagreements in a variety of areas may symbolize a growing disharmony in parental philosophy that might be greatly lessened with the help of a marriage and family counselor.

Another realm in which a child's initiative must be restricted is when he or she begins to interfere with the rights of others. All of us have been miffed by parents who allowed their child to do whatever she wishes, no matter what the consequences might be. Such children run wild during movies, charge up and down the aisles of meetings, and scream and cry in restaurants. All this occurs without any apparent adult restriction or concern.

Initiative needs to be encouraged, but only with consideration of the rights of others. Children this age are not naturally sensitive to others. Therefore, this is an area parents must often work on with their children at home—not in the restaurant, movie, or store. Although action-oriented techniques will be discussed later, as a general rule, parents should discuss expected behavior before entering a public place or visiting friends. If a child violates agreements, the child should be removed, without a lecture, from the situation. In this way, a child is allowed to exhibit initiative, but not aggression.

Occasionally one finds parents who are extremely threatened by the initiative of a child. They mistake the positive misbehavior for negative and useless misbehavior. Instead of working with the hope of encouraging initiative, they labor with the goal of suppressing the child's spirit. In one extreme case, I recall a parent I worked with who kept her child on a stake and chain so he would not "get into things" while she cleaned inside the house. When she related her practice to me, my well trained counseling facade betrayed me, and I showed surprise. Immediately, she assured me, "But I give him ten feet of chain." Similar sights, such as children on leashes in shopping centers, are not infrequent.

There are those who chain the body, and there are those who chain the spirit. Those who restrict and break the spirit do equal, if not more insidious, damage. Spirit enslavers always discourage children when children dream. "I'd like to fly to Mars and be an astronaut," imagines a four-year-old. "That's stupid," says the adult. "No one can live on Mars." Adults often are buried in facts. They lose the message of the child because they evaluate it rather than listen to it.

A neighborhood boy named Jackson somehow lost the playful luster so evident in children's eyes. He seemed apathetic, almost lifeless. Although he played with other children, he was always a follower. While others developed imaginary games with exciting plots and characters, he seemed to be more like a stagehand awaiting directions. One day I noticed that Jackson was taking part in a game with increased enthusiasm. As the day grew later, his parents drove by to take Jackson home. Apparently his play made him late for supper.

Despite the fact other parents were around, Jackson's mother immediately began to attack the youngster, "Where have you been? You are fifteen minutes late." Jackson replied, "I've been playing house with my friends." The mother retorted, "That is stupid. Boys shouldn't play house. You have got to stop wasting your time. Besides there is work to be done at home. You'll do it tonight before you go to bed. Now get in the car." Childhood is a time to dream and play. But this mother had not patience or time for imagination. She only understood the necessity for daily order. No wonder the light deserted Jackson's eyes.

Children need their dreams. Young people should plan trips, suggest silly places to eat, tell creative stories, and think of the impossible. To deny a child a dream is to deny a child a vision for the future. Never should a child be limited by ridicule and criticism. Adults, instead, should encourage the play and imaginations of children who follow a spirit not yet limited by life. Life itself will provide the necessary limitations to a child's dreams. It is up to parents to help keep the impossible probable.

Through actions and dreams, a child pushes the boundaries of life right up to the classroom door. Once she enters, she can develop those skills that will allow her to become her dreams.

ACCOMPLISHMENT VS. INFERIORITY: SCHOOL DAYS (5-11 YEARS)

There is far too much failure in our classrooms. William Glasser and Rudolph Dreikurs pointed this out decades ago. Yet, it still exists. The child of a friend of mine came home with a report card with 3 As, 6 Bs, and a D in math. The friend's immediate response was: "Why can't you do better in math?" The child hung his head and said: "I hate math..." After a moment, he added, "I think I hate school."

Like camera crews rushing to a catastrophe, concerned parents often are drawn to the weakness in their children's work. By dwelling on what is "wrong," they mistakenly emphasize failure. The result is the lowered head of a child who feels he is not good enough to succeed.

As Dreikurs correctly pointed out, children only grow through emphasizing the positive. Let's take the case mentioned above and rewind the cameras. How different the child's attitude would be if the parent said: "How marvelous to see how much you're enjoying school. Maybe someday you will enjoy math as much as your other subjects." No mention of the D in math is needed. The child is more aware of the problem than anyone else is. If encouraged, he may become more interested in math.

To emphasize the negative simply does not work. For example, how would you react if you were in a second marriage and, after sex, your spouse said, "You do better than my first spouse in everything but in bed. Why can't you do better here?" I doubt you would respond as the spouse may wish by saying, "Oh yes, I guess I could do better. I'll try harder tomorrow." Adults and children are similar in emotions and feelings. For most adults, pointing to their weaknesses rather than their strengths causes hostility and poor feelings. The same is true of children.

Early school years find the child surrounded with many possibilities, both for establishing competence or for failing. These years find the child challenged to read, learn mathematics, use computers, and build hundreds of academic skills. Socially, peers provide a constant testing ground for new interpersonal skills. Today, basic skills in sports are also being taught in these early years.

Encouragement from parents, as Dreikurs and Glasser note, is the main diet for children facing new challenges. If parents could treat every challenge as they did when their child first learned to ride a bicycle, then, in most cases, children would prosper. Remember that first bicycle! It was evident that the child wanted to do well. Equally, it was evident that it would require many falls and considerable frustration before the first successful ride.

Parents never consider discouraging a child in learning such a difficult activity. Every attempt is greeted with enthusiasm and cheers. Falls are taken in stride. Intrinsically, parents seem to know that the fall is penalty enough and should be ignored as a temporary setback. Naturally, the parents encourage the child to try again. Thus, the child tries repeatedly. Parents almost always take time to help and to show interest in the accomplishment without pushing or prodding. Parents know never to make comparisons in this particular circumstance.

Never have I heard a parent say, "Why can't you learn to ride as easily as your sister did?" There is an acknowledgement that the task is important and a confidence that it will be learned. Ironically, many parents find that, after all the time spent by parent and child with the bicycle, it is a neighborhood child who finally leads the child to success.

Children, if encouraged, will learn to read, to solve math problems, and to master other skills. Like riding a bicycle, there will be falls and setbacks, but success will come. The parents' proper stance is always enthusiasm, encouragement, and allowing time for helping. The skills learned in school are too complex for parents to push a child. Criticism of mistakes has no place in the learning process. Encouragement to try again has.

Two traits in some parents cause unnecessary problems for children: pride and ambition. Both traits cause parents to expect their children to excel rather than succeed. To excell means a constant evaluation of the abilities of children in comparison to others or to a mythical standard. Thus, the child is no longer thought of as in the process of learning to read but is considered to be ahead or behind the average child in the class. When such comparisons are made, the child often teeters on the brink of failure rather than on the threshold of success.

As a traveling tennis instructor in North Carolina, I worked with young players participating in tournaments around the state. One nine-year-old boy with exceptional potential was ranked in the top five in the state within his age group. His parents followed him to every tournament. His father sat behind the fence and questioned each shot selected. On two occasions, the dad stormed onto the court as the players were changing sides and berated his son for not trying harder.

Toward the end of the summer, the young boy began to look old and weary. He was tense and angry. None of his peers enjoyed him. His parents were overambitious. They did not want a son who was very good and enjoyed the sport. Instead they wanted a star. As the summer wore away, so did the young man's tennis. Players accused him of cheating. He was afraid losing would bring further criticism from parents. The next year, he did not appear at the tournament. His peers reported that his dad had forbidden him to play tennis again after he lost in the state tournament. "But," they reported, "he has a sister who plays well. Now they follow her around."

Young children experience stress that is largely unknown to their parents. The media brings violence, sex, and controversy into the home each day. Over 40 percent of all school children must adjust to living with a single parent who is trying miraculously to create a meaningful life in the hardest of situations. The economy often forces parents to work full-time and to live in a pressure cooker of bills, mortgages, and taxes. If children are not allowed to enjoy learning (such as they did when discovering success on a bicycle), a child's stress is increased. At best, children under stress become more temperamental, demanding, and perfectionistic. At worst, they become classroom losers — discouraged and withdrawn.

Parents who are confident in their own academic ability seem to understand children will be successful if encouraged. Both of my parents have advanced degrees from Yale. As a child, I never heard criticism of my work, although in elementary school I was the worst academically of the children in my family. My parents always showed interest in my pursuits. Never was there a need to compare me to my siblings. I was well aware of my poor status. After stumbling about for five grades, I was "turned on" to learning, finally, by a magnificent sixth grade teacher. The patience and confidence of my parents allowed this to happen.

I am convinced that each child creates images of her parents which influence her behavior for a lifetime. Sometimes we model after these images, and at other times, we strive to do the opposite. I can still see my parents after supper. Mother would be reading on the sofa while Dad typed in his study. I would walk into the scene and say to my mother, "I did lousy on the test today. So did everyone else." Still, I can hear her reply, "I don't care how anyone else did. If you did your best, that's all that counts." Their patience allowed me to find a teacher who showed me what my best could be. Their confidence gave me the opportunity to enjoy learning, rather than see it as an obstacle always ready to defeat me.

In this present era, I fear many parents who have an underachieving child try to find a physical cause. Too often, such children are given a label which may not truly fit, such as "learning disabled." There are children who are truly learning disabled and benefit from special attention yet others may simply be "learning delayed," as I was. Others may be "encouragement deprived." Unfortunately, the label may be one which prevents later "turn ons."

When an elementary school child carries the scarlet badge of LD (Learning Disabled) or ED (Emotionally Disturbed) or whatever, it may become a part of her identity and reputation. The labels may help a few truly disabled children, but for others they become a symbol of the increased stress placed on children whose parents and teachers push them to excel in this anxious age of ours.

Children are aware of the labels attached to their peers. However, they do not understand psychological rationale for labels such as LD or ED. Instead, they have their own interpretations of why people are removed from the regular classroom and given a label. Their impressions are often cruel. During the first month of school one year, I overheard neighborhood children talking about various members of the second grade class: "Yeah, Tommy (Learning Disabled) is in the dumb class. They're only doing first grade reading. We did those books last year. He must be really stupid." This was followed by a heartbreaking discussion about an ED child. "Jerome is in the ED class. I know that because he rides the school bus in from downtown. He always wears dirty clothes. Almost all of those kids bused in are in the crazy class."

The marvelous writer, Heim Ginnott, taught that "labeling is disabling." Nowhere can this be seen more clearly than in the school system. It is difficult for adults not to categorize children who are labeled as learning disabled or emotionally disturbed. But it is almost impossible for children to fully understand the implications. Once dropped into a childhood pigeonhole, it is tough for a child to make the climb back out.

If properly encouraged, children will become industrious. They will believe they can be successful in life by making positive contributions. If children become discouraged through criticism, pressure, and perceived failure, they may turn from the positive side of life. Those who suffer from inferiority need a gimmick to make them feel as important as successful individuals. Some turn to drugs, others to chronic misbehavior, and some to crime. The cost of failure is too high in our society. As adults, we must provide a safe, encouraging atmosphere that will foster success in our children.

Erik Erikson's ideas allow parents to have confidence in the face of healthy misbehavior. It is not only normal for children to misbehave in predictable ways at certain ages, but it is also essential for proper growth. The "perfect" children are not the ones that never misbehave, but the ones whose parents can guide them through the rough days to a sense of trust, autonomy, initiative, and industry.

Few of the outstanding people in our world were considered to be perfect angels as children. The same may be true of our children. Friends, teachers, and relatives may all criticize our children for their shortcomings. But if a strong foundation is laid and parents continue to support their children, then life can be lived to its fullest.

The biographies of Abraham Lincoln carry fascinating observations from neighbors and relatives who seem unified in their criticism of the young boy for his lack of desire to work. Said one, "He worked for me, (but) was always reading and thinking. . .I used to get mad at him. . .I say Abe was awful lazy. He would laugh and talk and crack jokes and tell stories all the time. . .didn't love work but did dearly love his pay. . .Lincoln said to me one day that his father taught him to work but never learned him to love it." (Beveridge, 1982).

But Lincoln had the basics, and later in his career, he looked back at his stepmother who had placed so much faith in him despite his imperfections and said, "All that I am or ever hope to be, I owe to my angel mother."

The goal of childhood is not perfect behavior but the development of trust, autonomy, initiative, and industriousness. No matter how rich or poor, successful or unsuccessful a parent may feel, the most important gifts they can give to a child are absolutely free.

ERIK H. ERIKSON

Erik Erikson has been the leading theorist in child development throughout the last half of the twentieth century. His life story proves fascinating reading in itself. Born in 1902 of Danish parents, he soon finished regular schooling and began traveling throughout Europe. His travels gave him time to consider how he might best fit into and contribute to the world. Although his family was not without wealth,

Erikson partially supported himself and fulfilled his creative needs by painting portraits.

As fate would have it, while touring Austria, Erikson met Sigmund Freud. As he painted a portrait of Freud's child, the two men entered into conversations which eventually led Erikson to join Freud at the Vienna Psychoanalytic Institute. He graduated from the Institute in 1933. Only this chance meeting between two great men of different generations enabled the world to benefit from Erikson's developmental ideas.

Erikson left Vienna to join the faculty of Harvard Medical School in 1934. From there, his research led him to Yale University (1936-1939), the University of California (1939-1951), and Austen Riggs Center. In 1950, his book **Childhood and Society** captured the minds of psychologists around the world and is now available in ten languages. It was in this text that he first outlined the stages discussed in this chapter. The impact of his theory was clearly seen as early as 1950, when the White House Conference on Children totally adopted Erikson's stages as accurately describing the stages of childhood and adolescence development.

In 1960, Erikson joined Harvard University as a Professor of Human Development. The appointment was intriguing because Erikson's education and training, although excellent, led to none of the official degrees so valued in American academic life. Erik Erikson became a full professor at Harvard and the leading child developmentalist in the world, without an M.D., Ph.D., or even an undergraduate degree. Erikson's notoriety has continued through the years. In 1969, his work **Ghandi's Truth** won the Pulitzer Prize and the National Book Award. Many books followed. Erik Erikson's life as well as his theories have taught the American people valuable lessons about the development and spirit of humankind.

RELATED READINGS

Beveridge, A. (1928). *Abraham Lincoln 1809-1858*. Cambridge: The Riverside Press.
Dick-Read. G. (1972). *Childbirth without fear: The original approach to natural childbirth* (Revised Ed.). New York: Harper and Row.
Erikson, E. (1962). *Young man Luther*. New York: Norton.
Erikson, E. (1964). *Childhood and society*. New York: Norton.
Erikson, E. (1964). *Insight and responsibility*. New York: Norton.
Erikson. E. (1970). *Ghandi's truth: On the origins of militant nonviolence*. New York: Norton.

Erikson, E. (1975). *Life history and the historical moment.* New York: Norton.
Erikson, E. (1977). *Toys and reason: Stages in the ritualization of experience.* New York: Norton.
Erikson, E. (1979). *Dimensions of a new identity.* New York: Norton.
Erikson, E. (1980). *Identity and the life cycle.* New York: Norton.
Erikson, E. (1982). *The life cycle completed: A review.* New York: Norton.
Gesell, A., et al. (1974). *Infant and child in the culture of today: The guidance of development in home and nursery school.* New York: Harper and Row.
Gesell, A., et al. (1977). *The child from five to ten.* New York: Harper and Row.
Ginott, H. (1969). *Between parent and child.* New York: Avon.
Karmel, M. (1959). *Painless childbirth: Thank you Dr. Lamaze.* Philadelphia: Lippincott.
Leboyer, F. (1975). *Birth without violence.* New York: Knopf.
White, B. (1973). *The first three years of life.* Englewood Cliffs, NJ: Prentice Hall.

CHAPTER FOUR

THE PREDICTABLE MISBEHAVIORS: COGNITIVE DEVELOPMENT

FROM SAND in the mouth, to doll babies that cry, to monsters from space, to tears over lost games—how beautiful are the worlds children enter and leave. But how frustrating to adults who do not understand the Three Worlds of childhood thought.

Children do not think like adults. They travel through Three Worlds, or stages of thinking, that are vastly different from adult thought. Fortunately, the work of Jean Piaget and David Elkind allow parents to add to their understanding of these worlds. Visiting each is like a journey to a foreign country.

The customs and practices are vastly different, but after becoming familiar with the culture it is thrilling and meaningful for parents to share these short-lived adventures. The secret to enjoying a child's thinking is to enjoy it as it is. Too often, parents try to pressure children into the kind of thinking that is far beyond their capabilities. Under normal conditions, the passing of time will take children from stage to stage, and eventually, most will reach a fourth stage, which is mature adult thought.

A child's travel through the Three Worlds takes time. There are substages, or small steps, within each of the three larger stages. No stage can be skipped, even by the brightest child, and although each world is visited in order, the arrival and departure times vary for each child. Some children will stay in one world longer than others. But when it is time, each child will move on to the next stage of thought.

Since each stage is rich and exciting, it is difficult to understand why anyone would wish to push a child prematurely into the next world. Many adults, both at school and home, pressure children to do work that is too advanced for their age and comprehension. Such impatience adds stress to a child's life, but it does not move her to a higher stage. Time will do this, as each mind progresses at its own rate.

Routinely, children attend my human development classes to display stage-appropriate thought with adults. On one occasion, an overambitious parent brought her five-and-one-half-year-old son, Jason, to class. Her husband was a successful scientist, and Jason was being programmed to follow his father's logical thoughts. The parents did not display a sense of humor or an appreciation of imaginative thought.

On this occasion, Jason was a polite, sophisticated child who displayed his parents' goal for him of being adultlike, rather than childlike. When our discussions wandered to jet planes, Jason began a detailed explanation about how a jet engine actually works. His father had taught him well, and Jason amazed us all with his complex explanation. Could it be that Jason had skipped the childhood stages of thought that Piaget describes?

Finally, I said to Jason, "I understand how jet engines work. But what makes a jet airplane go so fast?" Jason's eyes sparkled as he became a young boy: "I think there are chipmunks inside who ride bicycles. The more the pilots feed them, the faster they peddle and the faster the plane goes. I saw chipmunks like that at the fair."

A look of horror crossed his mother's face: "Jason, you know that's false. Tell Dr. West about jet engines, and this time, **think!**" He returned to his memorized account. But in his own mind, I am sure he sees a team of chipmunks peddling away.

Ambitious parents who push children often miss the joy of sharing the pleasures of childhood thought. There are so many years ahead for children to think like adults, and whether pushed or not, children raised in wholesome environments will reach their potential. The destination will always be the same, but the enjoyment of the voyage may be determined by the parent. Take it easy. Cherish these three childhood worlds. They disappear all too soon for most of us.

SENSORIMOTOR WORLD (BIRTH TO ONE AND ONE-HALF)

In the first month of life, a child's mental and physical abilities are limited. A playful kitten and an energetic puppy of the same age seem to far exceed the physical and mental abilities of a helpless infant; yet, by twelve months of age, a child can use tools and solve problems. Very few members of the animal kingdom will ever advance this far. Unfortunately, this marvelous mental growth is lost sight of within the whirlwind of changes a baby brings to her family.

The practices and customs of the sensorimotor are indeed foreign to the adult world. Not knowing how to speak, children must learn about their new world through physical actions. Their behaviors are creative and intelligent; yet since these are foreign to verbal parents, a baby's discoveries often go unnoticed.

For example, how can a child learn about unfamiliar novelties, such as sand, or toys, or sticks? She cannot formally ask her parents, "Pardon me, Mother, but could you please give me a comparative analysis of the texture of this finely granulated sand as contrasted with this rock I have just secured?" Since she cannot ask about it, she must explore and learn on her own. The most intelligent method of exploring new objects is to place them in the mouth. Once there, the texture of the sand, or sticks, or toy become obvious. The child has learned without help from an adult.

So many plans end in disappointment for new parents who are unaccustomed to how infants learn. Adults build sandboxes or plan beach trips for them. When they see their sensorimotor child place a handful of sand in her small mouth, parents usually look outraged. But for the child, tasting sand is much the same as it is for an adult enjoying a wine tasting. It is a marvelous learning experience. Some tastes are good and some bad. There is only one way to discover the difference.

The wind, rain, thunder, lightning, and nature's other phenomena are strange and challenging to young children. All require time for a child to understand. For example, gravity is a principle which makes no sense to a child. Watch a child seated in her high chair when she first discovers it. She may put a spoon or cup of milk in the air outside the perimeter of her tray. Her expectation is that the object will stay in the air until she returns for it, but suddenly she is betrayed. She hears the object hit the floor. When they hear the crash, most children grasp the side of the tray and stare below in amazement. Fascinated with the idea that things go down when released, the child then repeatedly drops objects from the table—still amazed at the result. In this case, the dropping of things is an act of intelligence—a scientific experiment. The results are fascinating! Should parents become frustrated with children dropping things from a high chair, the child then becomes equally amazed at her ability to control an adult's emotions. The world is a place of constant discovery.

In a restaurant once, I observed an ingenious young mother who was too resourceful for her child's own good. Obviously she was tired of picking up silver and cups from the floor, so she brought to dinner a high chair with strings ready to attach to the child's eating utensils. When the child threw down a fork, the mother simply pulled the string to retrieve it. The only problem was that, in several instances, the string was too short! The child would throw down his cup and — NO SOUND! For this child, the concept of gravity may develop slowly because there were too many strings attached!

Another difficult concept for children to learn is the "permanency of things." During their first two months, children have no idea that anything out of sight still exists. If Mom or Dad walks out of the room, to a child they are simply gone. "Out of sight, out of mind." By age four to six months the child realizes, "I can touch anything I see." Thus, a child begins to understand that everything seen is permanent enough to have substance. This discovery leads the child to grab anything — plants, pictures, glasses, and hair — with great enthusiasm.

The first purchase my eldest child made inadvertently occurred the same week that he began to grab everything in sight. Despite the fact that his grip on my hair led to several premature bald spots, I did not anticipate the potential havoc his grasp would bring. I found out in a flower shop. He was resting on my shoulder, when I bent over to look at a plant on the floor, but as I stooped, he grabbed a hanging plant. A crash followed. My son and I became the instant owners of a crippled spider plant!

For some time, a child thinks only those things she can see have surfaces that can be touched. If a child is reaching for a cookie and it is covered by a towel, the child will not search for the hidden object. Still, the motto is "Out of sight — out of mind." The adult idea that all things are permanent has not developed.

During this stage, our children fussed when they saw an adult with beverage or food. Even if they had their own drink or snacks, they, of course, preferred someone else's. This fussing made it unpleasant when guests visited. So when we served a beverage, we gave our friends a towel to cover it. Once the food or glass was covered, the child stopped complaining. For them, the drink was gone.

Similarly, a graduate student of mine had to pass through her child's bedroom to enter the only bathroom in the house. When the child saw her mother, she cried to be picked up. Knowing which stage the child was in, the mother began to travel through the room with a bag over her head. The child never cried, but was was greatly interested in the bag-headed body.

At twelve months, a child has learned much more about permanence. At this stage, when a child sees an object hidden, she will uncover it. Nevertheless, the concept of permanence is not fully developed. For example, while a child is observing you, take a toy and hide it under the same towel eight or nine times. Then, with the child still watching, hide it under a second towel. Often the child will look under the first towel.

By eighteen months of age, the mystery of permanence is solved for a child. Anything a child sees placed in a shopping cart will now be searched for at home. Drawers and shelves will be ransacked in the quest for hidden treasure. Children cannot be fooled now. A parent can no longer cover drinks with towels or walk unnoticed with a bag over the head, because the child has entered a new world.

At eighteen months, children also begin to be able to remember past events. They can copy behaviors observed days before. This would not have been possible a few weeks earlier. For example, a child can see another child's temper tantrum and reproduce it weeks later, when the mood strikes her.

We were ready for the first temper tantrum of our youngest child, Dustin! At eighteen months, he was worldly enough to have observed others' tantrums. The time was right. Soon he found the appropriate situation: He was denied candy for breakfast! Down to the floor he fell! He tried to coordinate pounding his hands, kicking his feet, and crying. But he forgot to cry. During the entire process, he looked up at us to see how he was doing. I winked at his older brother and sister. When Dustin was through, he looked around from face to face. We applauded his performance. Then he sat up and applauded himself. His experiment was over and rarely repeated.

Between eighteen months and two years, words begin to flow more swiftly. Learning can take place by asking questions and listening. Children are no longer confined to their five senses for learning about new objects. They are ready for a new stage—a new world of thought based on language and imagination.

SUGGESTIONS FOR PARENTS OF CHILDREN IN THE SENSORIMOTOR PERIOD

Throughout early childhood, young children learn best by playing and experimenting. The sensorimotor child loves to manipulate toys, play with pots and pans, and generally explore anything that can be touched. Encourage your child's activity. Try not to confine the child more than is necessary. Place valuable and breakable objects out of a child's reach. Baby-proofing the house frees the youngster to learn, and this also preserves a measure of sanity for parents. In fact, as a guest, one automatically knows toddlers live in a home if everything breakable is four feet above the floor. Visiting a toddler's home is like observing the beach at low tide, where one sees a wide space that used to be filled and will fill again. But for now, it lays barren.

Parents should play games that fit the child's stage of development. For example, peek-a-boo and jack-in-the-box are perfect for children learning about permanence. Watch a baby's face as you play peek-a-boo. When your face disappears, notice the child's intense look of concern. For the child, you are totally gone; it is as if you no longer exist. But look at your child's enthusiasm when your face reappears. Children literally jump with joy over the return! You were gone, but now you are there once more! Because time is required for a child to move up to another stage, these games can be played repeatedly with the same results.

Children do not profit from complicated toys at this age. Many companies put out useless toys designed to seduce adults into purchasing them, but babies rarely play with formal toys. In fact, most parents have seen children open an expensive toy and then play with the box. Mobiles are an obvious example of the toy industry's interest in selling to adults rather than in serving children. Mobiles often have brightly painted figures which can be seen only from the side. The baby sees only the bottom ridge of the figure. Mobiles are generally hung 24 inches above the baby, even though babies do not focus well at this distance. Some mobiles even have motors. In the past, mobiles moved only when the child discovered that by kicking her legs she could make something happen. This kicking and watching the results delighted the child and taught her the first lessons in cause and effect, but now children tend to passively watch. Mechanical mobiles may have become a training ground for later television watching. To be useful, mobiles should be about 18 inches above the child's eyes. The figures should be removed and replaced facing the child. Now, a toy made for adults can be enjoyed by babies!

Babies are our greatest explorers. Everything is new! Everything is exciting! No wonder having a baby in the house gives new life to adults. The First World of thought is a world of physical discovery. From absolutely no knowledge of how the world works, a baby moves, in a few short months, to being a young scientist. It is a marvelous trip through the First World and a short one.

THE PREOPERATIONAL WORLDS (AGES 1½ TO 6)

Like a butterfly in flight, the thoughts of preschool children flutter and float erratically through the air. Creativity soars. Unpredictability becomes the major rule of this new world. What a miracle it is that at the height of so many power struggles, a child's thinking is so entertaining. Parents who are looking for logic will miss the heart of this stage. Children in this stage are best at being spontaneous and creative. Logic and consistency are not yet available.

When Patrick was six, we looked forward to a morning of fishing at the river below our house. His job was to get the worms out of the refrigerator while I fixed the poles. When he showed up without the worms, I asked the obvious question: "Where are the worms?" His response was "They are not ready." Asked what he meant, he explained: "I put them in the microwave for ten minutes!" Charred worms do not catch fish! I suppose there was an element of logic there, but it was definitely preoperational logic — a different world of thought.

A growing vocabulary fuels the child's imagination endlessly and, with some, this leads to endless conversation! Suddenly, at about age two, a child seems to leap from saying single words to uttering complex paragraphs. By the age of five, most children understand the average adult's working vocabulary. For many children, the growth spurt in language can end months of frustration. Often, a child will be particularly fussy before the spurt begins, because they are limited in their means of communication; even though they understand langauge, they are unable to make their needs known. Once the language spurt begins, increased contentment usually results. Words can replace tears, and often charm develops along with the new facility with words.

It is this Second World of thought that has captured the love of adults through the years. It is a world not distracted by adult logic or concrete reality. In this world, Winnie the Pooh is alive and Superman is one of a host of superheroes. To a child, stuffed animals, trees, clouds, cars — everything around them — seem to be thriving with life. Dolls are popular with some, while the current line of soldiers or popular movie figures are collected and prized by others. If adults ever doubt a child's belief that their toys have life, they need only treat a cherished doll or stuffed animal improperly in front of its play-mother or -father.

Emily and I often play house with her dolls. Usually, I am the designated grandfather, who is given the task of admiring Emily's maternal nature. Almost always, I treat all of Emily's stuffed children with absolute respect, but one day I betrayed Emily, and I paid dearly for my error. In helping her clean her room, I thoughtlessly grabbed Mandy, her favorite doll, and threw her into a toy box. Emily shrieked when she saw her child violated by my vulgar hand. Tears followed. Mandy was gently lifted from the box, taken to the pretend hospital, and bandaged. No visitors were allowed. I was asked to leave the room and not to return until Mandy healed. I learned to be more sensitive.

Of course, parents can take advantage of a child's giving pretend-life to a doll. When a child has difficulty sleeping, their dolls and stuffed animals can become companions. When a child is given the responsibility of insuring a doll's sleep, she may insist that everyone remain silent to allow her doll to rest. With silence, sleep may eventually come to everyone.

Adults do not outgrow this tendency to treat objects as if they are alive: Some people talk to and punch vending machines that have stolen their money; others have long conversations with cars that won't start; athletes try to guide a golf ball onto the green by twisting their bodies and shouting instructions to the lifeless ball.

The creativity of children can be seen in their drawings and scribblings. The slightest scratch can blossom into life when given a child's amazing explanation. Adults who are careful never make the error common in dealing with children's art by saying: "I love it. What is it?" Such insensitivity to portraits bring aches to the hearts of young artists. Instead, a careful adult will make open-ended requests such as, "Tell me about your drawing." This allows a child to follow with her incredible interpretations.

A three-year-old visiting my child development class drew a maze of lines on the board that ordinarily would pass for scribbles. When asked to tell about his drawing, his excited explanation unfolded. Each line held a unique story: "This is Santa Claus. This is his beard. This is his fat stomach. This is his sack. This is his pipe. This is Rudolf. His arm is in a sling because he broke it playing reindeer games." Whether or not the drawing held the same meaning while he was creating it, I do not know. But open-ended questions allow preoperational children to create an adventure out of the commonplace.

For children this age, religious concepts are difficult to grasp and understand. For example, children generally believe all things are man made. When hearing about God, the creator of all things, children will think of God as an old man who somehow created trees and rivers through magical powers. Adult language, such as the "throne of God" and "sitting on the right hand of God," contributes to the child's assurance that God is simply an old, wise man. Religion and religious services are beyond comprehension for children this age.

Once I visited a protestant church where young children were expected to attend the formal church service. I sat behind a five-year-old who was having a rough time of it. He filled in every O in the bulletin with a pencil, then emptied his mother's purse of all it contained. The child was a volcano waiting to erupt.

Communion was served. The child grabbed a piece of soft bread from the plate. I watched as he squeezed and shaped the bread. Then, during the middle of the elder's prayer, it happened. The child created an airplane. Suddenly the prayer was interrupted by jet plane noises, complete with machine-gun fire. The parents and members of the congregation were horrified. But it was a wonderful demonstration of how futile it is to attempt to force a preoperational child to endure an hour of ideas meant for those capable of advanced thought.

Death is an equally difficult concept for children to understand. That physical death is irreversible cannot be fully appreciated until a child is in the eighth year; nevertheless, children are interested in death and try to understand it in their own way. I recall a dinner conversation with my three-year-old daughter during the main course:

Emily:	"Dad, is this chicken a bird?"
Dad:	"Yes, it is, Emily."
Emily:	"Is it a dead bird?"
Dad:	"Yes, it is, Emily."
Emily:	"Are you eating a dead bird's leg, Dad?"
Dad:	"Yes, I am, Emily."
Emily:	"Are you eating a dead bird's dead leg, Dad?"
Dad:	"No, I'm not, Emily. I'm not very hungry."

The net result of this conversation was that Emily finished all of the chicken.

The full impact of the death of a relative or a friend cannot be grasped at this age. Books and family discussions are of some help, but it is limited. Children, do, however, react to our emotions. They may cry or be sad when we react sadly. They are aware that death is an important human event. But it would not surprise them to see a dead person alive the next week. At this age, the mind is not ready to think of physical death as a permanent state of affairs.

It is not unusual for a young child to appear to understand funerals and grief. But an understanding of physical death is not established in the preoperational years. For example, after a grandfather's death, a child may visit his grandparent's house and be surprised not to find him there. Or, when visiting his grave, the child may wish to take granddad food or a blanket for warmth.

When Patrick was four, we took him to the home of Patrick Henry. As we walked about, Patrick repeatedly asked where Patrick Henry was. Finally, we showed him the grave of the patriot. It was Patrick's first encounter with a grave.

As our attention drifted to other things, we lost sight of Patrick for a few moments. What a mistake! When I looked up, I found my son dancing on Patrick Henry's grave. Fearing that we would be asked to leave if he were seen doing this, I rushed over to remove him, and senselessly, I asked for an explanation. Patrick simply replied, "I thought I might wake him up so he would come out and play." If adults would reflect on their own difficulty in understanding the death of a loved one, a child's preoperational confusion would seem inevitable.

One difficulty that active imaginations present for children is nightmares. Creativity does not sleep at night. Books about the "big bad wolf" and monsters in movies come back to haunt children after bedtime. Nightmares flourish between the creative years of two to five. Children respond well to being awakened and assured that the inventions of their imaginations have been banished from the room. If they are still afraid, children can be helped by the same imaginations that created the monsters. Heroes can be created to rid the bedroom-kingdom of monsters. If violent nightmares persist, or if a child consistently has difficulty awakening from a nightmare, a pediatrician should be consulted. In such a crisis, awaken the child, remove her to another room, and keep the light on until she regains composure.

Questions are common from children this age. There is so much to wonder about. Answers should be kept simple. David Elkind suggests that children ask questions with the belief that everything has a purpose. Questions such as, "Why is the grass green?" or "Why do leaves fall from trees?" are all asked with the belief that there is an explanation for everything. Adults should not give complicated responses. Remember, a child's world is not scientific.

Elkind suggests that when adults begin a reply with the word "because," they are often on the verge of giving a scientific response which is too advanced for this stage of thought. for example, an inappropriate response to the question, "Why do leaves change color?" is "Because in a leaf there are chemicals which. . ." Instead, replies should aim at a simple purpose. Beginning a reply with "to" seems to help. For example, "Why do leaves change color?" "To give us pretty colors to see." For the question, "Why do leaves fall?" an answer might be "To keep the ground warm" or "To make room for other leaves."

Humor at this stage often seems silly to an adult. Some humor reflects the two most important events that take place during this period: toilet training and a growing vocabulary. Children develop what has been called "bathroom humor." Nothing is funnier to them at this stage than to call someone a "pooh pooh head" or a "do do nose." In addition, "nonsense" words are created which often bring heavy laughter from children at this age. From the looks of public bathroom walls, many adults are still operating with the bathroom humor of a three-year-old!

As with "curse words" used at this age, a child is simply experimenting, not misbehaving. These words are not intended to offend others. The excitement for the child is in creating words which either have special meaning or which have a great effect on others. Parents should follow the suggestions given in Chapter One for discouraging the use of unacceptable words.

This Second World of thought still represents a tremendously self-centered or egocentric time in a child's life. It is difficult for children to consider the feelings or needs of others. But, whereas an egocentric adult chooses not to be interested in others, the egocentric child is that way by nature. This egocentrism will change only with time and experience; until then, children will believe that everyone understands the world through their eyes and ears. I recall getting a phone call at my office from my preschool son:

Patrick: "Dad, I painted a picture in school today!"
Dad: "Marvelous, tell me about it. . ."
Patrick: "Here, I'll show you first. Look—I have it held up to the phone. See, that's Superman knocking over a building and. . ."

On another occasion, I remember my mother showing a neighborhood boy the holes in our living room windows caused by his BB gun. She took him into the room, pointed to the holes and said with great displeasure:

"See the holes you made in the living room windows?"
Neighborhood Boy: "My Gosh, Mrs. West, you shouldn't sit in this room! It's dangerous."

A child's egocentrism causes problems for parents. Because a child cannot take another person's viewpoints, there is a tendency for her to want to do what she wants to do when she wants to do it. Unlike older children, she will not be able to accept the concept that it is best for the family to do anything that is contrary to her wishes. This, of course, leads to many power struggles.

Recently, our daughter Emily (age six) decided to make a cake. Of course, she wanted to do this immediately. My wife, Patty, rationally explained, "Supper must be cooked first, but I would enjoy baking with you afterwards." Not good enough! Patty left the room and immediately the cabinets were raided. She returned and declared, "Emily, not now. It's late and I need to cook supper. You can help with supper." Like a person in another world, Emily continued to pour flour into a bowl. With a fair amount of calm, her mother presented a choice: "Emily, you can stop or you can stay in your room until you can control yourself." Silently and undeterred, Emily reached for the milk. Before her hand could squeeze the carton, Patty picked the young cook up and led her to the bedroom. In ten minutes, Emily returned and exclaimed: "I'm not hungry and I want to cook a cake NOW!" Suffice it to say, my wife's response will not be quoted at the next Nobel Peace Prize Awards. The egocentrism of a child is a more powerful force than the logic of a parent. Frustrating moments are inevitable.

Another difficulty for some families is the tendency for children to talk constantly, without regard for another's right to talk or for the situation at hand. Parents who formerly were accustomed to discussing the day's events at supper are wise to choose another time for such sharing. Children will not recognize the parents' need to talk with each other. Even when the parents have an emergency to discuss, young children are not able to be empathetic.

Suppertime poses a particular problem for many parents. One father told our parenting class of an incident that had occurred the preceding night which seems characteristic. There had been an emergency at work, and he was anxious to talk about it with his wife. He arrived at home as supper started. But his four-year-old was determined to talk about a rat his cat had killed. The father implored his son to be quiet and explained the importance of the adults' conversation. For thirty seconds, the child was quiet. But soon he began rambling about the rat. The father exploded, and chaos reigned. The father's question to the study group was reasonable: "Can't one train a child to be quiet during meals?"

Of course, a child can be trained to sit quietly at the supper table. But to do so goes against nature. Children enjoy talking, even when no one is listening. Every family needs to decide on their own rules for mealtime, but consistency is needed. If children's talk is encourage on most days, then it is difficult to turn off upon request. If a true emergency exists, it may be better to make special provisions to allow for private discussion of the problem.

Preschoolers are equally self-centered. Although they enjoy the company of others, they will not interact smoothly. At best, they tend to play side by side, each involved in a personal interest. Talking follows this same egocentric pattern. Whenever a group of children gathers, they can be heard carrying on several different conversations at once. No one is really listening to the other. This tendency, called "collective monologue," is not unknown in adult circles!

Children at this age are able to focus on only one interest, desire, or thought at a time. Therefore, if a child wants a piece of candy, she can become "irrationally" persistent about it, refusing to take "No" for an answer. Parents who talk, rather than act, are often worn out by this focusing, or centering, tendency. At times like these, adults make statements such as, "I've told you one thousand times: NO!"

Once, I took my six-year-old to a college basketball game between two nationally ranked teams. On the way to the game, I mentioned to Patrick that he could buy a box of popcorn sometime during the evening. I was filled with excitement when we arrived and heard the crowd roar in response to the introductions. I was running to find our seats when a tiny voice asked, "Can I have my popcorn now?" A quick look showed the lines were long, and I put him off. We sat down as the first basket was scored. When I rose to my feet, I heard that voice again, "Could I have my popcorn now?" And so it continued, all though the first half. He was centered on the popcorn; I was centered on the game. Neither of us was flexible; therefore, we found each other to be irritating company! Children and parents both can be single-minded. For a child, it is a limitation of her developmental stage.

Another common frustration for parents is that children this age cannot generalize from a rule. For example, once after he hit his sister, I told my two-and-one-half-year-old son, Dustin: "No! You cannot hit Emily." Not two minutes later, he hit his brother Patrick. My immediate response was, "I just told you not to hit anyone." I was wrong. I had told him not to hit Emily. He obeyed my instructions. But he was not capable of generalizing from that rule.

When I realized my error, I tried to explain "not hitting" to him. The following series of questions shows the inability of a child to understand the principle behind a rule:

Dad:	"Dustin, you cannot hit Patrick, either. Don't hit anyone."
Dustin:	"Can I hit Mommy?"
Dad:	"No, you can't hit Mommy. You must not hit anyone."
Dustin:	"Can I hit Grandmommy or Granddaddy?"
Dad:	"No, you can't hit them. We do not hit people in our family."
Dustin:	"Can I hit Uncle Dwight?"
Dad:	"No, you can't hit anyone."
Dustin:	"Can I hit the kitty cat?"

My fear following this conversation was that anyone I left off the prohibited list was going to be pounded by the young slugger!

Preoperational children live and think in the present. The distant past and the future have little relevance to them. Children will not be surprised to hear that their parents crossed the Delaware with George Washington. The distant future is equally difficult to comprehend. Children cannot be convinced to save money for an event a month away, much less for future college years. What is important to them is NOW.

For a child, the present can seem like an eternity. Trips of any distance can try a child's patience. Every ten minutes, adults may be asked, "How much longer?" Even when a reward awaits the child at the end of the car ride or at the end of a wait in line, the present misery seems too much to bear. For adults, whose interest is invested in the past and future, the child's dedication to the present can be a positive challenge.

SUGGESTIONS FOR PARENTS OF CHILDREN IN THE PREOPERATIONAL PERIOD

Time will move a child from this creative world into a world of logic and rules. Until time passes, parents can cherish these short years filled by a child's imagination and growing interests.

Playing is vitally important for young children. As Maria Montessori said, and Piaget confirmed: "Play is a child's work." Encourage activities which the child enjoys. Don't forget that their tendency to center on things often make it preferable to do the same thing over and over. For example, practicing letters, numbers, and figures may be more beneficial for the child than learning something totally new.

Patience is often required. Adults grow bored with repetition. Children do not. Often a child will wish to read the same book night after night or enjoy hearing a record repeatedly. Adults need to take advantage of the child's enjoyment of repetition. Allow them, as much as possible, to follow their own inclinations. Try to focus on the child's needs, rather than your own.

Be careful that a child is not pushed academically during these imaginative years. Reading, math, and spelling are not compatible with this world of thought. Any human can be forced to learn reading or math early, but this usually serves only to meet overambitious parent's or teacher's needs. A child will learn to read; it is to the child's advantage to wait until she is mentally ready to do so. Adults may spend months pounding different skills into the mind of an unready child, yet those same skills will be learned in a matter of days by children whose parents wait for the right teachable moment.

A graduate student made an appointment with me to discuss the future of her four-year-old. According to the mother, her daughter could already read the newspaper. Her concern was that none of the local preschool programs could sufficiently challenge her daughter academically. She was hoping to find "a more serious preschool experience."

Since I am not a supporter of preschool kiddy colleges, I was of little help to the proud mother. But later in the year, this same mother returned with another set of problems. Her daughter was wetting the bed, had developed headaches, and refused to attend her preschool. This anxious mother was extremely angry because the pediatrician had suggested that the child might be reacting to too much pressure to achieve. The mother refused to believe that his diagnosis held merit.

Reading is an extremely important skill. Although this child learned to read early, others will learn more easily later. We hope that all children will enjoy reading as they grow older, but most will not have to suffer psychological side effects due to a parent's overambition. For a child, learning becomes easier with time. Skills should be taught when the child is ready to learn, rather than when the parent wants her to learn.

Instead of accenting academics, it is preferable for parents to spend time creating positive self-concepts in their children. Although children do not think like adults at this age, they do share similar feelings. Children become hurt, angry, confused, sad, and revengeful. Therefore, it is wise to treat a child with the same respect as an adult. For example, if you would not yell at you spouse for placing his or her feet on the furniture, being slow to dress, misplacing shoes, or being too talkative, then do not yell at your child.

Having said that, let me quickly admit to the impossibility for most parents of following this guideline perfectly. Recently, my son's Suzuki violin class was holding a concert. Everyone except my six-year-old daughter went early for the event. I was anxious to be on time, but my daughter refused to be budged. At first, I tried gently to urge her, "Come on Emily, we have fifteen minutes to get there." When I looked in her room a little later, I found that she had lost the shoes that moments earlier were in her hand. Because of my sense of urgency, I helped her find them, then nudged her on more adamantly, "Hurry, we have to leave." Two minutes later, I returned to find her absorbed with her dolls in a game called "picnic." At that point, I forgot my training and a shout rang through the house. Yes, children share our feelings, but few adults I know would dress slowly when time is an issue, or lose shoes in a period of sixty seconds, or become absorbed in playing with dolls while another person is being inconvenienced. A child's view of the world can often exasperate adults. Tempers will flare. Nevertheless, the feelings of a child should be respected as much as those of an adult.

Be sensitive to a child's limitations. Children this age are not able to assimilate complicated facts about human nature. For example, understanding the reasons for a divorce is complex for an adult and impossible for a child whose age is limited to another world of thought. Although children may parrot back what they hear, they often do not understand what they have memorized. Keep facts and ideas simple.

Tom and Martha Jackson planned a peaceful and cooperative divorce. Martha was appropriately worried about the separation's effect on her six-year-old daughter, Cindy. She did not want Cindy to take sides. She and her husband discussed the divorce with Cindy. No detail was spared when the complicated problems were explained to the child. The children in the family were not greatly involved in the parents' conflict.

Nevertheless, Cindy apparently thought she was the problem. After hearing the long explanation by the mother, the child's response was predictably self-centered: "If I had gone to live with Grandmom over the summer, like you and Dad wanted me to, this wouldn't have happened, would it?" Preoperational children cannot understand the complicated circumstances of adult life. Explanations of adult situations should be simple, honest, and brief. Feelings need to be especially considered and the self-centeredness of a child anticipated.

The Second World is an adventuresome one, full of imagination and life. But like the First World of the baby, this one is also short-lived.

THE WORD OF CONCRETE OPERATIONS
(7 TO AT LEAST 11)

Could this be the same child who lived in your home a few years earlier? All of a sudden, she has become a companion and, at times, a friend. Her thinking has become more consistent and logical. She can save money for adventures in the near future, although saving for college or the working years still seems too distant. There is a new found ability to help her understand another's viewpoint, although different views are not always appreciated.

Imagination sometimes seems totally lost in the child's fascination with rules and regulations. Children on the playground may spend more time arguing over the rules than actually playing. But in every game, each child has one rule which outweighs all others—**I must win.** To conform to this rule, chidren may stop in the middle of a game, or try to change the rules, or cheat a little bit when they think it necessary.

Playing the same game with children in different developmental stages is an experience in frustration. For example, in playing the game of Monopoly,® a preschool child will create her own rules. She may turn over dice to find the number she wishes, or she may skip over squares that do not suit. The older, concrete operational child playing with her may respond to the violations with outrage: "You can't do that. If you do that again, I'll quit." The preschool child may conform to rules made by the older child for a short time, but soon she will return to her creative rule making.

If the concrete operational child senses defeat is near, however, she too may change the rules to allow victory. For examples, "Whoops, the dice rolled off the board, so I get to do that over." Or, "Let's say that one person cannot own all of the railroads." While younger children feel no obligation to rules, older children will follow them as long as it is convenient for them to do so.

Lying is not uncommon at this age, but during this period, a unique problem occurs. If a child is backed into a corner and forced to tell a lie over and over, she will soon actually believe that the lie is true. For example, assume that a teacher sees a child take a pencil from another child's desk. Instead of acting to enforce class rules, the teacher makes the classic error of trying to force a confession. A typical conversation might go like this:

Teacher:	"Johnny, did you take Sally's pencil?"
Johnny:	"No. I did not."
Teacher:	"Well, Johnny how did you get it?"
Johnny:	"Sally gave it to me."
Teacher:	"Sally, did you give him the pencil?"
Sally:	"No ma'am. I didn't. He took it."
Johnny:	"You liar. I did not. You told me I could use it."
Sally:	"No, I didn't."
Johnny:	"Yes, you did."
Teacher:	"Johnny, see me after school."
Johnny:	"But that's not fair. She said I could have it."
Teacher:	"Johnny, you know that is not true. Now not another word."

Actually, Johnny does not know that his story is false. After repeating his lie several times, he has convinced himself that it is true. Of course, this is only the first part of the story. Johnny will return home to be questioned by his parents. That conversation may go like this:

Parent:	"Johnny, why are you late?"
Johnny:	"Because Mrs. Jones made me stay after class."
Parent:	"Well, what did you do?"
Johnny:	"Nothing."
Parent:	"You must have done something."
Johnny:	"No, I didn't. Sally told a lie about me and the teacher has it in for me. I hate them both. It's not fair."

And for Johnny, it is not.

Unfortunately, children this age often create rules about which they are mistaken. Once created, however, the rules are followed absolutely. For example, should a child believe "e" comes before "i" in most words, the child will spell each word using this incorrect rule. Mistakes in math are often caused because the child has formed an incorrect rule and uses it over and over. A competent teacher of young children is able to identify children's mistaken rules instead of simply marking problems wrong and indicating that practice is needed. More practice never helps a child who is working with faulty ideas. Rather, the faulty ideas must be recognized and corrected by the teacher, and then progress will be made.

One evening, an eight-year-old participated in a class demonstration. One of her tasks was to draw herself standing in front of her home. Typical of many eight-year-olds, this young lady began to erase each line she drew. For fifteen minutes she struggled. Each new line proved to be as crooked as the one before. Obviously, her rule was, "The line must be perfectly straight or I must start over." As time passed, her frustration mounted and tears began to appear. To relieve her of pressure, I only needed to change her rule: "Let's make a rule that no one can erase." A look of relief spread over the young girl's face and she was able to finish the project in seconds.

Parents may not find it easy to change rules a child has learned from other adults, such as teachers or coaches. For example, a child may ask for help in math. As the parent observes, an obvious error in procedure may be discovered. But after the parent suggests the proper way to solve the problem the child may reply: "But that's not the way my teacher does it." Even though the mistake is an obvious misinterpretation of the teacher's rule, the child cannot be persuaded. Once believed, rules are hard to change.

A major opportunity children have during this age is to form rules about themselves that are positive. Positive parents, teachers and coaches can help a child form rules such as: "I am a quick learner," or "I am going to be good in sports if I practice," or "Other children like me," or "I am going to be successful at whatever I try to accomplish in life." Of course, children can also create damaging beliefs about themselves. Negative rules, such as "I am not smart or pretty" can be tragic at this age. This stage of thought occurs during Erikson's Accomplishment vs. Inferiority stage. Failure at school is particularly harmful to a child this age and may lead a child to create rules that will continue to make success in life quite difficult.

William Glasser, the creator of Reality Therapy, believes that children create either a success or failure identity by the age of ten. If a child creates rules or beliefs that success in school and work is not possible, then failure may consistently follow. Once these rules are established during the elementary years, they become exceedingly difficult to change. Unfortunately, most failure identities are based on mistaken rules. Glasser suggests that parents and teachers need to make each child feel successful, no matter how limited or underdeveloped their abilities may be.

An exasperating discovery made by children that their parents are not perfect occurs around eight years. Upon learning this, the disillusioned child actually begins to act "superior" to the parent who has broken her heart with his/her fallibility. Often, children can be condescending and rude after they arrive at this realization.

When I was this age, I once asked my Dad, "Who plays third base for the Boston Red Sox?" Dad mistakenly named the starting third baseman for the New York Yankees. My world was shattered by his ignorance. For a time, his credibility ended. All of my friends knew the correct answer. If Dad didn't know, then this was probably just the tip of the iceberg. From then on, anything he **did** know seemed to matter little. I was most impressed by his ignorance.

This "cognitive conceit" in children makes it difficult for parents to teach or coach their own children. There is a tendency in children to believe that every adult must know more than mom or dad. A common reply to a parent's suggestions becomes: "Yes, but that's not the way my teacher said to do it." At this point, the best way to handle this is a short note to the teacher that indicates the mistaken rules under which your child is operating.

The child's humor at this age centers around broken rules and regulations, rather than silly words. Slapstick humor long has been the preference of young, school-age children. To them, nothing seems funnier than to see adults look foolish. If a teacher carrying a load of books were to slip on ice or fall down three flights of stairs and break every bone in her body, the children would laugh as she hit the last step. It is not that they are cruel but that they so enjoy seeing adults "goof."

SUGGESTIONS FOR PARENTS IN THE CONCRETE OPERATIONAL PERIOD

For parents in a more flexible world of thought, the concreteness of a child in this world can be frustrating. Again, adults need to take advantage of the attributes which come with the stage. This is the time to teach subjects with rules—like reading, math, or spelling. Activities such as taking field trips are still important. Also, children learn quickly by doing things with their hands. Experience is the great teacher for children this age. Words are less effective.

Many churches teach Bible stories to children through a "children's sermon" during the adult worship. Often, lay people are responsible for the service. Some are unfamiliar with children's thought. Although these teachers spend hours preparing an interesting lecture, children seldom remember the topic, much less the content, by the end of the day. Lectures help adults learn, but they do not benefit children. Other wiser teachers do not relay Bible stories but allow the children to act out the stories, and suddenly the characters and ideas are alive. Often, after a week has passed, children tend to remember the story. Children are active, not passive, learners. They learn best by participating.

Parents should not worry about accelerating conflict or stimulation. Except in deprived home environments, such children have enough stimulation for growth. Parents should spend energy strengthening the child's positive self-concept. Rules for a lifetime are being formed or confirmed at this age. Helping children develop positive feelings about themselves and their abilities is a major task for parents. Positive self-regard, developed now, may bring the child a lifetime of confidence.

THE WORLD OF FORMAL OPERATIONS

This is a later stage that usually is not reached by children until they are twelve years old. Some estimate that only 1 percent of twelve-year-olds and possibly as few as 50 percent of adults move into this new world. The formally operative person regains creativity and imagination. Rules are understood, yet new ways of doing things are explored. Adolescents in formal operations create ideal visions for how everything in society should be, but nothing in reality matches their visions. It is difficult for them to live in a world where they believe everything can and should be different! It is also difficult for parents to hear constantly about their own shortcomings. Formal operations is the final period discussed by Piaget.

Adolescents who have the aptitude for growth and consistent opportunities to solve age-appropriate conflicts will usually enter this world of thought — a world that differs radically from the Three Worlds of childhood.

COMMENTS

On the first day of school last year, our family enjoyed having a child in each of the three worlds of children's thought. Sadly, I looked over the yard played in so heavily that summer. The yard lay deserted, mute testimony to the three stages of childhood. I recorded in my journal:

"A plastic baseball bat lies on top of the hose leading to a Mickey Mouse Sprinkler for children. The ground on both sides of the sprinkler is worn from a summer of children jumping and running through the spray. A shovel and a half-filled bucket lay beside the sandbox. In the box, little toy figures still climb mounds of sand carefully shaped like cakes and pies. Emily's bicycle is rammed into a bush which already houses a large dodgeball, which caused as much anger as joy. A Hoola Hoop® is draped over another worn spot in the yard; it served as home base for a game I never fully understood. Only the oldest child knew the rules. No one else cared. An old refrigerator crate that served as a meeting house, army tanks, and stagecoach stands on its side. Inside is a hoe, some comic books, faded ribbons, and a few rusted cans. An old dump truck and a battered police car sit beside the cats' bowls on the front porch. The screen door stands ajar, as it has since the last child forgot to firmly close the door. The yard is littered with remnants of summer. Although all of us will clean it up together, only we parents will know how quickly it all is passing.

JEAN PIAGET

Born in 1896 in Switzerland, Jean Piaget displayed an early interest in nature and a remarkable inclination for academics. By the age of ten, he published his first scientific article about a rare albino sparrow discovered near his home. Not satisfied with the normal activities of childhood, Piaget, at eleven, became the laboratory assistant to the director of a natural history museum. At age fifteen, he was nationally known for his work on mollusks. At this time, a position as the curator of the mollusk section of the Geneva Museum of Natural History opened. Not knowing Piaget was so young, the museum's director offered him a job. When the director learned that Piaget was only a schoolboy, however, he withdrew the offer in great embarrassment.

Piaget's accomplishments continued at a rapid pace. When he was twenty-one, he completed his Ph.D. at the University of Lausanne. In addition to his formal academic work, he published twenty articles that established him internationally as a distinguished scholar in biology. Additionally, Piaget journeyed to Paris to work in the Alfred Binet Laboratory. While conducting intelligence tests, Piaget became fascinated with the wrong answers children repeatedly gave to questions at approximately the same ages. It was then that Piaget's research into how children learn and think began.

In 1929, Piaget returned to Geneva where he held numerous positions. He became a professor of the History of Scientific Thought at the University of Geneva, the Assistant Director of the Institute of J.J. Rouseau, and the Director of the Bureau of the International Office of Education. During his early career, his studies of children were mainly conducted in a clinical setting. The birth of his own three children, however, allowed him to make intricate studies of each child's cognitive development. His own children provided many of the ideas on which his theories rest.

Piaget's unique background, which combined biology, philosophy, and child development, led to his exciting theories. His insights so revolutionized psychology that many compare his contributions in cognitive development to those of Freud's in personality development. Unfortunately, Piaget's writing is extremely difficult to read. Parents and teachers are greatly indebted to scholars like David Elkind for making Piaget's ideas available to the public.

Although Jean Piaget died in 1980, it was not before the world had recognized his accomplishments. He was given honorary degrees from universities throughout the world. His appointment to the Sorbonne was the first made to a non-Frenchman since 1530. As many have suggested, once a person is familiar with Piaget's descriptions of stage-related thought, children will never be viewed in the same way again.

RELATED READINGS

Atkinson, C. (1984). *Making sense of Piaget: The philosophical roots.* Boston: Routledge & Kegan.
Boyle, D. (1969). *A student's guide to Piaget.* Elmsford, NY: Pergamon.

Elkind, D. & Flavell, J. (1969). *Studies in cognitive development: Essays in honor of Jean Piaget.* New York: Oxford University Press.

Elkind, D. (1976). *Child development and education: A Piagetian perspective.* New York: Oxford University Press.

Elkind, D. (1978). *The child's reality: Three developmental themes.* New York: Halstead Press.

Elkind, D. (1981). *The hurried child: Growing up too fast too soon.* Reading, MA: Addison-Wesley.

Flavell, J. (1977). *Cognitive development.* New York: Prentice Hall.

Furth, H. & Wachs, H. (1975). *Thinking goes to school: Piaget's theory in practice with additional thoughts.* New York: Oxford University Press.

Ginsberg, H. & Opper, S. (1979). *Piaget's theory of intellectual development,* 2nd ed. New York: Prentice Hall.

Glasser, William (1969). *Schools without failure.* New York: Harper and Row.

Glasser, William (1975). *Reality therapy.* New York: Harper and Row.

Inhelder, B., et al. (1973). *Piaget and his school: A reader in developmental psychology.* New York: Springer-Verlag.

Labinowicz, E. (1980). *The Piaget primer.* Reading, MA: Addison-Wesley.

Penrose, W. (1979). *A primer on Piaget.* Bloomington, IN: Phi Delta Kappa.

Piaget, J. (1965). *Moral judgment of the child.* New York: Free Press.

Piaget, J. (1962). *Language and thought of the child.* Atlantic Highlands, NJ: Humanities.

Piaget, J. (1962). *Play, dreams and imitations in childhood.* New York: Norton.

Piaget, J. (1965). *The child's conception of number.* New York: Norton.

Piaget, J. (1966). *Origins of intelligence in children.* New York: International Universities Press.

Piaget, J. (1974). *Biology and knowledge.* Chicago: University of Chicago Press.

Piaget, J. (1975). *Child's conception of the world.* Totowa, NJ: Littlefield.

Piaget, J. (1976). *Judgment and reasoning in the child.* Totowa, NJ: Littlefield.

Piaget, J. (1976). *The child and reality.* New York: Penguin.

Piaget, J. (1976). *The grasp of consciousness: Action and concept in the young child.* Cambridge: Harvard University Press.

Piaget, J. (1978). *Success and understanding.* Cambridge: Harvard University Press.

Piaget, J. (1982). *Adaptation and intelligence: Organic selection and phenocopy.* Chicago: University of Chicago Press.

Piaget, J. (1983). *The child's conception of physical causality.* Denver: Arden Library.

Piaget, J. & Inhelder, B. (1969). *Psychology of the child.* New York: Basic.

Singer, D. & Revenson, T. (1978). *A Piaget primer: How a child thinks.* New York: New American Library.

Wadsworth, B. (1979). *Piaget for the classroom.* New York: Longman

CHAPTER FIVE

THE PREDICTABLE MISBEHAVIORS: MORAL DEVELOPMENT

WE FIND it difficult to believe that Supreme Court justices used to sneak candy from the kitchen cupboard, just as our children do! You can bet each did.

You see children journey through the same stages of moral thought. Each is as unique and predictable as the Three Worlds of childhood thought seen earlier. Sometimes we forget that when we were children, each of us thought and acted much as our children do now.

Parents sometimes categorize children as either moral or immoral. There is a tendency to worry that a misbehaving child may never change. Therefore, it is often difficult for parents to relax with a child who has committed a serious offense. Although some individuals remain in lower stages because of limited potential or limited opportunities, most children with concerned parents advance to higher stages of moral thinking.

Nevertheless, parents remain inpatient, often ignoring the time required for a child's moral growth. A young physician and his wife, the Earlings, clearly exhibited this anxiety. Their four-year-old broke a valuable vase and hid the broken parts under his bed. When asked if he was responsible, the young boy insisted that someone else broke and hid it.

As Dr. Earling discussed the situation, he recalled, "When I was a boy, we knew right from wrong. I don't believe we ever lied like this. What are we doing wrong, or is there something wrong with him?" Probably nothing is wrong; it's that Dr. Earling's memory is faulty. Most adults only recall five or six specific memories of events that took place before the age of six. Therefore, many of our impressions are really from later childhood. When Dr. Earling was four years old, he probably behaved just as his son does. In fact, if Dr. Earling's parents were present, they would undoubtedly enjoy telling stories about their son's early misbehaviors.

Dr. and Mrs. Earling's son is developing normally. They only needed to be patient. Moral growth goes through age-related stages that cannot be hurried. Once again, time and experience become the allies of parents. In time, children begin to make moral decisions that are less self-centered and more caring. However, parents can affect their children's moral progression. The choice of discipline techniques used by parents can foster growth, or it can retard the child's progress toward higher moral levels. Parents can also affect their child's ability to carry through with moral decisions. It is not enough to be merely thinking on progressively higher levels of thought; the child must also develop the courage to act upon her beliefs. This courage is best learned by a child through her observation of her parents as they make important decisions that affect the lives of others. Children will grow. Parents can be confident that children will grow in the direction they are shown.

During a convention, I heard two counselors, both of whom were young fathers, discussing their income tax reports. One said, "Oh, I never report any of the money I earn doing workshops. There is absolutely no way that the government can track down that money." The other retorted, "But that's not the point. That is part of our income as professionals. I think it should be reported, and I do report it."

Both of these fathers are, or will be, concerned with the moral decisions made by their children. Both will tell their children to do what is right. But one is practicing what he preaches, while the other obeys the law only when he chooses to. As always, children are more influenced by what they see and overhear than by what they are told.

THE STAGES OF MORAL THOUGHT

Lawrence Kohlberg's work explains why children make specific moral decisions. There are distinct stages of moral thought. Although a child may make a brilliant decision occasionally, her moral thinking is generally limited to the boundaries of her life stage. Both children and adults have the ability to understand the moral thought of a person one stage ahead of them. Not only is the thought understood, but there is also a desire to begin to think in that advanced way. With the opportunity to practice and to observe decision making at a higher stage, one may soon enter into that stage.

Most adults have grown through the influence of a mentor whose thinking was respected and whose ideas were solicited. Generally, this person's thoughts were more advanced but were understandable. Adults usually continue to be influenced by people whose thinking they admire. Such a person may be a minister, teacher, writer, friend, or family member. But the point is that after ideas are exchanged, a person feels inspired to new levels of thought.

The mentors of children are usually their parents. If parents keep their thoughts challenging but within the reach of their children, growth will occur. If a parent's thought is too sophisticated for a child, she will ignore it, just as adults ignore a speaker whose terminology and thoughts seem needlessly obscure. On the other hand, parents should not dip down to their children's level by responding in kind to their actions and thoughts. Although some theorists believe it is proper to challenge from two stages above, it is probably better to remain a single level ahead of a child. The key is to challenge the child's thinking.

Moral thought and action can freeze in early stages. It is particularly noted that criminals and sociopaths seem to remain in those early stages of childhood thought. Also, some people who are mentally impaired may not have the potential to leave the lower stages; yet these are exceptions, and the vast majority will move to more conventional thinking.

PERIOD ONE: SELF-CENTERED THOUGHT

In the first two stages, or period one, thought is generally self-centered. The needs and feelings of others are rarely considered when decisions are made. Morality is usually based on the question: **How will this situation affect me? Or, what's in this for me? Or, will I be caught?** Kohlberg called this egotistical period of life the Preconventional Period. Children remain in this period at least through the age of seven. Some researchers believe that most remain there until the age of nine, or even eleven. But movement is individual, so knowing one's own child's moral reasoning is the key.

STAGE ONE — NO!

Moral thought may begin when a toddler understands the word "NO!" This may be particularly true when the word is accompanied by action. For example, parents may tell a nine-month-old who is about to stick a bobby pin into an electrical socket, "NO!" The child has no technical understanding of why she should not play with the socket. She is simply startled by the "NO!" and unhappy to be removed from the room.

After repeated "NO's!" coupled with consequences, children learn that if they do not do what their parents wish, they will experience negative results. Not wanting to be disciplined, the child begins to conform to the parents' wishes. Again, good behavior is not performed because it is "right" but to avoid parental displeasure.

Although children may be considered good or bad, judged by their actions, it is really the motives for their behaviors that display moral thought. For example, a young child who does not cheat on a test may appear to be good, but her reason for not cheating could be based solely on her fear of being caught, rather than on principles such as duty and fairness. An hour later, this same child may obey the orders of a playground bully by throwing rocks at a defenseless child. This time she appears to be bad, but the same motivation prompted both decisions. In the first case, she feared punishment from a teacher, and in the second instance, retribution from a tyrant is avoided. In neither case are sophisticated moral principles followed.

Some adults also do the "right thing" only because they fear punishment. Many will be careful not to drink and drive because they fear that the police may catch them. Others would not cheat on their tax returns because an audit is possible. In order to keep their jobs, some follow the instructions of bosses even when they know the instructions are wrong. In all of these instances, a person has made moral decisions solely to avoid being punished and experiencing the resultant negative consequences. There is no consideration of making the decision on the basis of whether it is essentially right or wrong. There is no thought given to how the decision may affect others.

With young children, however, this is a step in the right direction. To be able to identify an authority and to respect that person's wishes can save the child from danger and the family from potentially destructive situations. Because morality is not always based on inner beliefs or convictions, this level is a dangerous one for our world; it allows powerful people and governments to gain and wield too much control. This level of morality affirms the adage that "might makes right." Thus, the power of men like Adolph Hitler may go unchallenged, either on the national, local, or family level.

For a child, stage-one morality can lead to personal danger. A colleague of mine consulted me about bruises her child received in a daycare setting. When questioned, her child said, "I fell down." I urged the mother not to ignore her suspicions of foul play. She should try to insure that the setting was safe. The daycare operator convinced the mother no physical discipline was used.

Two months later, her child came home with lacerations and welts. After the mother assured the child she would never need to return to that daycare center, the child confessed that the woman in charge routinely spanked and 'switched' misbehaving children. When asked, "Why didn't you tell me?" the child replied, "Because she told me it was between the two of us and if I ever told I would really get it the next day." Unfortunately, sad stories like this are not uncommon. Adults can take advantage of a child's fear of punishment. To protect a child, parents must always keep in mind the child's limitations.

STAGE TWO—"SCRATCH MY BACK"

In the second stage, a child becomes interested in following rules in order to obtain a reward. "What's in it for me?" is a central theme of moral thought. As in stage-one, the stage-two thinker is egocentric, but now rules are followed, not primarily to avoid punishment but to capitalize on the potential benefits.

For parents, additional problems occur with the onset of stage-two thought. As children become older, they also become sneakier! Although older children still obey rules in order to avoid trouble, they will, on occasion, try to get away with breaking the rules. This is the stage when a child may break a window and blame someone else, or she may steal money from a parent's pocket or purse. The key is that a child actively tries to deceive the authority. Few behaviors antagonize parents more than willful disobedience. Kids will slip out of windows during nap periods, venture close to forbidden lakes, make deals with their siblings not to tell mom or dad, cheat at cards or other games, and generally try to beat the system.

A challenge for parents is to remember that children have not yet formed an inner code for what is right and wrong. Although they may be able to memorize the Ten Commandments or other rules for behavior, they do not understand the intentions or impact of such rules. They generally are able to consider only themselves.

A Sunday school teacher relayed her frustration in teaching first graders the story of the Good Samaritan. Her teaching strategy seemed ideal. Each child played a role as the class acted out the story. Afterward, the class members discussed the meaning of the story. Everyone seemed to understand the plight of the poor man who needed help. But before the class dismissed, the most unpopular child fell. His nose began to bleed profusely. Instead of feeling empathetic, the members of the class joined together in laughter. Openly, they made fun of the unfortunate child. The incident displayed that children's verbal skills, which allowed discussion of moral principles, exceed their true understanding and ability to apply these principles.

Since no inner code exists, guilt is also rarely present at this stage. Therefore, if a youngster eats an entire box of Girl Scout® Cookies and is not caught, she will not feel guilty about her actions. If caught, she may be upset only because she **was** caught.

When Emily was four, she reported that Patrick (six) was stealing a forbidden ice cream sandwich from the freezer. After being caught, Patrick's response was typically stage two: "Emily, you are not my best friend anymore. You can't play with any of my things." He proceeded to storm to his room, as if he had been greatly wronged. There was no consideration on his part of personal wrongdoing. This self-centered reaction is common in school-age children. Unfortunately for some, it continues into adulthood.

Adults whose actions remain in the second stage usually develop into good talkers who slide in and out of the law. They have a tendency to believe that money can solve all problems. I recall that during my college hitchhiking days I was picked up by a man who scared me to death by driving his elegant car twenty miles over the speed limit. Finally, a policeman pulled him over and gave him a ticket. After the episode and as we drove on, the driver looked over and said, "Don't worry. My lawyer will fix it. This is my fifth ticket this month." This driver never considered the necessary reasons that rules exist for not speeding. He felt no concern for the lives of others. Morality for him was based on the question: **"How can I do what I want to and get away with it?"**

Teachers often have students who live in this second stage. Unfortunately, many teachers still believe that students who cheat will be punished by "having to live with the knowledge that they cheated." This may be true with adults at higher stages, but for a person in stage two, guilt is not present. Such students will not monitor their own behavior.

When I worked with imprisoned heroine addicts, I found many adults existing within the stage-two world. Most showed no guilt for the robberies, shams, frauds, or other activities which supported their expensive habits. Many were still angry over the circumstances that led to their incarcerations. After talking to these prisoners, a stranger would swear each was one of the world's finest citizens. Everything said sounded right. Everything done seemed wrong.

Indeed, some adults do think like young children. But our children need not stop at this stage. For training purposes, parents need to remember that children only understand moral thought which is one stage above the one the child is in. Too often parents lose contact with their children by becoming too abstract. At a picnic, I watched a child sneak a piece of cake before supper. His father saw him. Then he began, as if by habit, a long lecture on morality: "Son, someday you will discover that people who do not follow the rules have to pay the price. It may not be in this lifetime, but sometime you will be accountable for your actions. . ." His speech continued for what seemed like hours. I was totally bored with the sermon, and I assumed that the child was also. My guess was confirmed ten minutes after the father left, when the child stole a second piece of cake. Parents need to avoid becoming too abstract with a young child. Instead, the simple ideas that reflect stage three, or "family morality," discussed below, will be more helpful to the child's continued growth.

THE SECOND PERIOD: CONVENTIONAL THOUGHT

The second period represents a tremendous leap from the two earlier stages. In stage three and four, individuals are able to take the desires and rights of others into consideration. The profound self-centeredness of the earlier stages is beginning to wane. Most American adults remain within the realm of conventional morality.

Debate continues among scholars concerning when the majority of children begin stage-three thought. Results of research vary. For many, stage-three thought will occur about the age of eleven, but most children tend to understand, and some appear to move into, stage-three thought during the early elementary school years. As always, what is important is what is true for your child, rather than the majority. Nothing substitutes for knowing one's children well.

STAGE THREE — "GOOD BOYS AND GIRLS"

Mom: "Johnny, you cannot call your neighbor, Suzie, an 'idiot'."
Johnny: "But why Mom?"
Mom: "Because it hurts her feeelings."

Johnny: "But why can't I do it? I can't stand her. Besides, Paul calls her an idiot, and his mother doesn't care."

Mom: "It doesn't matter what Paul's family does. You are a McGregor, and the McGregors don't do things like that."

The stage-three person regards the feelings and beliefs of those in her group as important. Family members are often the first individuals that children begin to respect. To be a part of a family, there are certain rules which must be followed. It is unimportant whether other children—or even others outside the family—act immorally. This unit has its own written, as well as unwritten, rules. Usually, an individual is proud to be a part of the special group and willingly follows its code.

In contrast, the stage-two person develops no loyalty to groups. She might verbalize loyalty to the family, but she would not act on it. Being a member of a group is important only for what the group can do for the person. When no longer needed, the group is discarded. Loyalty develops only when an inner code of right and wrong is established. The child in stage three **knows** what her family allows and does not allow, and there is pride in being part of the family. If the stage-three child violates a rule, there is guilt when misbehavior betrays the bonds shared by her family.

Although stage-two children will cheat on tests without guilt, stage-three children will feel guilty if cheating is condemned by the family or by a peer group of her choice. I can remember when I finally accepted that the West family did not cheat, lie, or steal. I can recall looking at someone else's paper one day in school, to get some help, and for the first time, I felt ashamed. I knew I had violated the rules of my family. I made an A on the test, but I felt dishonorable for weeks. I can never remember cheating again. The family's "shoulds" had taken over.

Most humans seem to need to belong to a group that they regard as made up of significant people. To be accepted by these individuals, one generally adopts the group's value system. How good this is for society depends on how positive the intentions and values of these groups are and how their values affect individuals throughout the world.

For example, some organizations insist that members conduct themselves in a manner that destroys the right to life and liberty of other people. An example might be the Ku Klux Klan or the legendary Mafia. To be a good member of such a group requires that a person accept traditions that violate others' human rights. In order not to be an outcast, rules are obeyed. Therefore, at its worst, stage-three morality profits a small group but endangers the rights of others. Nevertheless, parents need to help a child move from stage two by teaching each child what is right or wrong according to the family's own values, religion, and national heritage.

Stage-three people can display unbridled chauvinism. This narrow-mindedness became apparent in my own children during the 1984 Olympic games. While we all pulled for athletes from the United States, my children also pulled **against** athletes from other countries. Unfortunate injuries to foreign athletes were greeted with enthusiasm. Clearly, my children's values reflected a "We vs. Them" stance. The good of only a small number of the world's athletes was being considered. No sense of fair play for everyone was present.

International events provide valuable opportunities for parents to help expand a child's vision beyond the limits of his own family. By putting the child in the shoes of different people around the world, parents can help children reconsider their limited ideas. Personal, national, or world events are ideal opportunities for children to be exposed to a variety of different solutions to complicated moral dilemmas.

In 1985, devastating hunger resulted in the starvation of thousands of people in Africa. Individuals from around the world responded in ways that would alleviate some of the hunger. In a dramatic display of concern, famous singers from the United States released a song called "We are the World." Their influence on young people was seen as the record climbed to first place on record charts. Entertainers from other nations joined in influencing young people to consider the needs of others outside of their own limited associations. International events can also be used by parents to teach children about the less fortunate in our own communities, as well as in other nations. Children can contribute and collect money for worthy causes. The basis for such problems can become the focus of family discussions. Poverty and its problems may always exist on our planet, so opportunities for families to become involved will be present daily.

Many events in our world are controversial. Children can benefit from these hot issues. The more experience a child has in making decisions and hearing opposing opinions (or both sides), the more a child's thinking will grow. Conflict from others' beliefs is necessary for moral growth to occur. If parents accept ideas from people outside their most significant group, they will be able to lead children to the next stage.

STAGE FOUR—LAW AND ORDER

Not all adults move to the fourth stage. A host of productive and invaluable individuals remain in stage three. But many adults and some children enter the fourth stage when they realize that some rules must be followed for the good of all people in the world. Often, following these rules is not advantageous to the family or to a cherished organization, but there is a realization that if anyone could do just what she wished at any time, there would soon be chaos.

As children, we were always annoyed by adults in this stage. Invariably, after we tried to explain why we broke a rule, the adult would knowingly respond, "But what if everyone in the world broke rules whenever they felt like it?" There never seemed to be any way to respond to this argument. It was obvious that everything would be in chaos if **others** were free to break rules. Certainly, we felt capable of making exceptions, but not **others**!

Once a person believes that the world can survive best if everyone obeys the law, it is rare for that person to violate rules. Often, obedience to the law is required at great cost to the individual, her family, friends, or significant organizations. What is good for a small group is no longer the major criterion for action. Consistency and dependability are found in this law and order person. One does not wonder from moment to moment what behaviors or actions can be expected.

A law and order person develops an inward sense of duty which propels her to action. This feeling of duty overrides personal, family, and group considerations. For example, a stage-four adult might serve the military in time of war, even if he personally opposed the war. Taxes would be paid to the government, even when it would be impossible to get caught in a particular violation. Duty prevents this person from being impressed with the excuse that "everyone else is doing it." This simply means everyone else is exhibiting a lower level of moral reasoning.

Recently a colleague of mine was asked to review an article submitted to a prestigious journal. The authors of the article were two of his best friends, and the editor of the journal was the major doctoral professor of all three. It was obvious that the editor and writers chose my friend to evaluate the article because they anticipated that he would approve the manuscript because of their joint friendships. But the manuscript was bad—it met none of the criteria established by the journal for accepting scholarly work. The dilemma of my friend was clear; choose between supporting friendships or supporting the code of the journal. He chose to reject the manuscript. It was a choice which no doubt will be unpopular with his colleagues but, for my friend, his duty to the academic code of ethics was more important than breaking the code to insure friendships. A stage-three person might debate the issue of whether to reject the article or not. In the end, supporting relationships may outweigh legal considerations.

Difficulties occur when a person's dedication to obeying the law is greater than his dedication to what is morally right in a given situation. Often, there is a closed dialogue and a black and white treatment of all situations. Nevertheless, this is an advanced stage. All future moral growth will be built upon the basic truth and logic of law and order thinking.

Acting on the convictions of stage four requires courage. For those in the self-centered fast lane of stage two, law and order people appear dull and rigid. For those who place the interests of their own group first, law and order thinking can be considered cold and unfaithful, but the sense of duty to a higher order leads the stage-four thinker to live by rules on which the sanity of the world depends.

Søren Kierkegaard's two volumes entitled **Either/Or** feature a marvelous dialogue between a romantic youth displaying stage-two moral thought and an ethical judge who represents the law and order of stage-four. The young man enjoys living for his own pleasure, while displaying only slight regard for the rights of others. To him, Judge William lives a dull, predictable life. The young aesthete prefers the excitement and unpredictability of his own self-centered modality of living. Indeed, the youth may be partially correct about the judge's life. The person who bases his decisions on the rules and regulations of society is predictable. But Judge William's consistency allows order and fairness to exist in society. What the young man failed to see is that those who follow the law can also live exciting, enjoyable lives. One need not be morally self-centered to enjoy the pleasures of this life.

POST-CONVENTIONAL THOUGHT

Kohlberg suggests that there are stages beyond three and four. His work includes descriptions of stages four and one-half, five, and six, and a new stage seven is now being developed. In these stages, there is a belief that nothing is more important than an individual's right to life and dignity. How to conduct oneself when laws violate an individual's human rights becomes a primary consideration in each of these stages. These are not stages of childhood; only exceptional adults live within these worlds.

STAGE FOUR AND ONE-HALF — DISILLUSIONMENT

In late adolescence, young people often realize that the laws they obediently followed are not always essentially just. For example, sometimes college students learn that some rules are not to benefit students but in order to keep the alumni and trustees happy. For some who had blindly followed the law previously, anger follows. Instead of trying to change unjust rules, the adolescent response is often to break rules that seem unjust. "No one has the right to tell me what to do," is a common rationalization. Stage four and one-half behavior resembles the self-centered behavior found in stage two. The difference is that the stage four and one-half person still understands the necessity for following rules—if they are good rules. Soon this person should enter stage five to begin work within the system to change unjust laws.

A student whom I greatly enjoyed was arrested and convicted on drug possession. The offense was his first of any type. As his mother told me, "In all of his life, John was never so much as sent to the principal's office." Throughout his college years, John was a sensitive, dedicated young man who exhibited leadership inside and outside of the classroom. But he fell into a trap of stage four and one-half. For a few months, he, like a stage-two person, believed he could do as he wished and avoid punishment. This was a student who obeyed laws in the past and will probably obey them in the future. But the price he paid for his disillusionment with college and national laws provided to be a costly journey away from the legal path.

STAGE FIVE—SOCIAL CONTRACT

This stage emphasizes that laws were made for people and not people for laws. The quality of laws is judged and circumstances that might present special exceptions to the spirit of the law are considered. Poor laws are changed through peaceful means. In this stage, individuals generally prefer to work within the system to change unjust laws. Care is taken not to violate the rights of others when working toward change.

STAGE SIX—INDIVIDUAL PRINCIPLES AND CONSCIENCE

In the final stage, an individual develops principles founded on what is good for humanity. Self-chosen ethical principles are not based upon a clear code such as the constitution of an individual country may provide. Instead, general moral principles equally supportive of people in all nations are employed. For example, the Golden Rule—"Do unto others as you would have others do unto you"—is found in writings from every culture in the world. Yet, how one enacts this principle is not clearly stated. The stage-six person struggles to decide how to live and act to best serve all of humanity, based on universal principles.

The most influential critic of one's behavior is no longer family or society itself, but one's own self-criticism. To violate one's personal code of ethics would result in self-criticism far more painful than any punishment coming from outside oneself, including death. Examples Kohlberg cites of people who have acted upon such individual convictions include such world figures as Jesus Christ, Martin Luther King, and Mahatma Gandhi.

MORAL DEVELOPMENT AND DISCIPLINE TECHNIQUES

The dominant influence on the normal child's moral growth may be the discipline techniques used by parents. With discipline comes the truest modeling of how one human should treat another in times of stress. No longer are parents verbally teaching children about morality. **Now** they are showing them. Already it is widely known that children who have been emotionally or physically abused grow up to treat their own children in the same way. Likewise, discipline techniques used by parents to correct a child's misbehavior without damaging her self-respect influence the child's moral growth in a positive way.

Below, several major methods of disciplining children are discussed in terms of how their use might influence the moral development of children. Since other factors also influence the moral development of children, it is impossible to make an absolute match between moral growth and discipline, yet discipline may be a major predictor of the likely growth of a child.

GUILT

Guilt seems, for some, an effective method of influencing children to conform to rules. Many parents emphasize that a child is a "bad boy" or a "bad girl" if a rule is broken. Others respond in a hurt way, even weep, if a child violates a trust. Unfortunately, guilt is often felt by children after expressing hard feelings, such as anger, or normal curiosity, such as sexual exploration.

Many young children learn to feel guilty for expressing and/or feeling emotions such as anger. Traditionally, females were victimized by generations of parents who believed the display of anger by females was offensive. Anger is not an offensive emotion; it is a natural and healthy one. But the methods of displaying anger can be offensive. Therefore,

==parents need to teach children how to use their anger productively.== For example, the following dialogue is representative of families who view anger as a vice:

Cindy: "Mother, I hate you for not letting me go to the movie. Now get out of my room right now!"

Mother: "How dare you get angry at me and use that tone of voice. You should be ashamed of yourself. After all I have done for you, you have no right to get angry with me." (At this point, the mother may cry, leading the child to feel more guilt because of angry feelings.)

Let's replay this example of acknowledging anger in a more helpful fashion. Remember: it is not the anger that is mistaken, it is the presentation of the anger.

Cindy: "Mother, I hate you for not letting me go to the movie. Now get out of my room right now!"

Mother: "Cindy, I understand your feelings, but yelling at me is not going to get you what you want. When you are ready to talk about our disagreement, I will be happy to talk with you."

Many adults still suffer guilt feelings when engaging in activities they no longer believe to be wrong. Early moral training has a lasting influence. The Guilt Monkeys are almost impossible to get off one's back. It is as if parents were still giving disapproving signals to their grown children.

One young couple entered counseling because their sexual life was unsatisfactory. The woman was uncomfortable with sex of any type. The more she tried to avoid sexual interaction with her husband, the more the marriage suffered. I vividly recall her explanation for the difficulty, "When I was a little girl, my mother used to tell me sex was bad. She used to tell me that only animals should have sex. She never explained sexual intercourse to me. All she said was that sex is dirty and could ruin peoples lives if they had it before they were married. I never considered engaging in sex before we were married. Tom was really patient. But then when we were married, he expected me to be able to turn sex on. I just can't turn it on. For me, it is still as if my mother is in the bedroom telling me how disgusting it is. I just can't seem to get away from her." The intentions of this woman's mother are unknown. The mother may have been trying to prevent an unwanted early pregnancy, but the mother's use of guilt, rather than an educated conversation with her, handicapped her daughter's life. Guilt led to a needless struggle that threatened to destroy a young marriage.

The long term nature of guilt may attest to its effectiveness as a tool of conformity, but the limitation of this technique is its destruction of independent, moral thought. Guilt sometimes enslaves a child, and later the adult to the moral beliefs of their parents. The chains of guilt make it extremely difficult for a child to find her own way. It would appear that children frozen by guilt may remain in stage-three morality: Always there is a goal to please others, a belief that to be acceptable one must be a "good boy" or a "good girl." Unfortunately, what is good has already been predetermined by the parents.

Adult development specialists are discovering that many who did everything demanded or expected of them early in life are experiencing a crisis in middle adulthood called the "mid-life crisis." Some individuals may attend college, choose a mate, and enter a profession solely because they believe they should. But in the late 30s, these individuals often review their early decisions and find they are no longer satisfying. In this crisis, painful decisions are often made that reverse, or a least change, those commitments made early for the sake of others' approval. Being a "good boy" or "good girl" by following parents, friends, or society's wishes may indeed lead to despair.

PHYSICAL PUNISHMENT

The use of physical punishment may be linked to parents in any of the first four stages. But because of the physical pain involved and the fear children develop of being struck or getting in trouble, recipients of the punishment are often locked into the first or second stage. Intelligent children will often do anything to avoid being spanked or otherwise chastised. They either blindly conform, or else they tend to avoid honesty in order to avoid pain. Stage-one children may obey parents only because they fear punishment, and although their behavior is pleasing, it is based on hollow foundations. The consistent use of physical punishment as a primary tool of discipline seems too great a risk to a child's growing moral thought. Physical punishment highlights power instead of what is right and wrong in children's behavior.

The most sinister advice for parents I have heard came from a local, small congregation. The minister made a tape for his congregation, suggesting discipline techniques. He quoted such Old Testament passages as "spare the rod and spoil the child" as a basis for his advice. His tape instructed: "You must spank your child when he disobeys you. You must continue to spank the child as long as he cries while you are disciplining him. Crying is a further sign of disobedience, and the child must be freed of it. You should spank up to the point you see the blue of his marrow. For it is better for a child to feel the rod now than to experience an eternity in hell."

Such disciplinary techniques do not help a child grow in moral thought. These methods may destroy the spirit of some children and browbeat a child into apparent good behavior, but the obedience is a response to fear and intimidation.

Most parents who use physical punishment, of course, use it in a more reasonable fashion. But physical punishment never expands moral thinking. Although children who are regularly punished physically **can** advance to higher stages due to other techniques and attributes of parents, their growth occurs in spite of, not because of, physical punishment. Alternatives for physical punishment will be suggested in Part II of this book.

TALKING AND NOT ACTING

Children of parents who are generally permissive seem to congregate in stage two. They believe they can, and they usually do, get away with anything. Splendid oratory skills are developed which enable them to escape consequences. When children learn that they will not be held accountable for their behavior, they are encouraged to remain self-centered. There is no reason for them to be aware of the effect of their behavior upon others.

At a dinner, I observed a mother, who was a talker, interact with her son, who was still in Kohlberg's pre-conventional level. For a teenager, John's behavior seemed inappropriate and immature. He managed to insult almost everyone during the course of the evening. Following each insult, his mother replied, "Now John, you shouldn't say things like that. Be nice." John soon tired of insulting people and began to push and shove smaller children. At first the mother only watched. But then she called John over and continued to discipline with words, "John, try to remember these children are younger. Be nice." But John was not cooperative. He had learned over a period of time that he could do whatever he wished and not suffer any consequences. His mother never challenged his behavior; she simply interrupted it with conversation. Consequently, John's morality remained influenced by self-centered considerations.

INCONSISTENCY

Inconsistency from parents prevents children from building an inner code of right and wrong. Justice and punishment change radically as the parents' moods fluctuate. The child's attention focuses on the mood of the authority figure rather than on the moral situation itself. Therefore, children of inconsistent parents become more interested in reading an authority's mood than in reading themselves. Moral development may stop in any of the first three stages.

Once I taught a small class of six-year-olds who generally recognized and obeyed the rules that were necessary for maintaining class order. Most knew not to yell or run around the class or disrupt the work of others. However, one boy, Paul, lacked self-control. Instead, he literally looked at me after each positive or negative behavior. It was as if my response was needed for Paul to evaluate the propriety of his actions. Although the others in the class could have existed without a formal code of rules and consequences, such a system was established to help this dependent child move toward autonomous control.

By chance, I often was able to observe Paul interact with his parents. The parents held no consistent expectations for Paul's behavior. Instead, they parented by mood and convenience. The same act by Paul might be ignored, even laughed at, in one instance. But in the next, it could elicit an angry shout. Paul did not have rules to follow. Right and wrong for him was determined by his parents' reactions to his actions. Therefore, when with adults, he was constantly searching their faces in order to evaluate his behavior. He was morally dependent.

LOGICAL CONSEQUENCES AND FAMILY COUNCILS

The combination of discussion and action, which is encouraged by combining family councils and the use of consequences, provides wide possibilities for moral growth. Applying the concept of consequences provides flexibility for working with either very young, stage-one children, or much older, stage-four adolescents. For example, the toddler brought back inside for walking out into the street learns to behave in order to avoid the consequences. Likewise, the teenager who is allowed to develop her own consequences for violating jointly agreed upon curfews, learns to create and accept the consequences for her decisions.

With the use of family councils, children begin to learn that rules are made to benefit **all individuals in a family.** Having input into making the rules causes children to feel they are important and respected members of the family. By debating consequences, children begin to think more empathetically and with sharper logic. There will be a growing knowledge that the rules are made for family members and can be changed if they do not work well. If a child has the potential to grow, the family council will provide the stimulation and positive conflict needed to travel through the moral stations of development and growth. Guidelines for the use of consequences and family councils will be provided in Part Two.

THINKING vs. DOING

As the old timers used to say: "Knowing what's right and doing what's right are two different things. It takes guts to do what is right." Few people will claim they never knowingly did something wrong. As you drive to work today, observe the number of individuals who drift through stop signs, who don't stop before turning right on red, or race through a caution light, aware that it is about to turn red. These violators know their behavior breaks laws. If a policeman were on the scene, most of these same citizens would follow the law. But for personal reasons, they choose to create their own rules.

Although small daily decisions may or may not be significant to the workings of society, it is my belief that they form a model for the future behavior of children. How closely parents follow their own moral beliefs—particularly when it is difficult or sacrificial to do so—may well be the most important influence on how their growing children will confront moral dilemmas.

Americans know stories of patriots courageously acting in accord with their beliefs, despite criticism, and even in the face of death. President John F. Kennedy's book **Profiles in Courage** describes the lives of a number of people who acted courageously despite the influence of friends, family, political parties, or social pressure. But the most important examples for a child are those displayed by her own parents. Each of us has a personal example to follow. As a child, in the late 50s, I saw my father, who was a minister, resign from a church after the congregation voted to deny membership to Blacks. He did so at great expense to himself and his family. Yet it was his example—not the life of a national figure—that became the greatest influence in my life.

With proper discipline and dialogue, each child should reach her potential as a moral thinker. By modeling the ability to back moral beliefs with actions, it is possible for parents to give moral courage to their children. What greater gift can parents make to the world than young people with the ability to think and the courage to act. One of my proudest moments as a parent came when my own child showed his first moments of moral courage.

In our family, slapping and hitting are forbidden. Our children have grown to accept this principle, although they do not thoroughly understand it, as occasional violations display. When in the second grade, Patrick observed a teacher in the hall slap a disorderly student. He automatically said to her, "You shouldn't hit a child. It's not right." In anger, the teacher made Patrick stay in after school for "giving her lip." Certainly the teacher thought Patrick's behavior was a sign of poor training. As his parent, I believed it was a sign of a child's growing courage. He paid a price for what he believed to be right. Although morally unsophisticated, children can learn to stand up for their present beliefs. Parents need not only challenge limited thinking, but also they must support positive movements.

LAWRENCE KOHLBERG

Lawrence Kohlberg's life has taken interesting twists along the path to his current position as a professor and Director of the Center of Moral Education and Development at Harvard University. He delayed entering college to spend three years at sea as a junior engineer in the merchant marines. When he entered college, his academic ability was readily apparent. Remarkably, it took him only two years to graduate from the University of Chicago. He completed his undergraduate degree in 1949.

Due to his creative discoveries, Kohlberg's doctoral work required seven years to complete. While writing his dissertation, Kohlberg became critical of the standard explanations of how a child develops morality. Instead of continuing research based on trends and other traditional theories, Kohlberg created an entirely new model for explaining children's moral development.

Kohlberg's work is related to Piaget's in some ways. Each man believes stages cannot be skipped. Each stage becomes progressively more complicated. Kohlberg believes that the cognitive advancement described by Piaget is a prerequisite for growing sophistication in moral thought. For example, post-conventional morality is not possible until formal operations is present. But factors other than cognitive growth are necessary for moral growth to occur. For example, not all formally operative people reach the more complex stages of morality. Therefore, cognitive growth is necessary, but not a sufficient condition for moral growth.

Since the completion of his Ph.D. in 1958 from the University of Chicago, Kohlberg's career has blossomed. He worked for Children's Hospital in Boston, was a professor at Yale University, became a Fellow at the Institute for Advanced Study in the Behavioral Sciences in Palo Alto, and spent six years as a professor at the University of Chicago. In 1968, he became a Professor of Education and Social Psychology at Harvard University, a position he now holds. As Director of the Center for Moral Education and Development, Kohlberg has developed numerous programs which help foster moral growth. With the promise of increased moral development, the world may benefit from improved relationships among people and, we hope, nations.

RELATED READINGS

Duska, R. & Whelan, M. (1975). *Moral development: A guide to Piaget and Kohlberg.* Ramsey, NJ: Paulist Press.

Kennedy, J. (1956). *Profiles in courage.* New York: Harper and Row.

Kierkegaard, S. (1959). *Either/or.* Princeton, NJ: Princeton University Press.

Kohlberg, L. (1964). Development of moral character and moral ideology. In M. Hoffman and L. Hoffman (Eds.), *Review of child development research,* (pp. 383-432). New York: Russel Sage.

Kohlberg, L. (1969). Stage and sequence: The cognitive-developmental approach to socialization. In D. Goslin (Ed.), *Handbook of socialization and research.* New York: Rand McNally.

Kohlberg, L. (1976). Moral stages and moralization: The cognitive-development approach. In T. Lickona (Ed.), *Moral development and behavior.* New York: Holt, Rinehart, and Winston.

Kohlberg, L. (1981). *The philosophy of moral development: Essays in moral development.* New York: Harper and Row.

Kohlberg, L. (1983). *The psychology of moral development.* New York: Harper and Row.

Kohlberg, L. & Hewer, A. (1983). *Moral stages: A current formulation and a response to critics.* New York: Skarger.

Munsey, B. (1980). *Moral development, moral education and Kohlberg.* Birmingham, AL: Religious Education.

PART TWO
WORKING WITH MISBEHAVIORS

CHAPTER SIX

ACTIVE APPROACHES TO MISBEHAVIORS

"JOHNNY, I've told you a thousand times not to take your seat belt off when we are driving"..."Johnny, please put your seat belt back on"...Johnny, I mean right now...Johnny, you know how serious this is; I don't want to have to tell you again..." Suddenly, Dad swerves the car to a stop, reaches back, and slaps Johnny's hands. Johnny shrieks with pain. Mom feels hollow inside. Dad, not quite sure why anger got the best of him, silently speeds down the road. Ten miles later, Johnny unfastens his seat belt again...and smiles.

Most adults parent as their parents did. Our society has not yet responded to the challenge of training its citizens to undertake the most difficult and important task of life—parenting. Thus, new parents tend to use familiar techniques, those which they experienced in their own childhood. Even parents who swore they would not use certain tones of voice or harsh methods with their own children often find themselves, to their horror, repeating their parents' errors. Although parents may feel guilty when reverting to old methods, they cannot be expected to use techniques they have never experienced or learned.

However, by studying new methods, parents can add to their current knowledge, and before adding new ideas, it should be helpful to explore common methods of disciplining children.

TRADITIONAL DISCIPLINE: FLAPPERS, SWATTERS, AND MOODERS

Three common discipline approaches are often used by untrained parents. Each uses predictable behaviors when meeting the challenges of children. Flappers attempt to discipline by the tongue. Often flappers disclose their identities by using phrases such as "I've told you one thousand times," "How many times must I tell you?" "Wait until your Dad/Mom gets home!" or "When will you ever learn?"

Whenever you find a flapper, you usually find a "parent-deaf child." Such children craftily take advantage of parents who use words rather than action. Flappers' children obey only when the parent's anger grows intense enough to create action. These children keep a close watch on the adult's boiling point.

A cartoon passed around counseling circles shows a young girl playing outside with her friends. Her mother calls her to supper several times, but the daughter ignores her. Finally, the friend says, "Your mother called you five times, aren't you going inside?" To which the young student of parental nature replies, "Not yet. She isn't serious until she begins to scream." Children respond to parents when action by the parent is imminent. Flappers rarely act, so their children rarely react to pleas for appropriate discipline.

Generally, flappers are "good people" who want to be liked by their children and their friends. By rarely saying "No" to children and by creating few consistently enforced rules, flappers attempt to keep peace in the family, but outsiders gain the impression that the children are in control of these homes.

Youngsters raised in a permissive atmosphere frequently expect to be in total control. Temper tantrums are routine when limits are enforced. Rarely is disappointment or denial handled well. Unfortunately for them, much of life is spent responding to limitations and circumstance. Often, children of flappers develop grand oratory skills in an attempt to prevent parental action. An arsenal of ineffective verbal strategies may be used by parents in reply, including sermonizing, reasoning, warning, pleading, and granting "just one more chance!" Parents who prefer talk to action usually begin to feel over-burdened, out of control, and unappreciated. Relief from these feelings is earned as the parent begins to use Dreikurs's suggestion that "action, not words" is the key to discipline in a crisis.

For flappers, frustration can become intolerable. Nancy Johnstone expressed it this way during one of our parent study meetings: "It seems like I am always doing things for my kids. But they just don't appreciate it. I can ask them to do just one simple thing, like turn off the television and come to supper, and they refuse. They just sit glued to the television. Even when I talk to them until I am blue in the face, it does no good. They just do not listen to me. They show absolutely no respect."

Active Approaches to Misbehaviors

Nancy is right. They show no respect, but they do not lack respect for her as a mother. Instead, they lack respect for her ability to back her words with action. As Nancy began to talk less and act more, the children showed her the respect she earned.

Swatters tend to use fear and physical force to maintain rules in the home. There is a significant advantage to the swatter's method. It is beneficial **to act** when enforcing rules. Swatters tend to be less afraid to act and less dependent on the approval of others. However, swatting does have weaknesses. The use of power by parents promotes power struggles in the home and often creates an uncomfortable atmosphere. The majority of psychologists believe that consistent use of physical punishment inhibits the growth of internal moral control. Children continue to depend on authority figures for guidance. In addition, truthfulness is less consistently displayed by these children.

Maxine and Tom Bryant were a deeply religious couple, concerned about their eight-year-old son Jason's lying. Since lying was not tolerated by either parent, the Bryants were not sure how the habit began. As the Bryants discussed their philosophy of discipline, it became apparent that spanking was the parents' solution for most offenses. For example, Tom reported, "Yesterday, I found the handle broken off of the coffee pot. I was pretty sure Jason broke it, because he was throwing a ball up and down in the kitchen. I asked him to be truthful. He confessed, and I spanked him." What a price to pay for honesty! Jason lies to avoid an illogical, and possibly severe, punishment. If Jason could anticipate a logical consequence, like paying for the broken object, then honesty would increase.

A practical difficulty with physical punishment is its lack of effectiveness with rebellious children. Children who frequently misbehave expect physical punishment. Some even enjoy provoking parents into such humiliating situations. How often a power-hungry child is seen smiling as the parent delivers the first blow! Ironically, physical punishment only seems effective if used as a threat to cooperative children who rarely misbehave.

It is not unusual to find a swatter and flapper married to one another. In this parenting team, one talks too much and the other too little. Whether the flapper talks because the swatter is insensitive, or the swatter acts because talk does not work is of little importance. The combination creates difficulties both for parents and children.

The old policy "Wait until Dad gets home" often represents a union between a flapper and a swatter. Not only does it err in delaying the consequences, but it also makes Dad the designated bad guy. Mothers and fathers should speak and act for themselves. Parent educators are urging fathers to defy worn-out male stereotypes by sharing tender emotions. To be warm and close to children is difficult for a person who must also be the enforcer of family discipline. Parents should share the opportunities to both discipline and be tender with children.

A third group of parents use techniques of discipline that vary according to personal feelings. I call these parents "mooders." On a good evening, positive feelings may lead the parent to be tolerant of transgressions, or even to joke about problems. However, when the mood of the parent changes, so do responses to the same misbehaviors. If tired, depressed, or frustrated, the mooder may strike out at the child's mildest errors. Such parents are understanding one moment and inflexible the next.

Children of mooders are never confident about their behaviors. They are unsure how to act and tend to concentrate on how the parent is likely to react. Children frequently become what some have called "antenna people," who try to sense what mood the parent is in before deciding how to act. Such dependence on the parent's feelings robs children of spontaneity and self-confidence. Families who discipline by emotions often lack clear standards for behavior. Children may experience anxiety if there is uncertainty about the parent's reactions.

One nine-year-old boy in a group I worked with asked to speak with me privately. I discovered that Tommy had wrecked his bicycle when he jumped over a forbidden ramp. Although he was unhurt, the frame of his bicycle was badly bent. He was frightened to tell his parents. I asked, "What do you imagine will happen?" He responded, "Well, you never can tell what they are going to say. If Dad is in a bad mood, he'll 'tan my hide.' I wish I had been injured, then they wouldn't do anything to me." If Tommy's parents used logical consequences, he would be spared anxiety about his parents' reactions. Predictably, they would require him to be responsible for saving money to pay for the damage. But his parents' lack of predictability caused the child to panic. Family members experience less anxiety when reactions from one another are logical and expected.

Except when taken to extremes, nothing is critically wrong with any of these methods. Parents need not necessarily surrender presently used methods of discipline; instead, new approaches and techniques can be added to existing skills. Parents need to have as many options for methods of discipline as possible. Since one can always return to old

NATURAL AND LOGICAL CONSEQUENCES

Learning from one's own mistakes and misbehaviors is the best form of discipline. Never should discipline be revenge for disobedience. The goal of discipline is to help a child make better decisions in the future. Such choices should be based on sound judgment, rather than on fear. By learning to take the consequences for their decisions and behaviors, children begin to want to make helpful and productive choices. It is a slow but crucial learning process.

Adults in our society consistently take the consequences of their actions. For example, if a person is regularly late for work, a job may be lost. If one destroys another's property, restitution must be made. If money becomes scarce, belts must be tightened. Successful people living within the rules of a democracy generally understand the consequences of behaving appropriately or inappropriately.

Historically, some adults exist who use fear and punishment to force desired behavior on others. Such techniques are reported to be common among underworld organizations and delinquent gangs. Prisons were run on this theme in the past, but wardens have found it to be ineffective in rehabilitating prisoners.

Most parents wish to train their children to be contributors in a free society, rather than members of tyrannical groups. Freedom of choice, however, requires that a child be responsible for decisions. Just as adults do, children make errors; and like adults, children need to learn from their mistakes in order to profit from experience.

NATURAL CONSEQUENCES

Natural and logical consequences are powerful persuaders that help children learn responsibility. A natural consequence occurs when the parent does not intervene in a situation, but "allows the situation to teach the child." The technique is based on the adage "Every generation must learn that the stove is hot." Below are examples of common misbehaviors of children. For each misbehavior, several common parental responses are presented.

NATURAL CONSEQUENCES: EXAMPLES

SITUATION ONE

A three-year-old is playing with his food at the table. He refuses to eat.

Common Flapper Response. "Timmy, don't you want to try some of your beans?". . ."Timmy, please eat a little bit of everything on your plate." (Mother puts food on fork). . ."Timmy, let's pretent this is an airplane and your mouth is the runway—open up, here it comes!"

Common Swatter Response. "Timmy, quit messing with your food and eat, or you will spend the rest of your night in bed". . ."Your Mom spent hours making this meal. There are people starving all over the world and you won't eat.". . ."That's all, Timmy!" (Dad grabs Timmy's arm and drags him screaming to his room.)

Observation. The flapper's child learns that not eating can bring immediate parental attention. The parent is kept busy with the child. Not eating becomes fun for the attention or power-hungry child. The swatter's child can engage a parent in a power struggle at will. Not eating now becomes a weapon. Dinner becomes a battleground where Dad or Mom can be thrown into a rage by the child's simple refusal to eat.

Natural Consequences. Neither parent needs to say anything. At the end of the meal, plates are removed. Snacks are not allowed, and breakfast comes the next morning. Hungry children eat well.

Key to Natural Consequences. Parental agreement beforehand is important. There must be a family rule which allows no snacks between meals during the training period. Parents should never say to a hungry child later in the evening: "I warned you" or "I told you so." Instead, there is respect shown for the child's choice not to eat. Hunger is the consequence to be felt and should not be ruined by talking or "exceptions." Allow hunger to be the teacher.

SITUATION TWO

A first grade child loses her only baseball.

Flapper. "Mary, I told you to put the baseball up. You must learn to take care of your things. You wouldn't have lost the ball if you had put it in your closet. Are you listening? This time I will help you. But only this time. I'll buy another baseball, but I hope you finally have learned you lesson."

Swatter. "What do you mean you lost your baseball? That's totally irresponsible, Mary. I want you to spend the rest of the day in your room thinking about it. We'll talk about your irresponsibility tonight."

Observations. The first method teaches a child that the parent can be counted on to take the consequences of the child's behavior. After all, the parent bought a new baseball when the first one was lost. The second response leads a child into either a power struggle or revenge. The punished child concentrates on Dad's unfairness, rather than her own behavior.

Natural Consequences. "I am sorry you lost your ball. When you save enough money to buy a new one, I will be glad to take you to the store." The goal is to begin teaching the child to care for personal property. Although the parents express empathy over the loss, the child is allowed to learn from the consequences of her behavior. In some instances, if allowances are minimal, the parent may wish to pay for part of the purchase of the ball. Sometimes, children can pay parents back if a parent immediately replaces a ball. But no matter what arrangements are made, the child **and not the parent** needs to experience the consequences of her mistake.

LOGICAL CONSEQUENCES

There are times when nature's lessons are too severe. At such times, logical consequences for misbehavior must be developed. Particularly, this is true when harm can come to a child. For example, the natural consequence for a child wandering into the street without looking is that a car may run over the child. Obviously, no parent could allow such a harsh lesson. Thus, parents need to construct consequences that are helpful for the child's future decisions but that are less severe.

The secret of good consequences is the logic between the misbehavior and the consequences. For example, it is not logical for a parent to drive consistently to school to give a child a forgotten lunch box. In this instance, the parent takes the consequence for the child. What is logical is that the child goes without lunch or borrows money from the principal. In this way, the child learns from the error. Often it is difficult to think of perfect consequences, but with practice, such techniques become easy to master.

LOGICAL CONSEQUENCES: EXAMPLES

SITUATION ONE

A two-year-old runs into the street without permission and without looking for traffic.

Flapper. Runs after the child, grabs her hand and immediately begins talking. "Marcia, you scared me to death! Now you know you shouldn't wander into the street by yourself. I want you to stay in the yard. Remember: Don't go into the street! Promise?"

Swatter. The swatter runs after the child and spanks her immediately. The screaming and angry child is pulled back into the yard.

Observations. Once again, the two-year-old learned from the flapper that misbehavior is rewarded by undivided attention. Only the parent experienced negative consequences. The swatter created a power contest. When angry in the future, the child will look at the parent, dash into the street, and thus challenge the parent to act. In both cases, running into the street becomes a method of manipulating unsuspecting parents. It is a dangerous game children are learning.

Logical Consequences. If a child cannot play outside without venturing into the street, then she must return to the house. The parent can say, "If you go into the street, you are deciding to return inside." Every two-year-old tests parents. Soon the child will run into the street. The parent should quietly pick the child up and take her inside, despite the certain tears. Parents simply enforce the child's decision.

Observations. This method allows the child to make a decision. Children love to be outside. They soon learn that to go into the street is to give up the freedom and pleasure of being outside. Our eldest child took two weeks to learn this lesson. Finally one day, after being taken inside several times that week, he stood on the curb with his foot dangling over the street. He didn't look at his parents. Following some internal debate, he pulled his foot back from the edge and ran off to play. He had learned to make decisions, even at fourteen months. His thought centered on the consequences of his decision, rather than on how to control Mom or Dad. Two weeks is a short training period for such a crucial lesson.

SITUATION TWO

Dressing for preschool—Jack is a four-year-old who never seems to be ready on time. He dallies and will not dress.

Flapper. "Please, Jack, get dressed. You don't want to be late again. Here, I'll help you. Now, put your socks on. Jack, come back here. Right now! Jack, you're not even trying. You know I have to have you there on time. Please cooperate."

Swatter. "Jack, I want you dressed or I will spank your bottom. We have to leave. O.K. I warned you." A spanking follows.

Observations. Flappers again fall victim to the attention trap. Slow dressers learn how to control the adult's attention. And as usual, the power web entraps the swatter. An unpleasant home atmosphere persists, as parents always stand on the brink of warfare. In both cases, the child is more interested in controlling the parents than in dressing.

Logical Consequence. Tell the child's teacher that you are training your child to dress. Warn the teacher that it is possible that the child will come to school dressed inappropriately. The next morning, say to the child: "We will leave when the big hand is at the top of the clock." Nothing else is said. When it is time, take the child and the child's clothes into the car and start driving to school. Ignore protests. Respect the child's decision not to be dressed on time and allow her to experience the consequence of that decision.

Observations. If the parent can keep from turning this consequence into a power struggle by talking too much, the method should work quickly. The child may choose to dress in the car or she may arrive in pajamas at school. Her friends will then provide consequences. Two weeks of consistency with these consequences could prevent a lifetime of procrastination.

It is not always easy to think of appropriate consequences when first learning the skill. There will be times when parents grow tired of thinking in logical terms, and other times when laziness may lead a parent to use television or bedtime as a consequence. Mistakes will be made. But once a parent learns to use consequences readily, returning to former ineffective methods of discipline becomes unthinkable.

NORMAL MISBEHAVIOR AS AN OPPORTUNITY FOR LEARNING — STAGE-BY-STAGE EXAMPLES

Each new stage of childhood brings new misbehaviors. As one parent said, "Just when I found good consequences for one misbehavior, my child grows older, and an entire new set of problems begins." Logical and natural consequences are effective in each stage. As children grow accustomed to consequences, they can become more involved in creating their own. For younger children, parents may create logical consequences by giving choices. For example, one often used choice is: "Would you like to walk back to your bedroom, or would you like me to carry you?" Older children often are invited to create consequences: "What do you think should happen if. . .?"

Although misbehaviors change with age, many are predictable. In this section, predictable misbehaviors are examined and potential consequences discussed.

TRUST vs. MISTRUST

In the first eighteen months of life, prevention plays a significant role in reducing difficulties. For example, once the child begins crawling, the home can be "babyproofed." Valuables and delicate objects may be placed out of a child's reach so that she can explore in a relatively nonrestrictive environment. Babyproof latches for cabinets and stoppers for electrical outlets provide some safety for a child. Medicine, knives, machinery, gas, and other lethal household items should be locked away or placed out of reach.

Make sure not to expect too much of a child at this age. It is difficult, for instance, for a child to share toys or to wait for her turn. Toilet training seems inappropriate, in most cases, at this age. Language spurts generally occur in the next stage; therefore, pushing a child in language usage is not helpful. Remember, children develop at their own pace. While it is wise to encourage interests, it is unhealthy to push them. Childhood in our culture has enough stress without parents adding to it.

While misbehavior may not be as varied or as intense in this first stage, there are common challenges that parents will encounter.

OPPORTUNITY ONE: SLEEPING

Good sleeping habits begin about the fourth month, when a child is allowed to become independent upon waking at night. A discussion of this process was discussed in Chapter Three. Older children will display additional problems soon after learning to walk. Children may repeatedly leave the bedroom and try to join parents for the night. Often, magnificent power struggles take place over violated bedtimes.

Sample Consequences. Although parents may give the child the choice of walking back or being carried back to the bedroom, the rules must be clear: "It is bedtime. This is a time for resting. . ." When the child leaves her room, she should be taken back. Parents should not talk with the child. Acting is sufficient. The training period can be as long as two weeks or more, with the first nights involving fifteen or twenty interventions. Be prepared for this. Taking time now will save both time and recurrent problems for years to come. Children stay in their rooms when they realize that parents will act, rather than fight or talk. Later, a child may test the parent, but usually one step in her direction sends her back to bed.

OPPORTUNITY TWO: MEALS

Difficulties with children's eating habits occur at the end of this stage. The consequences of not eating were discussed earlier in this chapter. Remember, rarely is there a young child with eating problems who does not have a parent who either attempts to "talk" or force food into the child.

Children exhibit a natural tendency, called cafeteria feeding, to choose foods needed by the body. This means that if parents offer a variety of nutritious foods, an appropriate diet will be selected. Parents should take note of a few tendencies displayed by most children. Food preference may radically change. A favorite food one week may be avoided the next. Also, the same amount of food is not eaten during each meal. Lunch or dinner may become the time when the heaviest intake occurs. Snacks may be required to tide a child over between meals. It is important to provide a variety of fruits and raw vegetables for snacks instead of less healthy options, such as candy and ice cream. Snacks should not be given in the last two hours before a meal. Remember that young children tend to take a long time to eat; at least twenty minutes, and preferably thirty, should be provided for meals.

The dining table can become one of the great battlegrounds for families. Respect your child's natural inclination to eat appropriate foods; be tolerant of the expected idiosyncrasies in eating; avoid unhealthy snacks and apply natural consequences when a child uses food as a weapon in power struggles.

OPPORTUNITY THREE: BITING, KICKING, AND HITTING

All of these aggressive acts are natural responses from a frustrated child. Although natural, they are not acceptable.

Sample Consequence. Whenever a child bites, kicks, or hits, it is best to take her to an agreed-upon place until positive behavior returns.

"Time out" places include bedrooms, living rooms, sofas, or wherever a child can be separated from others. A simple statement should be made, such as "We do not bite in this family. Please stay in your room until you can keep from doing this." Once this rule is made known, action from the parent should follow the misbehavior, since words from parents usually escalate the difficulty. On second offenses, an agreed upon amount of time usually works best. If this happens in public or at a friend's house, take the child home. Yes, this will inconvenience parents. But it will show the child the parent's firm intention to act. Time spent at the onset of this problem will minimize future combat and public embarrassment.

Inconvenience to parents is a price paid for proper training. After Christmas, I looked forward to taking my children to a toy store to spend their Christmas money. I was as excited as they. Before we entered the shopping center I said, "If there are any fights or disruptions, we will go straight home. Do you agree?" They did. But suddenly Emily became frustrated because she didn't have enough money to buy the item she wanted. Her brother, enjoying her dilemma, teased her in a brotherly fashion. She responded by punching his arm. A crisis for me was at hand. I wanted to stay. After all, it was time-consuming to make such trips. But a deal had been struck. In order for them to know that consequences are serious agreements, we had to leave. Was I frustrated! The next day we returned. The same consequences were set and this time obeyed. Training children requires a sacrifice of time and often causes disruption of plans. But such sacrifices are essential for children to learn to trust their parents' intentions to act. Once children are confident in a parent's will to act, incidents of misbehavior are reduced.

OPPORTUNITY FOUR: MINOR INJURIES

During this stage, children suffer many minor injuries. Injuries do hurt. But it is crucial for a child to learn to overcome setbacks and to try again.

Sample Consequence. A child who is hurt needs comfort. But overconcern or too much sympathy leads a child to be timid, lacking confidence in her own ability to be active in the world. Overcautiousness encourages uncertain behavior which leads, ironically, to more injuries. A few children may even find that injuries become enjoyable because they lead to the predictable overinvolvement of a protective parent. Too little attention is equally devastating. Ignoring a child's pain may lead the child to withhold information about potentially serious injuries. The most helpful approach is to acknowledge the injury with concern, but encourage the child to be assertive again as soon as possible. Small injuries heal more quickly than growing fears.

During my first summer as a little league T-ball father, I observed a game featuring a team mother who was overly concerned by minor injuries. Twice in the first inning, balls took bad bounces, then struck her players' shins. Immediately, she ran from the bench and comforted the players whose pain seemed to increase because of her concern. Our team mother handled similar incidents with recognition, then encouragement. After one child was hit in the stomach, she said, "Ouch, I know that hurts, but shake it off." She was aware the injury was not severe.

After an inning or two, I said to the father sitting next to me, "If this team mother keeps overreacting to injuries, they'll soon have more injuries than hits." Sure enough, a month later I saw this team play again. Every inning was stopped due to an injury. In no other game was play stopped by casual accidents. This team mother taught her children that the consequence of injury is not only pain but a load of attention.

OPPORTUNITY FIVE: BABY-SITTERS

Don't forget, a child develops a fear of separation that may stretch to the second birthday, but this should not become more than an inconvenience. Parents need to leave home and spend time together alone. Children need to learn to conquer personal challenges and uncomfortable life situations.

Sample Consequence. Try to find a baby-sitter the child enjoys and whom you trust. Do not return if the child cries when you leave. Returning makes your eventual leaving more difficult for everyone. Teach your child that she can prosper on her own. Showing overconcern to a child's objection leads the child to believe that there is a good reason to be upset when the parents leave. It may be logical during this period to limit the use of baby-sitters, if possible. Don't forget that the passing of time is the greatest remedy for separation anxiety.

AUTONOMY vs. SHAME AND DOUBT
(18 MONTHS – 3 YEARS)

This is the stage of epic power struggles. Parents who have a strong need to be in control struggle through the period. But consequences can help maintain peace and order in the home. Children routinely should be allowed choices. Whenever possible, a child should be given the responsibility of planning consequences for present or potential misbehavior.

Fostering autonomy also will lead parents to follow Rudolf Dreikurs's rule—"Never do for a child what he can do for himself." Parents should encourage children to dress themselves, clean their rooms, and become increasingly responsible. Over-protective friends and relatives often do not understand this. As one distressed grandmother said to her daughter-in-law: "I can't believe you sit there and don't help him tie his shoes or get dressed. It's just too much to expect of him on a school day. When my children were that age, we did everything for them." Parents often must do what is right rather than what is popular.

OPPORTUNITY ONE: USE OF SEAT BELTS

Most children occasionally decide to liberate themselves from seat belts while the parent is driving. They do so with the complete understanding that this violates family rules.

Sample Consequence. When a child's seat belt is removed, operating the car becomes dangerous. Drivers should pull the car to the side of the road and stop as soon as possible. Say briefly, "We will sit here until the seat belts are fastened." Then remain silent. Usually it will take two or three such experiences to influence the child to keep the belt connected. The longest wait I have experienced was 15 minutes. It seemed an eternity to me, but longer for the bored child. Children cannot tolerate inactivity. After two or three occasions, the problem is solved. Certainly, waiting is inconvenient. But it takes time to train a child. Parents who don't make the time generally continue to have the problem.

Children learn to enforce family rules quickly. I first realized this on a trip across town, when our two-and-one-half-year-old exclaimed: "Stop the car, Dad! Mom is out of her seat belt." She was and I stopped the car. Our children have taken over the enforcement of family rules such as "Everyone wears a seat belt or the car stops." Children particularly enjoy catching adult violators!

OPPORTUNITY TWO: DRESSING AND BATHING

It is normal for children to experiment in resisting both of these activities.

Sample Consequence. Earlier, suggestions were given for reverse psychology and games with autonomy-seeking children. Such indirect methods avoid power struggles. For consistent resisters to dressing, it was suggested above that a child be allowed to go to school in the condition the child chose at departure time. Others stress prevention by encouraging the child to join in the process of choosing daily clothes. The child may choose unusual color combinations, so a parent's creativity and humor are a necessity. While bathing, many parents transform bath time into an enjoyable event. Guessing what color of food coloring is about to be added to the water or playing exciting games with simple toys changes a demanding routine into an exciting adventure. There are countless possibilities for avoiding power struggles through the creation of situations. Severe consequences should be used only when creativity ends.

OPPORTUNITY THREE: PUBLIC MISBEHAVIOR

Grocery stores, shopping centers, and other public areas provide children with exciting opportunities to misbehave. Parents are most vulnerable in public, and children recognize this. It is very unusual to have a child who never asserts her will enough to misbehave in public, but a child must learn that going into the outside world is a privilege that is earned by good behavior.

Sample Consequence. Setting up consequences in advance is the key to public sanity. Before entering a store, a parent might say, "We will go into the store, but if you do not follow my directions, we will return home." Usually, it takes two or three training incidences to help the child decide to behave. Again, leaving will be inconvenient for parents, but it is essential in helping a child learn responsibility. If the situation has reached a difficult level, another consequence may be added. For example, "You may go with me to the store. If you do not follow directions, we will go home, and next time I must leave you with a baby-sitter." Save your most competent but unappreciated sitter for such a learning experience!

No matter how successful parents are, public embarrassment will be experienced. It is a part of parenthood. In any public place, at almost any time, children can be seen misbehaving. Parents who use consequences will be embarrassed as they carry a screaming child from a grocery store or shopping center. But take comfort in knowing that your embarrassment will bring improved behavior in the future. Parents who have no contingencies planned for their children's public displays are doomed to live with the problem repeatedly. Embarrassment cannot be avoided. But it can be reduced in the future, when misbehaviors become opportunities for training.

Note. When your child asks for toys or money in stores—Handle this contingency by agreeing **before** going into the store on what, if anything, can be purchased. "We cannot buy anything this time," or "As we leave, you may choose a piece of gum." It is not a good precedent to later change this agreement. Never give in to repeated demands that violate agreements. Consistency is the key.

Parents who behave like slot machines eventually give in to a child's persistent demands. By giving in, parents teach children to be relentless beggars. In a department store recently, I heard a parent say, "I've told you one thousand times that you cannot have any candy." Five minutes later she said with anger: "OK! But just one piece. Now don't bother me again!" Bingo! The jackpot! The child learned that if mother's lever is persistently pulled, she will eventually pay off. Children will quit begging only when convinced that the parent's will cannot be swayed.

OPPORTUNITY FOUR: PUBLIC MISBEHAVIOR IN RESTAURANTS

This problem is similar to one found when visiting stores. However, training at home can prepare a child for eating away from home.

Sample Consequence and Note. Children must be encouraged at home to practice what is expected of them in restaurants. Only when a child can stay in her seat at home and refrain from yelling or running about can a parent expect similar behavior when she eats in a restaurant. Put on a special tablecloth, candles, and fancy napkins to create enjoyable practice sessions. Allow the child to earn the privilege of going to a restaurant with grown-ups by showing her best behavior at home. Children should know when they enter a restaurant that their misbehavior will be met with immediate removal. Again, a baby-sitter next time you go out may be used as an additional logical consequence.

Again, the obvious must be considered. During training periods, parents are often inconvenienced. On three occasions, I left an inexpensive but greatly desired meal to enforce the rule: "If anyone misbehaves, she or he will have to leave the restaurant." Each child tested the rule once. Each was removed while the rest of the family finished dinner. It was a sacrifice to miss a meal. But afterwards, major problems did not reoccur. When I witness children repeatedly misbehaving in the presence of their frustrated parents, I realize those few frustrating occasions were worth the inconvenience.

Active Approaches to Misbehaviors

OPPORTUNITY FIVE: TEMPER TANTRUMS

At about eighteen months of age, children become more sophisticated in experimenting with temper tantrums. Adult responses to temper tantrums will show the child how effective emotions will be in controlling parents.

Sample Consequence. When possible, ignoring temper tantrums is best. When a child has a tantrum, leave the room. Often the child, still screaming, will "follow" the parent around the house. If personal anger mounts, go into the bathroom and lock the door. The bathroom should remain a sacred place for privacy. It may take time to outwait tantrums; but never give in to the predictable coercion. Instead of the parent leaving, it may be best, at times, to remove the child and say, "You may have a temper tantrum in your room, but not here," and then take the child to her room.

In public, parents need to follow the guidelines suggested above. Tantrums require the child's removal from a public place and, possibly, the future use of a sitter. The key is: Never be drawn into emotional blackmail. Consequences or avoidance, rather than power, are most effective.

Some parents are easily manipulated by children's public temper tantrums. Parents who are high in the need to control situations and people are humiliated by public displays of emotion. Sometimes, instead of using consequences, parents utilize power. As Chapter One suggests, power struggles with children are always lost by the parent. Do not try to reason with a child who is having a tantrum. Generally, children will become even more irrational in order to overpower a parent's verbal weapons. Either walk away from, or remove, the child. Above all, avoid overtalking and physical punishment. Both lead to complications.

OPPORTUNITY SIX: TURNING OFF TELEVISIONS AND RECORD PLAYERS

This is a common ploy practiced by children in order to involve the parent by gaining attention or beginning power struggles.

Sample Consequence. As with other inappropriate behavior in the home, it may be best to send the child to her room. "You may come out when you can keep from turning off the television." The training period may require many trips, but after two weeks of consistent discipline, the child's experimentation is over. If, during a short span of time, the misbehavior continues, some adults prefer to place a timer outside the child's room. When the chimes are heard, the child is free to return.

This works, but it also can lead to power struggles that can lengthen the process. Whatever variation a parent chooses, what is required is action and consistency. Remember, parents should keep quiet when enforcing consequences. Words lead to more severe power struggles.

OPPORTUNITY SEVEN: THUMB-SUCKING

This is a common experiment of children, which often begins quite innocently.

Sample Consequence. Thumb-sucking is best handled by ignoring it. Children will not suck thumbs or fingers long, unless the activity becomes a major issue. If a parent attempts to force a child to stop the habit or ridicules the child, then a power struggle will begin. Power struggles can continue for years. Frequently, the best consequence is to do nothing and allow time to take its course.

The Wilhelms had a kindergartener, Mary, who was still sucking her thumb after five years. In response to a question from a member of the parenting class, Mrs. Wilhelm listed their fruitless attempts to stop the habit. "We painted her thumb. We removed five cents of her allowance each time she sucked it, and later we gave her a quarter a day for not sucking it. We put a substance on her thumb which was suppose to taste awful, and we sent her to her room for as long as an hour per offense. I am embarrassed to say this, but we even made fun of her. Finally, we eliminated her Saturday morning television. Nothing worked."

Well, of course not. Mary Wilhelm's thumb-sucking turns the entire house inside out. What power the parents have given the small girl! By doing nothing more than sticking her thumb in her mouth, Mary can control her parents' emotions. Why would a child give up such power for nickels, television, or solitary confinement? After following the study group's suggestion to ignore the thumb-sucking for six weeks, it stopped. Not only did Mary lose control of her parents, but also she was teased by her classmates. Peers often train children who retain immature behaviors. Parents must avoid prolonging habits by using techniques that are well intended but are poor solutions.

OPPORTUNITY EIGHT: WHINING

This is another common behavior indulged in by children. Most often adults find whining to be disruptive.

Sample Consequence. It is best to say, calmly: "I cannot understand you. When you choose to talk in a normal voice, I will be able to help you." Ignore continued whining. Never allow a child's persistence to lead to a power struggle. Try to keep from becoming emotional! If whining has no obvious effect on an adult, it will soon stop.

All parents have areas of weakness. One weakness is to allow a habit that is temporary to bother us. Our reactions can transform a passing fancy into a major problem. My wife and I both experienced a failing in this area. For my wife, it was my daughter Emily's whining. I could ignore whining, knowing it was a temporary challenge, but my wife could not. As soon as my daughter found whining gave her power over her mother's emotions, Emily used it as a weapon. What was a short experiment became an engrained characteristic which took almost a year and one-half to end.

My weakness was my son's rabid materialism. Although I realized it was a natural interest for a child his age, I was disgruntled with his monetary fascination. Soon, Patrick realized that money was a subject that aroused my temper. Whenever he wanted to see me irritated, he simply began counting his pennies and discussing ways to spend them. In both instances, our children capitalized on our weaknesses. What may have become a temporary experiment or interest became a thorn our children cleverly injected in our sides. Ignore that which will soon pass.

OPPORTUNITY NINE: CLEANING BEDROOMS

This age-old problem is discussed in every parent group. Unfortunately, it is difficult to resolve in a manner that completely pleases both parents and children.

Sample Consequence. The younger the child, the more difficult it is for her to respond to the directive, "Clean up your room!" For younger children it helps if you make small and specific requests. For example, "Please put the books on your shelves." Total cleaning may require help from parents, and it can become a joint adventure. For older children, it is usually best to allow the bedroom to become the child's own territory and responsibility. Thus, it becomes the child's decision in regard to cleaning the room. Parents react to these decisions. For example, adults may choose not to go into a dirty room to say goodnight, to read, or to retrieve dirty clothes. Should the room become too dirty, a decision could be made not to allow the child's friends to visit because of possible health hazards! Keep responses logical and influence the child's decisions indirectly.

Some parents are not comfortable about allowing a child to have total control of her bedroom. Often, they give children the right of first cleaning. For example, my brother-in-law gives his children a reasonable amount of time to clean bedrooms. If they decide not to clean, then he cleans in a manner which leaves the children unable to find prized possessions for days. As long as the father is willing to allow the same privilege to his children when his study, workroom, or bedroom is considered to be in an unacceptable state, then the rule seems fair. Different agreements work for different families. However, as children grow older, their bedrooms become more sacred. Intrusions of any type may be met with strong opposition.

OPPORTUNITY TEN: SHARING

Children at this age do not share well and will not readily learn this difficult social skill.

Sample Consequence. If two children fight over a toy, put the toy away for the day. "If you cannot share, we'll put the toy up. Neither of you will be allowed to play with it." Fights are eliminated and the idea has been introduced that sharing is desirable.

INITIATIVE vs. GUILT (3–5 YEARS)

To imagine a child seeking initiative visualize her running, skipping and jumping, attempting dangerous feats, saying anything that comes to mind, and testing every limitation in her path. In one moment she is confident, and in the next she's insecure. Power struggles during this stage shift to the child's increased testing of the rules and boundaries of life. When rules are made, it is important that consequences after violations be clearly agreed upon. As the child's creativity increases, new problems arise. Below are some of the opportunities to teach children that are experienced by many parents.

OPPORTUNITY ONE: DESTRUCTION OF PROPERTY

Often, children treat property roughly. Toys may be destroyed or tools misused and broken.

Sample Consequence. If a child breaks a toy, it is gone. To replace the toy for a crying child only shows the child that property is easily replaceable. Children should save their own money to replace broken items. If tools are misused, they should not be used again for a specific period of time. For example, when scissors are used for cutting hair, they can be removed for a week. Crayons used to write on walls should be taken away, and the wall can be cleaned by the child. Allowances, if given, can be a great advantage in helping children learn the value of property. When children can add and subtract, they are ready to manage an allowance.

OPPORTUNITY TWO: SEXUAL INTERESTS

Children's interest in sex is natural. Playing doctor and attempts to masturbate are normal and healthy.

Sample Consequence. A parent's overreaction to natural sexual interest is a mistake. If children believe that parents are anxious about sexual exploration, then they often hide sexual questions and problems. In later years when advice is needed, such parents are rarely asked for help. Discuss sexuality openly with children. Be careful not to give more information than is requested. Parents may explain to children that personal exploration should be done in the privacy of the bedroom: "There are some things that are private." Their play with friends who may be sexually aggressive should be curtailed by close supervision. Parents should prevent the occurrence of situations that may push a child into feelings and behaviors which are difficult for young children to handle. Let common sense and sensitivity be the guide.

As with all parenting, what techniques are chosen is not as important as the spirit in which they are shared. Parents need to indicate to children that sex can be frankly and easily discussed in the family. Using correct terms for sexual organs can enhance a parent's attempt to show openness in discussing sexuality.

In my locality, this often is not done. Children frequently have neither a penis or a vagina. It is a strange phenomenon. Instead, boys have what parents call "ding dongs" or "hot dogs." Girls' sexual parts generally remain nameless. How can children talk comfortably about sex to parents who are uncomfortable using anatomically correct language? Using appropriate terminology is a first step toward honest discussion of a child's sexual inquiries.

Parents need to prevent potential problems and avoid overreacting when problems occur. A colleague's eight-year-old spent the night with six other boys. The hosts, mistakenly, allowed one eleven-year-old to join the group. During the evening, the mother heard silence from the boys upstairs—a sure sign of trouble! She sneaked up the stairs, plunged into their room, and found the boys nude in a circle. Each was stimulating the penis of the boy to his right. The mother panicked and began yelling at the children. Each child was put into an individual room. Parents were called, told of the incident and asked to retrieve their sons. An incident that could have been avoided became a neighborhood scandal. Children will experiment with sex. It is important to monitor them more closely, not to mix ages, and not to overreact to experimentation.

OPPORTUNITY THREE: TELLING LIES

Lying for children this age is not the serious violation that it is for teenagers and adults. As a child's imagination grows, lying increases. As discussed earlier, most "children do not lie if they are not afraid to tell the truth," but fear is not the cause of all lying. Children may lie to exaggerate or to practice using the imagination.

Sample Consequence. Prevention is important in reducing lying. Lying does appear to escalate with children who are harshly punished. For them, lying does not seem evil but is viewed as a practical way to avoid pain. If lying occurs, check consequences to make sure they remain logical and fair. If a child escalates lying, evaluate the atmosphere of the home. Increase her involvement in creating consequences for potential misbehavior. In most cases, confronting a lie is counterproductive. A parent who sees a child misbehave should never force the child into a corner by asking the obvious: "Did you just do. . .?" Spirited children may deny the obvious and throw the parent into a large scale power struggle. Older children, in concrete operations, soon believe their repeated lies are true. If a lie is frivolous, ignore it, or joke about it in a knowing way. If you are positive the child is guilty of a major infraction, present the facts, and then act.

OPPORTUNITY FOUR: NIGHTMARES

Nightmares are common at this age. The chapter on Piaget discussed some causes and some techniques for handling nightmares. If nightmares are violent and persistent, consult a pediatrician.

OPPORTUNITY FIVE: FEARS

Fears often develop in young children. When a child experiences fear, acknowledge it, but do not dwell on the difficulty.

Sample Consequence. Paying too much attention to a child's fear may reinforce it. The more one talks about the objective of fear, the more the fear seems warranted. Some fears are difficult to remove. For example, fear of the dark is a common problem. Allow the child to use a night-light. But do not stay up through the night with the child. Scare away ghosts, but do not become an armed guard in the room. As a rule, do not allow a child to sleep with you in order to protect her from an imaginary fear. The more parents give attention to minor fears, the greater the anxiety becomes. For fears such as fear of water, discuss the fear, then have the child **slowly** experience the object feared. Never force the child. Move by small increments. For example, encourage the child to dangle her feet in the water on one day and then to stand in the water the next day. If a child becomes anxious, retreat and try again later. Most fears will leave a child within a year if the fear is not overindulged or ridiculed by a parent. Make a special effort to show a child you are confident in her ability to handle the situation.

Several years ago, a mother whose child was taking swimming lessons reported an instructor's potentially hazardous policy. Parents of preschool and elementary school children were forbidden to observe swimming lessons. Her child, who feared water, was repeatedly immersed in an attempt to break her of her fear. Instead, the child became hysterical. The instructor understood that children should be exposed to the objects of their fears, but she did not understand how to expose a child in small increments. When a child expresses anxiety, exposure should be stopped. Later, the child can probably be persuaded to try to go slightly further, but the child must be the brake! Respect for children as equals should be the governing norm. Adults do not like to be forced past a comfortable anxiety level; neither do children.

As a footnote, parents should protest actively against any program which prohibits parental involvement. Professionals need to learn to work with parents. Potential inconveniences created by a minority of parents do not outweigh the potential for abuse that unsupervised people and situations can present.

OPPORTUNITY SIX: STEALING

Children do not understand the concept of personal property, a concept that all humans slowly learn to understand; therefore, stealing does not, for a child, seem the social evil that it does to adults. Instead, it is a chance to learn to respect the rights of others.

Sample Consequence. Always have the child make retribution for a stolen object. During quiet moments, explain to a child why people do not take the belongings of others. Additional consequences are usually unnecessary. Again, allowances can be used to help pay for replacing belongings. Avoid power struggles over stealing when possible.

OPPORTUNITY SEVEN: STUTTERING

Many children stutter for a short period of time.

Sample Consequence. Never direct attention to stuttering. Particularly, never ridicule it. Do ignore it. As long as the child does not become self-conscious about stuttering, she will soon abandon it. Be patient. Treat the child as you would wish to be treated if you experienced a temporary speech difficulty.

Most adults have experienced the torment of self-consciousness. Some feared errors and then made them in oral presentations or before audiences. Others may have been tongue-tied during interviews or when meeting admired individuals. Recently, we had a large gathering of people in our home. I worried about forgetting the names of little-known guests. All went well until I came to the wife of one of my closest friends. Nothing could break through my nervousness and enable me to recall her name, although I have known her for nine years. Children are the same way. When stuttering or other potential difficulties are brought to their attention, they become anxious. When anxiety is near, whatever is feared lurks close behind.

OPPORTUNITY EIGHT: CURSING

Children invariably experiment with cursing. Experimentation increases when school days begin. Children enjoy seeing the effect certain words have on parents. Rarely do young children understand curse words or the reasons for not using them.

Sample Consequence. Help children understand why cursing is not allowed. Keep explanations simple. Some recommend an explanation like, "There are some words that make people feel good and some words which make people feel bad. This is one which makes people feel bad." If cursing continues, a child can be sent to her room until her language can be controlled. Never allow cursing to become a weapon the child knows will rattle parents. If cursing is treated as no big deal and reasonable consequences are built in, then cursing seldom becomes a problem. Incidentally, if a parent curses, the same consequences should be followed which are required for the child. I once said a prohibited word while watching the end of a televised conference championship, and I was sent to my room by my five-year-old! I missed the deciding play of the game. But I did learn from the consequences of my misbehavior!

Of course, curse words find their way into your home at the most embarrassing moments. Patrick's first curse word came at the dinner table, when his grandparents were visiting. He was two years old. Suddenly, he dropped his fork and without hesitation said, "Damn!" Everyone was astonished! For him, the word "damn" probably meant "whoops!" Patty and I immediately tried to blame the television for poor modeling. But in reality, we learned to become better models. Embarrassment at times is a good teacher.

ACCOMPLISHMENT vs. INFERIORITY (AGE 5–12)

School days bring problems of increasing complexity. At this age, it is essential for children to begin developing their own consequences. If logical consequences have been used by parents up until this age, then children are likely to think in similar terms. If a child refuses the invitation to help set a reasonable consequence, make one for him that is fair but tough. Next time, the child may wish to join the process.

As explained in Chapter Three, the goal of this stage is for the child to feel competent. This means developing a confidence in handling not only academic problems but also social situations. As the next chapter will stress, encouragement is the key. However, problems will occur for all children. Below are some of the major challenges brought to parenting classes.

OPPORTUNITY ONE: ONE CHILD EXPERIENCING SCHOOL PROBLEMS

See the chapter on ordinal position and sibling rivalry. This is a common but complex difficulty.

OPPORTUNITY TWO: HOMEWORK

Many children do not do their homework, or they postpone doing it.
Sample Consequence. A family rule might be developed which creates a quiet time for the child to do homework. However, if the child does not do homework after you provide the time and encouragement, then it becomes a teacher-student problem. Properly trained teachers should create consequences for their students, as well as provide inspira-

tion that makes learning enjoyable. Parents should provide the child the opportunity to study and the encouragement to work. Know the limitations of your influence and insist that school personnel use the influence of their positions.

Most teachers work well with parents. A visit or call can often lead to the creation of successful strategies for motivating children. Logical consequences for school difficulties can be discussed, but remember that homework can become the source of power struggles. As suggested in Chapter One, if a power struggle develops, then efforts by parents to make children work will backfire. The best solution in such struggles is to withdraw and allow the child to experience the teacher's consequences.

OPPORTUNITY THREE: MISBEHAVIOR IN THE CLASSROOM

Often, a teacher calls to report a child's misbehavior in her class.

Sample Consequence. Always acknowledge the problem and thank her for her concern. Then ask her what she plans to do about it. Try to support her plan. Do not allow a poorly trained teacher to try to force you to "do something about Johnny's behavior in my class." The problem is a teacher-student one. You are not in the class; therefore, you cannot respond immediately to the misbehavior. Competent teachers should have classroom consequences for misbehavior, as well as for academic problems. Parents should try to support the teacher's attempt to reasonably discipline children.

OPPORTUNITY FOUR: BAD TEACHERS

Although there are more good teachers than poor ones at every level, there are bad teachers. Often, everyone is aware of the negative teacher, but no one seems to be able to do anything about the situation. Unfortunately, it appears that many of the poorest teachers choose to work with young students.

Sample Consequence. Discuss problems with the teacher first. If no solutions are met, give the principal a specific complaint in writing. Then meet with the principal. If no help is forthcoming, never be reluctant to report the situation to the superintendent of public schools or to the director of elementary schools. Too many parents are afraid to make waves. Such reluctance allows teachers who discourage good learning practices to remain in place. If the teacher's problems are severe, try to have your child transferred. If they are not severe or you cannot have the child transferred, try to make learning at home as enjoyable for the child as possible. Don't add to the child's problems by emphasizing the teacher's difficulties. However, do not deny the teacher's shortcomings if the child brings them up. Assure the child that she can overcome the situation. The greatest encouragement for a child at this age may be to find that her parents support her and that education is not confined to the classrooms. Parents remain a child's most influential teachers.

Early in his school career, my son experienced a teacher whose incompetence was legendary. Parents whose children suffered from her work warned new generations of parents about her inability. In private, her colleagues, and even her principal, agreed she was a poor teacher. Attempts to have her removed were unsuccessful because of politics and tenure.

Patrick did fall behind. But we tried to compensate by educating him outside of the system. Our goal was to keep alive the natural joy of learning exhibited by children. We read together daily, took family field trips, and supported his interests. We quietly listened to his complaints about school, without fanning the flame. The quality of future teachers allowed him to compensate for his wasted year. It is sad to see that, in a field dominated by excellence, a few rotten apples exist. But it is comforting to know that with parental support a child, in time, can survive a poor teacher.

OPPORTUNITY FIVE: BAD GRADES

Although it is questionable that giving grades to children under nine or ten has any positive value, it is a practice that will continue. Competitive parents insist on seeing grades, despite being aware of their limited value. Children are keenly aware of the meaning of grades. Poor grades discourage them. Good grades may encourage some students. But often, grades cause students to be more interested in the evaluation than in the learning process.

Sample Consequence. Never make a big deal over grades with young children. Negative comments are rarely needed, since children often punish themselves most harshly for bad grades. Give only encouragement. Place your emphasis on enjoying work rather than on the grade or the teacher's evaluation of work. Children who are properly encouraged will enjoy learning. Never give rewards for As. Again, this emphasizes external rewards rather than the enjoyment of learning.

Children who are pushed to make good grades often fail to realize that there is much more to learning than receiving good grades for the minimal work required.

One parent in our program paid each of her three children fifty cents for each A. At first they worked hard for the As. But soon they asked for more money. The parents refused, so the children refused to study. In a sense, they went on strike until their demands were met. The problem is obvious. Arrangements that basically pay children to learn, detract from the true goals of learning. On the college level, many of us are concerned with students who respond to suggestions to read marvelous literature with such statements as "Will I get extra credit?" Education is its own reward. Payment for grades is counterproductive.

OPPORTUNITY SIX: SPORTS

Earlier and earlier, our children are encountering organized sports being taught at a sophisticated level. Contemporary sports can increase stress in a child's life rather than decrease it. Parents whose misguided ambition causes them to overreact to the performance of their children can create a negative atmosphere.

Sample Consequence. Allow the child to choose her own activities. Never push the child. Make the sport enjoyable, and be sure that practice is fun. Do not add to stress by discussing winning and losing. Instead, discuss what happened in the game. Don't allow society's transitory values to interfere with the true purposes of sports in young children's lives: friendships, fun, and exercise. Parents who are highly competitive should make sure their energy is being channeled appropriately into personal accomplishments. If it is not, there is a tendency to allow their personal ambition to be transferred to the child's life. No child deserves the pressure of a parent's unfulfilled dreams.

In sports, as well as in other areas, parents must conquer feelings of disappointment that may occur. My father and I were state father-and-son tennis champions in North Carolina five different years. Our play together remains among my fondest memories. I looked forward to someday sharing a similar experience with one of my children. It never occurred to me that none of them would pursue my interest in tennis. But none has. Each has a unique world in which many of my major interests may never fit. Knowing their choices are healthy does not relieve me of disappointment, but it does show me that the problem is mine, not theirs. Many parents' disappointments in the area of sports come from their own creation rather than from their children's.

OPPORTUNITY SEVEN: CHORES

All children need to have chores to do. Each should feel their contributions make them part of the working family. A list of chores should be set up and consequences should be discussed at a family council (discussed in the next chapter). Make sure chores are reasonable. Allow children to rotate chores each week.

Sample Consequence. The family council can decide on the consequences of failing to do chores. There are many. One standard is: "If you do not take out the trash and do the chores you chose, I will have to finish them when I normally have time to take you to gymnastics (the movies, etc.)."

As always, consequences created by children work best, even when the logic is not ironclad. For example, our children heard a rule in school that they adopted for failing to help set the dinner table, "He who does not help does not eat." This worked well for a couple of weeks. Then they changed it to "He who does not help has to eat alone in the kitchen." I never liked this rule because I was required to eat in the kitchen first. But for them the consequence was a success.

OPPORTUNITY EIGHT: SELECTING FRIENDS

This can be a major dilemma for many parents. Children often pick friends who seem to pose potential problems.

Sample Consequence. Picking friends is like choosing a spouse. To deny a child access to a friend often seals the friendship. It is best to allow a child to choose her own friends. How many times have you heard a parent lament: "The second I told her I didn't like her date, she fell in love with him." Or, "When I told him I thought she would be a poor wife, he immediately married her." Unfortunately, the lust for forbidden fruit is a common characteristic. Children particularly are attracted to the untouchable. It is easier to work behind the scenes to make preferred friends more accessible than to oppose unwanted friendships. As usual, dwell on the positive rather than the negative.

Friends who last over a period of time generally share the major values of the child's family. Often, what is different are minor differences, such as speech, interest, fads, etc. It is also best to permit children to terminate friendships on their own volition. Exceptions to this should be rare and then only in highly threatening situations.

Perfect children do not exist. Instead, like the child in the nursery rhyme, "When they are good, they are very, very good. But when they are bad, they are horrid." Parents all share in the frustration that misbehavior elicits. Fortunately, many misbehaviors are predictable. As long as parents treat moments of misbehaviors as opportunities to teach children to accept the consequences of their behavior, then parents are doing an excellent job. Parental guilt should have no place in these adults' lives. Guilt should be endured only by those who cling to the myth of childhood perfection, are irresponsible as parents, or fail to help children become responsible, loving individuals.

RELATED READINGS

Brooks, J. (1981). *The process of parenting.* Palo Alto: Mayfield.
Canter, L. & Canter, M. (1982). *Assertive discipline for parents.* Santa Monica: Canter & Associates.
Christensen, Oscar C. & Schramski, Thomas G., eds. (1983). *Adlerian family counseling.* Minneapolis: Education Media Corporation.
Dinkmeyer, D. & McKay, G. (1982). *The parent's handbook: Systematic training for effective parenting.* New York: Random.
Dodson, F. (1973). *How to parent.* New York: Prentice-Hall.
Dreikurs, R. (1972). *Adult-child relations.* Chicago: Alfred Adler Institute.
Dreikurs, R. (1972). *The challenge of child training.* New York: Dutton.
Dreikurs, R. (1972). *Coping with children's misbehavior.* New York: Dutton.
Dreikurs, R. (1974). *Discipline without tears.* New York: Dutton.
Dreikurs, R. (1979). *Challenge of parenthood.* New York: Dutton.
Dreikurs, R. & Grey, L. (1968). *Logical consequences: A new approach to discipline.* New York: Dutton.
Dreikurs, R. & Soltz, V. (1964). *Children: The challenge.* New York: Dutton.
Gesell, A., Elg, F. & Ames, L. (1974). *Infant and child in the culture of today.* New York: Harper and Row.
Grey, Loren; (1982). *Discipline without tyranny.* Wooster: Social Interest.
Grunwald, Bernice & McAbee, Harold. (1985). *Guiding the family.* Muncie: Accelerated Development.
Kvols-Riedler, B. & Kvols-Riedler, K. (1978). *Parenting guidelines.* Boulder: RDIC Publishing.
Mosak, H. (1980). *A child's guide to parent rearing.* Chicago: Alfred Adler Institute.
Painter, G. & Corsini, R. (1984). *The practical parent: Solutions to the everyday problems of raising children.* New York: Cornerstone.

CHAPTER SEVEN

DARING TO BE CLOSE: ENCOURAGING AND COMMUNICATING WITH CHILDREN

FIVE-YEAR-OLD Johnny ran into the house carrying a messy looking cardboard box with bugs and butterflies taped to the cardboard. "Look, Mom! I've started my first butterfly collection."

Mom quickly looked at the project, then said, "Johnny, who gave you permission to use the scotch tape? You know you shouldn't get the tape without asking me. Besides you shouldn't tape the bugs to cardboard. You should use a different type of background and attach them with pins."

Johnny's voice lost its enthusiasm. He replied, "Yes ma'am, I'm sorry about the tape," then left the room.

Mother bragged to all her friends about Johnny's collection. But later in the day she could not understand why Johnny lost his initiative to search for new specimen.

Discipline is only one part of the art of raising children. While it does teach a child to understand the consequences of choices, it does not create enthusiasm in a child. Enthusiasm for life and fascination for the wonder of life develop in homes that nurture a child's natural curiosity and desire to explore.

Sharing a child's inner world is an adventure that creates intimacy between parent and child. Young people offer continuous opportunities for parents to share and further inspire their inner worlds. Parents too concerned with rules and order may miss these promising occasions.

To be intimate requires taking risks. Often, being close brings criticism, pain, and disappointment, but the pleasures more than compensate: they provide a lifetime of memories and good feelings. It takes courage to dare to be close to children. Parents who begin to see the daily possibilities for inspiring children can quickly add to their existing abilities to enter a child's world.

ENCOURAGEMENT

Critics in life are plentiful. Those who possess the rare ability to encourage others are few. Looking back in time, most of us find that the individuals who made the greatest contributions to our lives were those who knew how to be positive toward others. At all ages, people are attracted to those who make them feel strong, important, intelligent, competent, and needed.

Parents can fulfill this role. Also uncles, aunts, neighbors, teachers, or acquaintances can. Everyone needs at least one person who listens to them, praises their ideas, and genuinely enjoys their company. Often, encouragement comes from unexpected sources. As a child, I experienced support and enthusiasm from a woman named "Irene," who worked for my grandmother. She was a person of limited education, but always she seemed thrilled with the presence and contributions of grandchildren in the family. Because she was supportive and positive, we stayed close to her. Soon we began to believe we were important. Irene helped us feel that way. It does not take education to love life and people.

It is difficult to dwell on the positive in our society. Many ambitious and competitive people reach for perfection and criticize that which falls short. Childhood is a time for falling short. These early years are filled with learning to master literally thousands of activities—from talking, to walking, to reading—and they are also filled with spills and errors. The potential for adults to be negative about children is always present. Unfortunately, children never grow from criticism.

Encouraging children is a way of living that requires a distinctive set of skills and beliefs. Parents who are truly encouraging labor to concentrate on the positive side of children's behavior and thoughts. But for some, personal pessimism about life makes the encouragement of others a difficult challenge. Positive and negative mind sets are represented by the old example: "Optimists look at a glass of water and say it is half full, while pessimists see the same glass but believe it to be half empty."

Any parent may experience a situation which renders him or her temporarily half or totally empty. A loss of job, death of a loved one, or marital stress can rob a person of the ability or desire to give. It is to be hoped that such situations will be transitory and that soon the giving to others will become easier. But for some, life always seems empty and nonrewarding. The addition of children to this person's life appears to sap any remaining optimism. Many who abuse their children seem to suffer from a rather static emptiness. Because they are empty, they feel they possess nothing to give others. Their concentration is centered on being self-filling. In contrast, parents who live fulfilling lives find it easier to help fill others' lives.

Children grow stronger by believing they are becoming "full." In schools, there are a few special teachers who can transform a failing child into a successful one by encouraging the positive. Instead of the words spelled wrong, the words spelled right are stressed. Rather than pointing to the child's negative behavior, successful contributions are highlighted. Although such teachers generally follow consistent and clear guidelines for discipline, their emphasis in class is, predictably, the success of the child. Parents need to be like good teachers.

Outside of family members, the most influential person in my first twenty years was a sixth grade teacher. Known as a strict disciplinarian, Mrs. Cross was popular with adults and administrators. Children loved her for her extraordinary ability to find something precious in each of them.

For a project, I once turned in a Viking ship constructed from part of a tree limb, Popsicle® sticks, and acorn caps. Little did I know it would change my life. Instead of simply telling me it was good, Mrs. Cross immediately sent me to the principal's office to display the project. So many times before, I had sat outside of the powerful one's office awaiting punishment! But now I was distinguished in a positive way. Mrs. Cross "Caught me being good." She took this single incident of academic achievement and transformed it for me into a broad enthusiasm for learning.

Correcting misbehavior does not build success in a child. Success builds success. There are teachers and parents who are good disciplinarians and weak encouragers; such adults tend to see, first, what goes wrong and, last, what goes right. Their children behave but lack confidence in their own ability to act and be productive.

Encouragers look for what is right first, and handle what is wrong second. If one could be positive all of the time, misbehavior in children would be reduced dramatically, but no adult is a perfect encourager. Nevertheless, each adult can add to existing abilities to encourage.

Encouragement is so predictably successful that one can easily test its effectiveness. If for one day a parent begins to use constant encouragement, ignoring as much misbehavior as possible, positive changes in both children and the home atmosphere should take place by nightfall. Before attempting this test, parents should be sure the contrast between discouragement and encouragement is clear.

OPPORTUNITY ONE

A two-year-old tries to make his own bed. He covers the pillow with his sheets, but every blanket is winkled, and the job is generally messy.

Discouragement. "Johnny, that's not quite the way to do it. You need to pull the blankets tightly. Come try it again."

Comment. This approach highlights the child's shortcomings rather than the positive intentions of the child to help. The child will now avoid initiating helpful activities in order to avoid making more mistakes.

Encouragement. "Johnny, I'm so pleased you wish to make your room look nice!" (Gives Johnny a hug.)

Comment. This stresses the effort and intentions rather than the outcome. Initiative is encouraged.

OPPORTUNITY TWO

A three-year-old tries to write her name. She writes "Mary" but turns the "r" backwards.

Discouragement. "That is a good job, Mary, but you have the "r" turned around. Try it again, but make your "r" like this."

Comment. At the moment the child showed her writing to the parent, she was proud of her efforts. This is not the best time to teach. The parent has months to practice making letters with the child. Again, weaknesses were pointed out, rather than strengths. It is possible the child will lose interest in writing, or worse, she may stop showing her work to her parents. The parent "lost the forest in the trees." Leave details alone and comment on the positive intentions. There is always time to teach later.

Encouragement. "Look at you! Learning to write already!"

OPPORTUNITY THREE

Johnny is learning to catch a baseball. But he misses it almost every time. Dad keeps throwing but becomes increasingly frustrated. Throwing and catching is not coming easily to the youngster.

Discouraging. "Johnny, if you just tried harder you could do it. You are not concentrating enough. I know you can do better."

Comment. Dad's frustrations ruined the game. Dad was overambitious, and his overambition discouraged his son. There are few comments more disheartening than being told one is not trying hard enough. Dad meant "You are not doing well enough to please me." Johnny understands the hidden message. Throwing with Dad now becomes work, rather than fun.

Encouraging. "Johnny, I am so glad you enjoy playing baseball with me." Make no comments that evaluate the quality of the performance. Patience is required when encouraging children.

It is not always easy to be encouraging. Parents are often tired or distracted. And often, children wear thin the best parental mood. Fishing trips are often my downfall. I recall one in particular when frustration feasted on every moment. As Patrick and I reached the river, he discovered the fishing worms had been left in his bedroom. Why his bedroom? Who knows! Still in a vacation mood, we retrieved them while I showed exemplary patience.

To the river we returned. His first cast hooked a sprawling oak tree. Before I could intervene, he jerked the line, and the tree immediately owned the hook, line, and sinker. As he fished with my pole, I fixed a new line for him. Before I could finish, the youthful fisherman caught a submerged stump. Again he snapped the cord. After all, as he reminded me, I told him not to yank a hook caught on a tree. I never mentioned stumps. Again he fished, as I repaired a line. Finally, I was ready for my first cast. The bait hit the water at the moment Patrick yelled to announce his discovery of a bee's nest. Fish wearing ear muffs would have been frightened away!

Still, I held my temper, but I was not enjoying the afternoon. The next cast of Patrick's led to my final undoing. As if in slow motion, his hook floated toward me. Unable to move or speak, I watched it lodge in my shirt. Yank! Once again he snapped the line. My shirt and nerves were victims. Patrick caught a tree, a stump, a shirt, and my temper, all in one half-hour's time. Encourage each and every time you can, but don't feel guilty over our mortal limitations!

OPPORTUNITY FOUR

A first grader has saved his money to buy a long desired toy. He takes the toy to the cashier and counts his money. Unfortunately, he forgot about taxes and falls fourteen cents short. He returns in tears to his parent.

Discouraging. "You should have thought about the taxes in advance. I'll give you the fourteen cents, but I can't believe you didn't think about it yourself."

Comment. The importance of the effort of the child in saving money and in taking the responsibility to buy the toy with his own money is lost. All that is emphasized is the single miscalculation.

Encouraging. "That's too bad about the taxes. But I'm proud of the way you saved and counted your money. It won't take long to save fourteen more cents. I promise to bring you back when you're ready."

Comment. This parent dwells on the positive, even in a difficult situation. This response allows the child to learn about his money from observing natural consequences. Variations of this response can be helpful and less stringent. For example, parents may prefer to loan the child fourteen cents and have the child pay back the loan. The major object here is to be encouraging and to allow the child to learn from the experience.

OPPORTUNITY FIVE

A second grader comes home from school and declares: "I hate reading. Those books we have to read are dull. It's awful. I can't stand it."

Discouraging. "If the teacher says you have to read them, you must read them. It doesn't matter whether you enjoy the books or not. Now, did you bring the books home to practice, as she said? Good! Besides, I don't think they are so boring."

Comments. This type of response is discouraging for many reasons. First, it does not acknowledge that many school books are dull. Whether it's enjoyable to the parent or not is not the point. It is boring to the child. Second, the response implies that reading may always be dull. Third, it leads the child to believe that adults are not empathetic and will form a united front against his feelings.

Encouraging. "I'm sorry you are not enjoying these books yet. I enjoy listening to you read. Why don't you pick out one of your favorite books and read it to me tonight?"

Comment. Here, the child's feelings are acknowledged, but in a manner that allows for future change. The parent encourages the child about his reading, then allows him to practice with a book which is more enjoyable.

Opportunities to encourage children occur daily. Many of them will be missed by all parents. Life is difficult, and perfection is unattainable. But if parents train themselves to look for the positive and to ignore small errors, children will blossom. Parents should look at the effort and intentions of a child first. As long as they are not discouraged, young people will strive to model parental behaviors and actions in order to improve. If the spirit to succeed is nourished, the details will be mastered eventually.

LISTENING TO CHILDREN

From hour to hour, children rush through intriguing emotions and enchanting thoughts. Despite the fact that this process fascinates, how rare it is for a person to possess the listening skills needed to share this part of a child's life. Listening is not a natural ability. Think about the hundreds of people you may know at this time. How many of them are really good listeners? Probably few are.

Listening is one of the most effective methods of encouraging others. When one attends to a child, her thoughts and feelings are affirmed as important. This is a luxury for most children in our culture. Because adults lead hectic lives, children are generally only half heard. Their concentration is split between the child and the parents' own tasks which seem to constantly demand attention. Parents cannot create more time. But they can use the time spent with the child more effectively.

Listening, like other forms of encouragement, is a delicate art which requires people to do what seems unnatural. Carl Rogers has been particularly helpful in developing "reflective listening" skills in therapists through the years. These techniques are equally useful for parents.

The first requirement of parental listening is the desire to know what the child is feeling and thinking. To attend to another, one must listen "actively," trying to avoid sharing personal opinions and comments which might discourage discussion. Understanding a child requires a parent to "get into his skin" or "to walk in his shoes," as Rogers said. Think of those people you know who are good listeners. They probably display an intensity in listening which makes you feel valued, as well as understood. To listen with concern, interest, and empathy is a skill. Few possess it naturally. All people can develop it. To become an active listener, one needs to be aware of the pitfalls to listening. Below are some common errors to avoid when talking with children.

OPPORTUNITY ONE

Child: "Mom, I really hate school. It's dull and boring. I can't stand to go back anymore."

Limiting Response. Mom: "I used to feel that way too. But I changed and began to love school."

Critique. This response is a conversation stopper. The parent changes the subject from the child to the adult. There is a strong message that school must be loved. The feelings and thoughts behind the child's statement are lost to the parent.

Reflective listening requires a person to show that the child's position is understood. This encourages her to continue discussing important issues. To reflect, one attempts to return the child's message in a brief summary. Being brief helps prevent the parent from taking control of the conversation. Rephrasing the message can also aid the child in developing her thoughts more precisely.

Reflective Response. Mom: "It sounds like you aren't too pleased with school right now."

Comment. Whether one's response here or elsewhere is perfect is not important. What is crucial is allowing the child to know you are trying to understand. Sincere concern is enough to encourage the child to continue talking. By talking, children may be able to work through difficult problems.

OPPORTUNITY TWO

Eight year old: "Dad, I hate Johnny Brown. He is the meanest kid I ever met. I just hate him."

Moralistic Response. Dad: "Mary, it is not right to hate people. You don't really hate him. Hating is not good for anybody."

Critique. Mary is told her feelings are wrong. This does not miraculously remove her hatred. But it does teach her to feel guilty about her hard feelings. She will probably avoid talking to Dad in the future when she has similar feelings.

Reflective Listening. Dad: "You seem to be having some real difficulties with Johnny. . ."

Comment. An open-ended response allows Mary to continue, while showing that Dad is willing to listen. Notice Dad chose not to use her word "hate." His response allows the child to think more in terms of the problems which are allowing this feeling to emerge.

OPPORTUNITY THREE

"Mom, it's not fair. You gave Johnny some sandals and didn't give me any. You always give him more. He gets whatever he wants, and I get nothing."

Shaming Response. Mom: "I'm disappointed in you. We work hard day and night to make your life better. You should be appreciative of all you do have. Other children would be pleased in your situation."

Comment. Many parents find shame to be a powerful ally in suppressing undesired feelings of children. By shaming a child, parents force them to hide feelings. The minimum price for this silence is the momentary end of communication and honest sharing. The maximum cost is the formation of long-lasting resentments that are difficult to resolve. Many adults still harbor old feelings of having been treated unfairly by parents.

Reflective Response. Mom: "You're feeling that things are not fair for you right now. . ."

Comment. This parent showed the courage to investigate a challenging situation. It might be temporarily easier to overwhelm the child with guilt and end the discussion. But by discussing the situation now, the parent may avoid complex problems in the future. Parents must be willing to evaluate whether some of the child's criticism is valid. If so, the parent may need to make changes.

OPPORTUNITY FOUR

Another pitfall in listening is to switch from a hot topic to an unimportant one. Child: "Mom, why is it that you and Dad yell at each other so much?"

Avoidance Response. "Jimmy, we don't have time for that now. Let's get some ice cream at the store before it closes. Come on! You'll have to hurry."

Reflective Listening. "It seems to you that we yell often. . ."

Listening is difficult. It requires time and exceptional effort; yet nothing bonds people more closely than feeling truly understood. It is a risk to listen to children. Sometimes their messages can hurt. That too few take the risk can be seen by the number of adults who report, "My parents never really understood me." Any amount of energy expenditure seems worthy of hearing one's child make the opposite statement: "I always felt that my parents understood me. They always made time to listen."

OBSTACLES TO COMMUNICATION

RELUCTANCE TO TOUCH

Communications are often limited by what parents do not do, rather than what they do. For example, some adults lose priceless opportunities for closeness by not touching children. Children need to be held, hugged, kissed, and squeezed. Being close physically can become the most dynamic method of sharing a message with a child. Instead of just saying how pleased you are with her, give her a hug. Instead of telling him how much he adds to your life, give him a tight sqeeze and a kiss.

For many in our culture, it has been traditional for males not to express themselves physically with other males. How sad for a father and son to be robbed of these pleasures! Dads need to hug sons as well as daughters. In discipline, it was seen that actions speak louder than words. In communications, the same is true.

One son in a family with whom I worked shared a heartbreaking story previously unknown to other family members. We were all touched by his emotion in relaying his pain. Instinctively, his mother moved to touch him. Equally, the father wished physical contact, but he was frozen. Tenderness was his wife's domain. I asked the mother to stand beside the son while the father comforted him. As if relieved to be given permission, the dad walked over and held his son. The encounter did not solve the problems of this family, but it opened new possibilities for the sharing of emotions and feelings. Courage was required by the father in the act of becoming physically close to his son.

Frequently, both parents are uncomfortable in expressing tender emotions through touch. Often this discomfort has been learned from one's own parents' reluctance to be physical. It takes courage to do things differently. Remember, however, that children may not be aware of your discomfort. Act as if you are comfortable touching and hugging, and soon you will be. Dare to be close.

"MINDREADING"

John Gottman discusses a problem between couples called "mindreading" that also separates many parents from their children. Mindreading is a lack of communication that is based on the faulty assumption that one already knows what another thinks or feels.

The following discussion is characteristic of a father who mistakenly believes his son understands his intentions. Also, it shows that our behaviors often fail to relay our feelings. This father is unhappy because his son wishes to spend Saturday afternoon with a friend:

Dad: "But we always watch the baseball game together on Saturdays."
Son: "Are you kidding? All you do is sleep. Then I have to be quiet."
Dad: "But I really enjoy the time with you."
Son: "Then, why do you sleep?"

For a long time, the father had believed that his son appreciated their time together. But the opposite was true. An act intended to show love was interpreted as boredom. Neither person could read minds. Unfortunately, it took a minor crisis to allow clear communications to be established.

The feelings and attitudes of humans change frequently. To know a child one month does not insure understanding her the next. Routinely ask children questions. Give them a chance to share their feelings or views on any topic. Be careful not to assume that the behavior of a child always reflects what is happening inside. Be assertive in soliciting communications and making your thoughts and feelings known.

NONVERBALS AND TONE OF VOICE

Sometimes parents say the right words, but their tone of voice and nonverbals give a contradictory message. How often I have heard parents apparently give a child freedom of choice but in a tone which demands "You better do what I want." For example, "Yes, you can spend the night with Tommy instead of going to Grandmother's with the family. It's up to you. I KNOW YOU WILL DO THE RIGHT THING." One's tone of voice is more important than what is said. Parents need to make sure the tone of voice used with children is not angry or dictatorial when the child is expressing opinions that may differ from those of the parent.

Body language can also give away one's true thoughts, particularly when one is talking with children. For example, a parent may say, "Go on and talk to me, John. I'm really interested in what you are saying." But if at the same time the parent continues watching the news on television or does not put down the newspaper, a different message is given the child. The message is, "But your ideas are not worth my full attention."

Another contradictory message is given by parents who utilize the evil eye. This is a look which says, "You'd better step in line right this instant or you are in deep trouble." Often, the look is accompanied by pleasant-sounding public phrases such as, "This is my daughter Cathy; we're very proud of her." Anger, joy, humor, concern, hope, disappointment—the body can show any human emotion. Try not to let the body make a lie of what comes from the mouth. Double messages are confusing and unfair. Honesty, is, as usual, the best policy.

SPEAKING FOR OTHERS

An accepted rule of communication is "only speak for yourself." There is a tendency for parents to speak for each other or for their children. For example: "Mom, can I go to the movies tonight?" Mom may reply, "It's okay with me, but I'm sure your Dad will not approve." Poor Dad isn't even allowed to be the bad guy by his own choice. Not only do parents often speak for each other, but other children may speak for their siblings. Particularly, this seems true of older children speaking for younger children. For example, "Tommy, how old are you?" Older brother answers, "Tommy is five." Often this allows the younger to become dependent on others to speak for him. At its best, speaking for another is disrespectful. At its worst, it robs individuals of the responsibility to stand on their own two feet. Not only allow but insist that others speak only for themselves.

Example. Child: "Dad, is it okay with you and Mom if I go to the lake with Tommy and take Mom's fishing rod?"

Speaking for Another. "Yes, I'm sure it's fine" or "You can go, but Mom wouldn't want you to use her equipment."

Speaking for Self Only. "It's okay with me if you go, but I don't know what Mom will think. You'll have to ask her."

LABELING

Many nonproductive techniques must be avoided when discussing family problems. One of the most common mistakes is using labels to characterize the person with the problem. Children have been called lazy, rebellious, stupid, inconsiderate, mean, or irresponsible simply because they failed to do the dishes. Labels are usually exaggerations and are almost always discouraging. Heim Ginott's phrase—"labeling is disabling"—is as true now as in the year he wrote it. A child who is labeled lazy soon begins to live up to the title. Whatever parents expect of a child is what the child will begin to expect of herself. Be careful of the use of labels, even when they are positive.

One mother of my acquaintance tried to encourage her children by giving each a positive label. She introduced her four children, starting with the eldest and moving toward the youngest. "This is my daughter Emily, who is our good student. This is our daughter Sarah, who is the artist. This is our son Matthew, who is the athlete. And this is our daughter Marcey, who is our comedienne." The mother was trying to point to a strength in each child. But in reality, she limited each to a single area while unconsciously discouraging the others to share the strength.

OVERLOADING

Often frustrated people store their criticism of children until the cork pops out and all of their complaints rush forth at once. For example: "You never clean up your room, or take out the garbage, or help in the kitchen, or do anything for anyone else in the family." Such overloading does little good. Each problem should be discussed as it occurs, or in routine family meetings. If a number of difficulties occur at once, handle only one at a time. If overloaded, children break down and do not respond well.

How ironic it is that many parents may not notice that they are overloading a child but are outraged when a boss or friend overloads them. Imagine how the average adult would react to this boss's evaluation: "You never turn in complete reports, or take the initiative to create new ideas, or spend extra time with employees, or do anything unless your direct supervisor tells you to." My guess is that discouragement and anger would reign. Children have similar reactions.

PROBLEM SOLVING

BEING SPECIFIC AND USING "I" MESSAGES

A problem-solving formula cited by Gottman is helpful in handling problems productively. Although awkward at first, practice will allow a parent to find his own style.

The formula is: "When you do ___X___, in situation ___Y___, I feel ___Z___." For example, a father may say, "When you yell at me in front of my friends, I feel embarrassed and humiliated." This statement tells the child exactly what she is doing to embarrass the parents. Also, the parent is sharing his feelings with the child. Sharing those feelings allows a child to understand why the action is undesirable.

Be sure "I" statements are intended to increase dialogue. Some adults become so intent on sharing their feelings that they slip into long, dull monologues. Children quickly lose interest in such verbage. Many adults are unaware that they are overtalking. Be sensitive. If the child looks bored or shows no emotion, the point probably was not succinctly made. "I" statements are the first step in problem solving, not the last!

WE HAVE A PROBLEM

Misbehavior and poor choices made by children affect other people. When the child is rude in public or fails to do household chores, it is a problem for the family. The mutuality of the problem needs to be presented to the child. Children are more likely to join in solving the difficulties if they do not feel cornered and if they understand that a solution benefits everyone.

Example Opportunity. Johnny fails to take out the trash.

Faultfinder. "Johnny, you didn't take out the trash. That's your job. Don't use excuses. It's your responsibility. Take the trash out now."

Mutual Response. "We have a problem with the trash in the kitchen. It's really in my way."

Asking the Child for Help. Parents too infrequently take advantage of the goodwill of youth. Children enjoy helping adults. It is well known that if a teacher begins a class by saying, "I am not feeling well today, and I need your help," children generally rally to support her. School-age children, in particular, will do the same for their parents. This desire to help extends far beyond emergencies.

Helping adults makes a child feel needed. Too often they feel coerced and directed by parents; therefore, they resist orders disguised as requests. I have seen children repeatedly respond positively to requests such as: "I need your help. I feel really overloaded in the kitchen." Or, "I have a problem I need help with. I feel uncomfortable taking all of you to the grocery store." Allow children to solve the problem at hand. Children follow their own suggestions best. Although it may be unnatural to ask a child for help, it is often successful. As the old maxim suggests, "if you want to make a friend forever, allow her to do you a favor."

BEING FLEXIBLE

Children often make suggestions and plans which do not please adults. It is important to respect a child's right to think differently. Although the ideas presented by children may not be the best, it is important to allow them to try out their plans. The worst that could happen is that children will learn from their experiences. The best is that children will gain confidence in themselves because of your respect and support of their ideas. Certainly, children's solutions cannot always be followed. Many need to be amended or denied. But when reasonable, allowing children to think for themselves will create confidence for the future.

As communications and problem solving improve, parents may find that they occasionally make errors. When this happens, never be afraid to admit to a child that you were wrong. Adler called this "the courage to be imperfect." Children need to see that it is okay for others to know that one is not perfect. Such honesty allows others to feel closer and to be more honest in communications. Also, it prevents children from entering the painful and self-destructive world of perfectionism.

In class, parents often ask, "How can I relieve my child of her need for perfection?" As the parenting classes continue, I notice how perfect the questioning parent is. Perfection in dress, manners, emotions, and completion of assignments is consistent. So how can these parents help their children avoid perfectionism? They should become imperfect themselves.

Take risks. When risks are taken, errors are made that children can observe. Play games in which children excel, but the parents do not. Jump rope, roller skate, or play soccer. Become engaged in life in the areas where mistakes are inevitable; then laugh about the mistakes and enjoy the activity itself. Nothing cures perfectionism like imperfection. Nothing cures children modeling perfectionism more than a parent's mature acceptance of personal setbacks.

FAMILY COUNCILS

Children cherish opportunities to sit down with parents to discuss family concerns and to create family plans. Rudolph Dreikurs's family council is a marvelous way to insure that families communicate routinely. Such family meetings have become even more crucial in the age of television, travel, and cluttered schedules. So often, modern families are separated throughout the week. The family council provides one hour per week to which everyone can look forward. Joining together in discussing family life becomes an anticipated event.

The family council is a meeting which allows each member to discuss concerns, make enjoyable plans, and divide family tasks for the week. The council allows complaints but never becomes a gripe session. The guiding attitude is "yes, that is a problem. What can we do to solve it?" Decisions which affect the entire family require a majority vote. Rules made in the council stand for one week. Sometimes rules are made which do not work out well for children or parents. Nevertheless, under normal circumstances, the rule will stand for the week. At the next meeting, another solution can be found to replace the faulty one. Members who are not present must abide by family decisions.

A distinct advantage of family meetings is that everyone is aware that there will be a definite time to discuss problems. It is against the rules of most councils to nag or complain between meetings. Thus, if Dad is concerned about Johnny's not taking out the trash, he must wait until the next week to discuss it. At the next meeting, the difficulty can be explored and a consequence created by the family. Knowing a time exists to discuss problems enriches the family atmosphere and prevents the hostile feelings that can result from criticism and nagging.

People often wonder when it is best to begin family meetings. "Immediately" is usually the answer. It is beneficial to begin meetings even before having children. Couples who practice cooperative problem solving before children are born will find it an easy transition later when they add children to the meetings. Children as young as one year may benefit from being in the room with parents who are reasonably and cooperatively discussing family life. First impressions of family atmosphere are long lasting. Modeling positive communications is an important contribution to young children's growth.

As early as two to three years of age, children can be allowed to attend meetings as long as their attention span holds. If parents allow children to plan at least one enjoyable event during the meeting, they begin to look forward to the planning sessions. With young children, it is often helpful to present a list of household jobs which require attention. Children enjoy selecting chores more than having them assigned. Parents also should choose jobs from the list so that children can begin to develop an appreciation for the amount of work that parents contribute. If children do not wish to make their own selection of chores, parents also can choose not to select chores. Very early in life, children grow to understand the cooperative nature of work.

There is a chart on the next page which could be used by a family. Our family will use a long list such as this one only when children begin to lose the notion of the family's work being a cooperative venture. In such cases, we are careful (as parents) not to volunteer our time to transport children to their favorite activities. When an explanation is demanded, the reply is: "I would like to take you but during that time I'll have to wash dishes and take out the trash." Children quickly catch on to this simple logic.

The order in which participants choose jobs rotates every meeting. Charts for checking off the completion of chores, or other unique ideas, create more enthusiasm in children. Should a task not be completed by a parent or child, the council should wait to discuss consequences the next

WEST JOB CHART

	Sun.	Mon.	Tues.	Wed.	Thurs.	Fri.	Sat.
Cook Breakfast		K					
Set Table		E					
Wash Dishes		P					
Cook Lunch		P,E,D					
Set Table		K					
Wash Dishes		M					
Cook Dinner		M					
Set Table		D					
Wash Dishes		K					
Laundry		K					
Fold & Put Away Clothes		M					
Vacuum		E,M					
Clean Tubs		P,K					
T-Ball Transportation		K					
Swimming Lesson Transportation		M					
Cut Grass		K					
Earn Money		K,M					
Feed Cats		D					
Feed Fish		P					
Take out Trash		E					

Chairman ___Emily___
Secretary ___Dad___

K - Dad
M - Mom
P - Patrick
E - Emily
D - Dustin

week, if possible. Always use encouragement in the meetings and highlight success. Expect positive results and be generous in noting accomplishments, and cooperation will usually improve. Also be flexible. Children may prefer to draw slips out of job jars or to make trades. Whatever system works well for the family should be adopted. Changes in the system of choosing jobs may be desirable to avoid boredom. Do not overload children beyond their capacity.

Chairmanship for meetings should rotate. Parents need to be careful to use their best listening skills to prevent dominating the meetings. The most important outcome for the family is for each person to develop a spirit of cooperation. Family councils can represent an exciting experience in family harmony if they are conducted properly. In this age of busy individuals, times together for talking and planning must be established.

Several common difficulties challenge the effectiveness of family councils. Possibly the most frequent failure is scheduling. Some families cannot find thirty minutes per week to share. When a family encounters severe time problems, the following question should be investigated: "What does it say about our family and our values that we cannot spend thirty minutes of our time together per week?" It is a sad commentary on the state of any family if members are repeatedly unable to spend time together.

Another difficulty is lack of self-discipline in calling regular meetings. In most families, children are the first to call for meetings. Meetings give them an opportunity to discuss important parts of their lives. Talking with their parents and actually influencing a family's life leads a child to feel significant. Parents need to follow through on a child's request to meet. If, by chance, children do not enjoy the meetings, then parents need to examine the tone of the event in order to insure that meetings are enjoyable. Planning more entertaining events and less problem-solving ones may be in order. Soon a balance between the two can be struck.

Most adults are cautious. Occasionally, one parent may avoid making changes in the family's decision-making policy. Although cautious, the majority of individuals will experiment if properly motivated. The parent desiring change needs to explain to the parent who is skeptical how the addition of family councils will benefit the family. Once the joy of working together as a family is experienced, parents generally are hooked and fears are forgotten.

Learning which agenda items are appropriate for discussion and which are not takes time. Parents need to consider each topic with this question in mind: Am I willing to openly discuss this? If the answer is "No," then postpone handling the item until discussion is possible. Parents who do not really wish free discussion will end up dominating a meeting; instead of discussing problems, they will dictate solutions. Parents must be honest and say "NO!" to children who present untouchable topics. Otherwise, the meetings will end in mutual frustration.

As the years pass, family meetings become a part of family life. Problems and anger rarely occur during the sessions. A common response of parents who use meetings is: How did we survive before we regularly talked about our problems and our plans? While it does take time to develop family meetings, the results are well worth the effort. Good communications and shared responsibility are within every family's grasp.

Communications are challenging and difficult. Adults can quickly add to their skills and abilities to communicate. Sometimes, increased communications may lead adults to discover shortcomings in themselves. This is a risk, but the benefit may be increased closeness for a lifetime.

RELATED READINGS

Becvar. R. (1974). *Skills for effective communication: A guide to building relationships.* New York: Wiley.

Brazelton, T. (1981). *On becoming a family: The growth of attachment.* New York: Delacorte.

Briggs, D. (1970). *Your child's self-esteem: The key to his life.* New York: Doubleday.

Carkhuff, R. & Pierce, R. (1976). *Helping begins at home.* Amherst, MA: Human Resource Developmental Press.

Faber, A. & Mazlish, E. (1980). *How to talk so kids will listen and listen so kids will talk.* New York: Rawson Associates.

Ginott, H. (1969). *Between parent and child.* New York: Avon.

Grodon, T. (1970). *Parent effectiveness training.* New York: McKay.

Gottman, J. (1976). *A couple's guide to communication.* Champaign, IL: Research Press.

Harris, T. (1969). *I'm OK — You're OK.* New York: Avon.

Lester, G. (1981). *When it's time to talk about sex.* St. Meinrad, IN: Abbey.

Robson, J. (1981). *Parents, children and sex.* St. Paul, MN: International Marriage.

Satir, V. (1972). *Peoplemaking.* Palo Alto: Science and Behavior.

Schaefer, C. (1984). *How to talk to children about really important things.* New York: Harper and Row.

Sluzki, C. & Ranson, D. (1976). *Double bind: The foundation of the communication approach to the family.* New York: Grune and Stratton.

Spock, B. (1978). *The problems of parents.* Westport, CT: Greenwood.

Sundene-Wood, B. (1978). *Messages without words.* Milwaukee, WS: Raintree Publishing.

Watzlawick, P., Beaver, J. & Jackson, D. (1967). *Pragmatics of human communication.* New York: W.W. Norton.

PART THREE

THE SITUATIONAL MISBEHAVIORS OF CHILDHOOD

CHAPTER EIGHT

WHEN THE MARRIAGE IS WEAK

NORMAL MISBEHAVIOR is common in all healthy children. But some families experience misbehavior in children that is not shared by other families. Often this unique misbehavior is disruptive to the entire family and/or to society at large. Why do such misbehavior patterns occur?

The following two chapters will discuss situational misbehavior from the viewpoint of family therapy. Family therapy is a relatively new field that has distinguished itself by treating an individual's difficulties as a symptom of more complex family problems. Family therapists' ideas have revolutionized the field of therapy and challenged the thinking of professionals and parents. By helping families to make changes in their relationships and the use of power, therapists have enabled children to give up situational misbehaviors and return to normal misbehaviors, which are expected in healthy children.

This chapter will concentrate on the husband and wife relationship. The parents' relationship provides the foundation on which individual family members grow. When the foundation is strong, all family members will benefit, but when the relationship of parents is weak, individuals in the family may experience problems in normal growth. Although marital difficulties may lead to a wide variety of problems in all family members, this chapter's emphasis is on some of the ways in which children may be affected. There are many excellent family therapists. Three of them are featured in this chapter: Salvador Minuchin, Carl Whitaker, and Augustus Napier.

Each of these therapists emphasizes a different aspect of living together as a family; yet their ideas blend to give readers an understanding of how a marriage may influence a child positively or negatively. Whether the reader is more interested in children who are displaying normal or situational misbehavior, understanding the ideas of family therapists will challenge parents to examine their influence on each child. By reevaluating relationships in families and by reconsidering the distribution of power, parents can strengthen areas of weakness and add to areas of strength.

MARRIAGE: A FOUNDATION OF ROCK OR SAND? (NAPIER AND WHITAKER)

The most important relationship in any family is between the husband and wife. This bond is the foundation on which the entire family's growth rests. It is a bond which may endure after each child passes through childhood and leaves the home. Marriages which give families solid support come in thousands of different varieties. There is no single model of strength. But common threads in sound marriages do exist.

Erik Erikson maintained that before a successful marriage can take place, two people must establish individual identities. In their marvelous book **The Family Crucible,** Carl Whitaker and Augustus Napier expand Erikson's idea by explaining that establishing an identity requires a person to live comfortably, using personal resources. The individual who succeeds without dependence grows confident and strong. In other words, they have **self**-confidence, **self**-awareness, and **self**-loyalty. The person who is individually successful develops a sense of security in life (Napier and Whitaker, 1978).

Ideally, marriage joins two people who have established individual security and autonomy. Each comes to the marriage with personal strength. Both bring something unique to the relationship that makes living together more enjoyable than living separately. Because marriage alters one's way of life, the decision to give up independence may be difficult. But once a union is decided upon, the couple is ready to forge a new life based on cooperation with respect for the individual identity of each member.

When identity is not developed before marriage, an individual may feel incomplete and emotionally empty. Living alone is an uncomfortable task, an overwhelming challenge. Another person is sought whose responsibility it will be to bring security and fullness to an otherwise stagnant life. Marriage becomes a simple solution for complex problems in living. A spouse is required to fill the loneliness, provide security, create sexual and romantic love, soothe the hurts of past wrongs, and offer a sense of meaning and direction to life. Instead of two strong wholes anticipating the sharing of life, two incomplete people dream of what marriage should do for them. These demands on the marriage and marital partners are unrealistic.

The famous family therapist, Murray Bowen, believes that people of similar maturity levels attract one another. People with strong maturity levels attract one another. People with strong identities seek out strong partners. Likewise, immature people attract partners from the same developmental level. Immaturity manifests itself in different ways. For instance, a highly emotional person may marry a person who exercises almost no emotionality. Both are equally out of balance. Or, a driven extrovert with little power for introspection may marry a closeted introvert with little apparent social interest. Again, they are out of balance. While mature marriages frequently occur between people who bring different attributes to marriage, immature marriages often bring together extremes. Despite the variations, the major point is that people of equal maturity levels attract one another. The emotionally mature attract the emotionally mature. The emotionally immature attract the emotionally immature.

Great passion often accompanies the marriage of people who have not established a secure identity. For a while, each may feel whole for the first time. At this point, the marriage can be red-hot, like molten lava. But time, the enemy of such marriages, inevitably passes.

When the demands on marital partners are too unrealistic to be met, the marriage soon begins to hint of imperfection. Situations may occur which prevent the partners from serving each other's needs. At that point, the marriage suffers a shock. Life may become highly emotional as each partner feels betrayed because the other did not meet the impossible dream. A quick divorce is possible.

But more often, the partners are too dependent to give up the legal arrangement. The prospect of being alone is terrifying. Therefore, they continue the arrangement and usually ignore the existing problems. There is a quiet but desperate hope that things will improve with time.

Marriages between most couples change with time. Normally there are ups and downs. In marriages between two mature individuals, the expectations and demands made upon each are not extreme. Each member looks equally at what can be contributed as well as gained from the cooperative venture. When problems arise, each feels responsible for jointly creating a solution. But in marriages between dependent people, attention is focused on how the other has failed. Emotions grow intense.

There is no cooperative movement toward solving problems. Each looks to the other to change.

The hot marriage begins to cool. Each partner becomes disappointed in the other. Few humans can tolerate such deathly coolness. Warmth is sought. When the marriage does not seem capable of providing the heat necessary for vibrant living, another source of intensity must be found.

Most marriages are enriched by the exitement found in interests outside of marriage. These opportunities are healthy because they add to the existing richness of the marriage. But when interests are pursued because the marriage is floundering, the interests substitute for the vitality needed in the relationship. The partners do not jointly gain from the involvement; instead, they jointly suffer as the neglect of marital weaknesses continues.

Usually it is the partner who is least comfortable with the existing marriage who finds the third source of excitement. This source becomes the third leg of a triangle. It represents a crutch which allows the marriage to continue standing. The third leg can be a sexual affair, heavy drinking, immersion in athletics, total dedication to the job, endless volunteer work, overinvolvement in graduate study, or any one of numerous possibilities. Each selection provides the passion the marriage lacks.

Into such unstable marriages, many children are born. Through fate, these children are destined to be entangled in the struggles of the parents. In such situations, the children may become that third leg of a wobbly relationship. Unfortunately, the pressure causes some to develop problems which provide the heat that preserves the parents' marriage. Several of the common ways children become entangled with their parents will be discussed below.

FAMILIES BUILT ON A ROCK
(SALVADOR MINUCHIN)

Each family organizes itself in a distinct way. Certain people have more power; some relationships are closer than others. As time passes, a pattern or blueprint of the family's structure can be created. This structure is consistently played out in daily life.

There is no single healthy structure or model for distributing power and communicating within the family. There are countless variations which prove successful. Occasionally, people with an extremely unusual organization will create exceptionally healthy family members. But when families do seek family therapy it is often because at least one member is experiencing problems. Frequently this is due to the dynamics within the family.

In such cases, Salvador Minuchin suggests that the family's structure be analyzed, then changed to allow optimal growth for each member. To help create such changes, many therapists share an ideal structure for families. Below is a diagram of a healthy family structure:

HW
FM
— — — —
Children

In this structure, the husband (H) and wife (W) are close together. This represents a basically cooperative and peaceful marriage. It does not mean that the couple does not have disputes and challenges to be handled. As one therapist observed, "Whenever a couple claims they never fight, it generally means one person is doing all of the thinking." Instead, the closeness means that the difficulties the couple experience are contained within the marital relationship.

Whether disagreements arise concerning in-laws, money, social manners, ambition, the ebb and flow of intimacy, religion, or other adult issues, the couple does not involve children in their disagreements. As was suggested earlier by Piaget, children are not cognitively capable of handling the complexity of adult problems. They should remain free to face the significant challenges of childhood.

The mother (M) and father (F) symbols are also together and represent parents who equally share the responsibility of parenthood. Although parental roles vary from family to family, each partner needs to be committed to being a parent. Ideally both should provide discipline and nurture for their children. Each should experience both the pleasures and headaches of raising children.

Perfect agreement on childraising is not necessary, but a joint commitment is. Parenting courses are extremely successful for parents who share both a strong marital bond and a dedication to raising children but who differ in their approach to discipline and communication. It may be that parenting courses are least effective when the husband and wife relationship is weak. In such cases, raising children becomes a side issue which continues the marital struggle.

Betsy and Bob were a couple raised in very different family atmospheres. They joined our parent study program and presented the image of being loving parents who were seeking a common ground on which to raise their children. But on one occasion, when discussing their application of logical consequences to a rather typical misbehavior, it became apparent that their differences involved more than simple technique. Bob reacted to Betsy's handling of the situation: "Well, the consequence was set up, but Betsy didn't follow through. Of course, she never follows through on anything, so I guess I can't expect her to with this." Betsy's response showed hurt and hostility toward Bob: "Yes, and when you responded to the same problem, you did it like a hurt child. Instead of acting, you ranted and raved and made a big issue out of nothing. You never are able to look at things in our lives objectively." At this point, the parenting course was not proving helpful. Instead, it became a battleground for two hurt and disappointed people.

The spaces in the above diagram between the parents and the children represent a relationship which allows access to the parents but displays a distinct separation of authority between the parents and their children. Parents cannot be effective disciplinarians and also act like one of the kids. Instead, adults must assume responsibility for the development of the children, while at the same time allowing comfortable communications.

The solid dashes also display limitations in the communication process. For example, while discussions in family councils may include almost any family issue, children do not have the right to make decisions about parental concerns. For example, they do not have the right to order a parent to resign from a job, or for the family to relocate in another city, or for parents to increase their frequency of sexual intercourse. Likewise, children have the right to privacy in their own lives.

In some families, one may find a parent who has dropped below the line and actually supports a child's misbehavior. In this case, a child may become a tyrant who runs the family, to the dismay of the responsible parent who is undermined by the spouse.

Mark and Tina entered the parenting program because they had an "uncontrollable" three-year-old. By their report, he never responded to discipline and did as he pleased all of the time. Occasionally, fate allows an outsider a perfect view of the problem. It so happened that I was able to see this family perform at a local mall. As I walked through a store, I heard a disturbance in another aisle. There was Mark crawling down the aisle behind his son. Both were making loud disruptive animal noises. As the mother approached, Mark looked at his three-year-old and said, "Oh no, here comes the big, bad Mom to tell us to behave." In this case, the mother was trying to provide discipline for two beastly children. But each time she tried to discipline the child, the father successfully undermined her. This particular case exemplified Minuchin's picture of children who become tyrants by standing on the shoulders of one of the parents. Below a diagram of this structure is provided. The dotted line between the father and child displays a lack of appropriate separation.

```
        Mother
    — — — — — — —
              •
Father   •   Child
              •
```

FAMILIES BUILT ON SAND

Unhealthy family structures can arise for many reasons. This section will focus on difficulties caused by marital problems. As mentioned above, weak marriages cannot stand without help. Often, the third leg which balances unstable marriages is some type of affair. Although sexual affairs can serve this purpose, it well may be that the largest number of affairs are not sexual.

For example, as weak marriages cool, some men begin an affair with their work. As Minuchin implies, the husband's career provides the excitement, companionship, optimism, and support that his marriage lacks. As the heat of career making builds, work becomes the husband's true passion. Home becomes a stopover between business dates. On paper, the spouse is married to his wife. In truth, he is emotionally married to his career. This affair can occur either before or after the birth of a child.

Where does this leave the wife? She also has a need for passion and meaning. She also wishes to feel competent and needed. But she has been emotionally abandoned by her spouse. How will she fulfill herself? All too often, a child becomes the object of her unfulfilled needs. The child is expected to provide all of the passion her marriage lacks. The mother begins an affair with the child.

Soon the mother becomes overinvolved with the child. Like a plant given too much water in too small a planter, the youngster is smothered by the mother's attention. There is no room for the roots of individuality to spread. Every emotion and behavior of the child is responded to by an overly concerned mother. Every weakness of the child is explored and emphasized. Family therapists call this overinvolvement between mother and child enmeshment.

The child's normal misbehavior and problems resound like sonic booms through the family. The intense scrutiny of the parent begins to imprison the child in the name of love. Not being allowed to create autonomy and initiative freely, the child may soon display personal and social disabilities. Some children become pampered monsters, expecting and receiving a response to every whim and desire.

Unfortunately, others begin to emphasize the behaviors that get a reaction from the enmeshed parent. A normal problem becomes a major emotional issue. For example, a child may develop an assumed learning disability which has no organic base. Particularly, this occurs if the parent is both ambitious for and disappointed in the child's academic progress. If the parent becomes overinvolved in the child's misbehavior, then the child may be labeled a problem child at home and emotionally disturbed at school. Actually, his original behavior was disturbing the emotions of the parent, rather than his being emotionally disturbed himself. Other children may retreat into physical illness in an effort to find sanctuary from the parent's overconcern. These children soon begin to be considered "sickly."

After a child is given a label, the parent's overinvolvement becomes more justified. The child is watched closely for specific disabilities and, of course, they are found. Soon the child begins to believe the designated problem is real. She acts as everyone expects her to. The vicious cycle is in full force. The irony is that the actions of the parents are all based on love. But it is a love which is too intense for a child to bear.

  H/W

    F (work)

  M

  · · · ·

Children

The diagram above represents a typical problematic family structure. The H/W represents the emotional distance between the husband and wife. Since Dad is essentially out of the house due to his affair with work, he has surrendered the parenting obligations to Mom. In the diagram, only the mother appears in the parenting position. Her relationship with the child is no longer represented by solid dashes, but dots. The dots represent the enmeshment or overinvolvement of the parent with the life of the child.

Because the structure provides each parent with emotional heat, the marriage can remain intact. Both parents are satisfied with the arrangement. In fact, dad will privately encourage mother's overinvolvement, since it allows him to avoid the difficult task of investigating the problems with the marriage. It would be a marvelous arrangement, except that the child must pay too severe a price.

Sid and Sylvia entered counseling because their six-year-old daughter Pam was wetting the bed and experiencing disruptive behavior problems in school. During the first session, the mother maintained a constant vigil over Pam. Every action by the child drew a reaction from Sylvia. During the session, Sid retreated into what appeared to be a thoughtful but observant world of his own. He never entered into a relationship with his daughter but showed support for his wife and her concern about Pam's behavior.

An example of this may be found in anorexia nervosa. Potential anorexics may not appear to be different from many others their own age. At first they become very weight- and figure-conscious. Diets begin. But long after appropriate amounts of weight are lost, the anorexic continues, even intensifies dieting. Soon they have wasted to a point where they have a skeletal appearance. Nevertheless, they still hold fast to their strict diets. Without intervention, from 10 to 20 percent may die from the condition. Ninety percent of those who suffer from anorexia nervosa are women.

While the success rate of therapists is generally around 50 percent, Salvador Minuchin's therapy has brought health to 86 percent. Minuchin treats anorexia as a family problem, rather than an individual difficulty. Minuchin discovered that the condition generally occurs in tightly enmeshed families. Because of the overprotection and overconcern of parents, children are unable to create a strong, individual identity. Anorexic families tend to avoid overt conflict. Particularly, parents may avoid working through their conflicts and problems. Instead, they direct their energy toward the problems of their children.

Minuchin attempts to free the child of the family's enmeshment. Conflict is brought out in the open. Consequently, the child gains a new freedom to establish a personal identity. No longer must the anorexic seek control in life through the narrow area of weight loss. No longer can the family be blind to interpersonal conflicts by focusing total attention on the symptomatic child. By opening the family, Minuchin allows everyone to grow through meeting their personal challenges in a more appropriate manner.

Soon the cause of the problem sounded all too familiar. Sid and Sylvia both came from broken homes. Both hoped for better things in their marriage. But Sid did not know how to love or maintain closeness to another person. When life at home became frustrating, he quit his well-paying job in order to open a private business. The business took him away from home several nights a week.

Sylvia was left with unfilled time and unfulfilled dreams. Her child became the object of her attention and affection. But Sylvia's overconcern caused her to overreact to normal misbehavior. She was constantly correcting and scolding her daughter. Pam soon began to believe she could do nothing right and began to play the role of bad child; thus, a vicious cycle of negative interaction was established. It was not until the parents' relationship improved that Pam was allowed the space to create her own positive identity.

This particular paradigm is one of literally thousands of variations. Nevertheless, the principles remain the same. If the husband and wife's relationship is not solidly grounded, their children sometime pay the price. But overinvolvement is not the only way that children can be victimized by the unresolved problems of the parents. In some instances, parents may blame a child or children for their marital disharmony. Particularly, this occurs if couples cannot make the adjustments necessary when a family adds another member.

In such cases, parents may build a wall between themselves and their children. Neither parent assumes the parental responsibility for nurturing children. Emotionally, they withdraw from the relationship. This movement is called disengagement. Instead of being smothered by too much attention, the child is starved. Feeling desperate to receive recognition, a child may react inappropriately in order to force parents to enter a relationship. A child's bid for recognition may manifest itself in behavioral problems, emotional difficulties, school failures, or a host of equally disruptive possibilities.

When Pete met Jennifer, she became thrilled with Bobby, the four-year-old son from Pete's first marriage. It was Bobby she talked about to friends and relatives. Everywhere the couple went, Bobby tagged along. Soon after Pete and Jennifer married, Jennifer was surprised to find she and Pete shared no common interests. They really did not enjoy living together.

Instead of trying to create a better marital relationship, Jennifer began to blame Bobby for the couple's problems. The past angel now descended to the rank of devil. "If it were not for Bobby, we would have a good relationship," she was often heard to say in front of the child. Every week Jennifer and Pete became more detached from Bobby, although their relationship did not improve. Bobby became the scapegoat who allowed the marriage to drift through time. He elicited the passion and fire that the marriage lacked. The couple united against a child, now designated as the common enemy. Such a family might be diagrammed:

   H/W
   FM

   Children

The solid line between the parents and child represents the disengagement present in the family.

In other cases, the warfare between parents draws the child directly into parental fights. For example, one common triangle requires a victim, persecutor, and rescuer. Often the child sets herself up as the victim by drawing Parent A into a power struggle. Parent A disciplines the child, who then howls for help. To the rescue comes Parent B (rescuer), who saves the child (victim) from Parent A (the persecutor).

Jason and Betsy seemed to share little joy in life. They took turns slyly degrading each other but were careful never to express anger. They seemed to believe that as long as they held their angry feelings toward each other inside, the relationship would continue painlessly. Their five-year-old son, Tommy, sensed that his parents were vulnerable. Tommy began to defy his father's instructions. Feeling humiliated, Jason would respond by spanking the child, although he knew his wife opposed physical punishment. Tommy would scream as if the world was ending. Knowing what the cry meant, Betsy would fly into the room and berate the father for his actions and then hug poor little Tommy. Dad responded by leaving home for the evening.

Anger always finds an outlet. In this case, Tommy was in control of the floodgates. Unfortunately, the system the family developed never allowed the source of the problem to be explored. Anger would rebuild until Tommy once again provided the temporary release.

Children can be dragged into parental fights in a multitude of ways. Often a child joins in a full partnership in one parent's war against the other. This scenario can be diagrammed:

```
    M ⎫
· · · · ⎬ F
    C ⎭
```

Once I counseled a family composed of a teenage daughter, Mary, and her parents, Becky and Fred. The father was twelve years older than the mother. Following retirement, the father's energy seemed to wane. Sex between the couple became infrequent. Fred showed no interest in joint friends, hobbies, recreation, or other activities. Most of his time was spent in front of the television or working in the yard. Becky's religious tenets led her to believe that it was wrong to show her discontent with her husband. Instead, it was her duty to love, honor, and obey him. Becky's energies needed an outlet. Therefore, Mary soon fell under the intense scrutiny of her mother. On cue, Mary began to perform far below her ability in school. The family came to counseling, due to Mary's academic problems.

In subsequent sessions, it became apparent that the mother's vow of silence did not extend to Fred's parenting. Becky lambasted Fred for his lack of interest in and enthusiasm for Mary. Her complaints were the same as those she had felt toward Fred in marriage. Mary joined in the attack by describing her loneliness and desire to be close to Fred. She cried desperately in the sessions.

Fred vowed to do better. He created plans to be close to Mary the following week. But, you guessed it! No matter what he tried, it simply was not good enough. Becky and Mary would join forces the next week to attack Fred's parenting weaknesses. The coalition continued for as long as the parents avoided their own problems. Mary was always recruited by mother as a comrade-in-arms, but since a fictive battleground was chosen, no victories were possible for the family.

Although this section's focus has been on family problems caused by marital disharmony, difficulties can arise due to other flaws in the family structure. For example, one frequent structure which promotes difficulty involves what Minuchin calls a "switchboard Mom." In this structure, the mother serves as a go-between for the father and his children. She expresses his feelings and thoughts to the children. The children, in return, begin to use her as a switchboard to relay their feelings to the father. Such statements as, "Your dad really loves you, but he just doesn't know how to show you," or "Your dad really is proud of you" are representative transactions.

The tragedy in such a situation is that children need each parent to share his feelings directly. Many children deprived of a parent's emotional support search fruitlessly throughout adulthood to find the magic formula that will bring an aging dad or mom emotionally closer. But without work, most structures will not change. As long as the mother (or father) is enjoying the power of the switchboard, neither the children nor the detached parent will learn to speak for themselves. Someone must have the power to bypass the switchboard by using direct communications. Beware, however! Systems such as this resist change!

Other structures which are frequently seen include the "accordian family" and the "shoe family." In the first, there is often a parent (traditionally the father) who travels. When the traveling spouse is outside of the home, the remaining spouse is the sole authority. But when the voyager returns, the entire structure of the family changes, depending on the amount of power that is shifted. In the shoe family, reminiscent of the Old Woman Who Lived in a Shoe, there are many children present. But in this case, the mother does know what to do. She elevates one or more of the older children to parental status. The parental child helps raise the younger children. The role of the parental child is discussed later in the special chapter on single parent homes.

Each family has a unique structure. Uncommon misbehavior in a child may be a symptom of a family with broader problems. Should a child encounter problems more serious than the normal misbehaviors described in earlier chapters, parents are wise to inspect the foundations on which the family rests.

The marriage is a good place to begin exploration. Check the temperature of the marriage. Is it hot enough to survive without outside support? Could it be that children have unconsciously become involved in adding needed heat? If parents are not sure of answers to these questions, a marriage and family counselor can help. They are skilled in reviewing structures, identifying triangles, and helping couples add vitality to their relationship. The kitchen of marriage needs heat, but the parents should be responsible for stoking the fires. The heat of the marital kitchen is not a place of child's play.

STRENGTHENING THE FOUNDATIONS

By choosing to read this text, individuals may have already displayed the dedication necessary to enrich relationships in order to prevent stagnation in adult life. To continue growing, husbands and wives, as well as parents, need to continue adding to the positive parts of relationships. Unfortunately, most people know couples who have stuck their heads in the sand, refusing to nourish their relationships. Inactivity usually leads to stagnation. Although many of these lifeless relationships endure through time, all that exists for the couple is a pseudomutuality or an appearance of closeness. Life is too short to surrender vitality to the forces of inertia.

Individuals and couples need to seek new ideas, new ways to create meaning and enjoyment in life. This quest can find many sources, including counseling, enrichment experiences, and self-help programs. Marriage and family counselors are trained to help couples understand and expand their relationships. Often, couples are too embedded in life to gain an objective view of how relationships might grow. Counselors can provide a clearer understanding of the relationships. Positive suggestions for movement can be expected. In my opinion, it is healthy couples and families that seek counseling. They have the desire and courage not to remain the same throughout life.

Some couples may prefer less expensive alternatives. Enrichment programs for parents and couples can be found in most localities. Such opportunities are usually educational and/or experiential in nature. Often, programs are connected with colleges, hospitals, churches, mental health associations, or other sponsoring organizations. Interaction with trained leaders and peers experiencing similar challenges in life can be inspiring and encouraging. Whether the courses of workshops focus on marital relationships, sexuality, communication, or parenting, such programs can be of great help in enriching the lives of couples.

In addition to counseling and group enrichment experiences, many individuals enjoy self-directed searches. Couples can grow through reading one of the many self-help books available in bookstores. Additionally, personal and couple creativity can lead to exciting new experiences and increased enjoyment of each other. Below are a few ideas I have found helpful to couples who wish to add to their existing happiness in marriage.

LEARNING FROM PAST SUCCESS

Although many would suggest burying the past, I believe it may hold some suggestions for future happiness. Many enjoyable, creative, and romantic moments are found in the early years of a couple's relationship. High points are scattered throughout their past. Rediscover those past events. What was once successful may be helpful again. Never bury successes.

1. **Recall the days when you were first dating your spouse:** Make two lists.
   a. List four things you did to try to attract your spouse to you.
   b. List four things your spouse did which attracted you. Exchange lists with each other and discuss. Think of whether **you** could do similar things now to be romantic!
2. **List the four most enjoyable times you have spent with your spouse:** When and where did they occur? Exchange lists and discuss. Are similar experiences possible now or in the future?
3. **List four life challenges (births, deaths, loss of job, moving, illness, etc.) you successfully faced as a couple:** What did your partner do to contribute to the success? Exchange lists and discuss.
4. **List four attributes of your spouse which you have most admired and respected through the years:** Exchange lists and discuss.
5. **Add to any of these discussions** by sharing positive feelings, memories, and observations you carry from past years.

   Remember: Dwell only on the positive!

ENRICHING THE PRESENT

1. **Spend short times together regularly:** Many couples look to big events which require hours of time together. Have a night, or nights, each week when you share 15 minutes together while the children are asleep or in school. Take a walk, eat a snack, share a drink, or just sit and talk about the day. Keep the time short so it is reasonable to schedule such times frequently. These "little times" may pay big dividends.
2. **Spend time together away from the children:** Leave the children with friends or relatives and spend time together. Don't take friends along. Instead experience being with each other alone. It is not necessary that a couple has a lot to say or has a marvelous time on such occasions. Just being together alone is important.
3. **Spend time together with children:** Plan an event together which your children will enjoy. Surprise them, if possible. Concentrate on their happiness. At the end of the day, find some time to discuss the events you remember most.

4. **Return to romance:** Review the ideas from the past. Ask your spouse for a date. Plan events he or she will like. Concentrate on your spouse's happiness. Try to take tips from your early relationship. Have the courage to act young again!
5. **Add a new interest neither has developed:** It does not matter what it is: jogging, bowling, opera, music lessons, wine clubs, church groups, or whatever. Experience newness together.
6. **Special topics nights:** Have a night when you discuss "hot topics." For example, talk about sex. Share what turns you on and off. Talk about desired sexual frequency, sexual positions, and fantasies. You may wish to study together one of the books available on human sexuality.
7. **Show your love "correctly":** Certainly, it sounds strange to think there is a "correct" way to show love. But many lovers do things to show love which are not appreciated by the spouse. Separately,
    a. List in order the eight most important ways you show your love to your spouse.
    b. List in order the eight most significant ways you **wish** your spouse would express love to you.

    Exchange lists and discuss. Often the lists do not match. For example, a spouse may have cooking special meals high on the list for how love is shown, say #3. But if that activity does not appear high on the spouse's list, then it may be best to pick a higher rated activity. Don't spend your time giving your spouse #8s on the list, if giving #1s is possible!!
8. **Do what is hard for you:** Take a chance. If you are the initiator in the family, allow your spouse to plan some events. If you are more often the thinker and your spouse usually the emoter, then take some chances in expressing your feelings. Learn to express feelings which are difficult for you! Have courage.
9. **Do not avoid conflict:** It is easier to solve many small conflicts than one large one. Have problem-solving meetings, when problems can be freely discussed and common solutions found. Do not allow problems to escalate. Remember the communication skills discussed in earlier chapters. A helpful attitude is: "This is a problem for me; what can we do to come to a solution?" Never be afraid to say "I want this from you." Let your wishes be known.

CREATING AN EXCITING FUTURE

So often our busy days are overwhelming. We can become lost in the necessities of the present. Couples can profit by planning future events which liberate them from daily responsibilities.

1. **Plan an event for the near future** — spend time together discussing an event or trip to be shared in the next week or two. Review past events which brought enjoyment. It can be as simple as a night out or as complex as a weekend's travel. Alternate planning interesting occasions for each other.

2. **Plan a large event for the future** — look down the road and create a "dream" plan. Create a plan for something you have always wanted to do, but have not. For example, go camping for a week, take a long trip together, or travel abroad.

3. **Look at life after the children leave home** — what dreams that are impossible now, due to the restraints of family life, will be possible when the children leave home. Plan for those years when you have fewer obligations. We can only do that which we dream. The future should draw couples toward it, rather than frighten them.

Many couples can profit through self-help efforts. But if a couple becomes stuck or there exists a lack of cooperation, outside resources should be utilized. Almost all couples can profit from educational opportunities, including counseling. Those who work to grow stronger usually do. Those who do nothing but let time pass, simply grow older and more stagnant.

SALVADOR MINUCHIN

Salvador Minuchin was born in Argentina. He completed medical school in 1947 at the University of Cordoba. In 1948, Minuchin joined the Israeli war effort as a volunteer army doctor. Following his efforts in Israel, he came to the United States to study child psychiatry at Bellevue Hospital in New York City. Upon completion of his studies, he returned to Israel to become Psychiatric Director for the Youth Aliyah, Department for Disturbed Children. His work during this period brought him into contact with displaced children of the Holocaust and with Jewish immigrants from the Arab countries. His experiences with these individuals led Minuchin to begin working with the entire family or individuals experiencing life problems. Minuchin returned to the United States and began developing his therapeutic ideas into what is now called Structural Family Therapy. Many of Minuchin's specific techniques were created in his work with black and Puerto Rican delinquents who attended the Wiltwychk School near New York City. From 1965 to 1975, Minuchin's creative leadership as Director of the Philadelphia Child Guidance Clinic led to the expansion of the staff from 10 to 225 people, making the clinic the largest facility of its kind in the world. The clinic, connected with the University of Pennsylvania, still serves a population predominantly from ghetto areas. Currently, Dr. Minuchin is a Research Professor at the New York University Medical School and Clinical Professor of Child Psychiatry at the University of Pennsylvania. His writing, lecturing, and travels still carry him around the globe.

CARL WHITAKER AND AUGUSTUS NAPIER

Dr. Carl Whitaker has long been held as one of family therapy's most innovative and exciting therapists. He is Professor of Psychiatry at the University of Wisconsin Medical School. Augustus Napier is in private family practice in Atlanta, Georgia. Their book **The Family Crucible** is a marvelous view of one family's travel through family therapy. Knowledge of Dr. Whitaker and Dr. Napier's work will prove helpful to parents who are struggling to enrich their own marriage and family life.

RELATED READINGS

Ard, B., Jr. & Ard, C. (1976). *Handbook of marriage counseling.* Palo Alto: Science and Behavior.

Barker, R. (1983). *Treating couples in crisis: The fundamentals and practice of marital therapy.* New York: Free Press.

Bowen, M. (1978). *Family therapy in clinical practice.* New York: Jason Aronson.

Broderick, C. (1983). *The therapeutic triangle: A sourcebook on marital therapy.* Beverly Hills: Sage.

Chesser, B. & Gray, A. (1979). *Marriage: Creating a partnership, an experiential approach to the study of marriage and the family.* Dubuque, IA: Kendall-Hunt.

Fitzgerald, R. (1973). *Conjoint marital therapy.* New York: Aronson.

Gurman, A. & Rice, D. (1975). *Couples in conflict.* New York: Aronson.

Hall, M. (1983). *The Bowen family theory and its uses.* New York: Aronson.

L'Abate, L. & McHenry, S. (1983). *Handbook of marital interventions.* Orlando, FL: Grune.

Lasswell, M. & Lobsenz, N. (1977). *No-fault marriage.* New York: Ballantine.

Libermal, R., et al. (1980). *The handbook of marital therapy: A positive approach to helping troubled relationships.* New York: Plenum Pub.

Minuchin, S. (1985). *Family kaleidoscope.* Cambridge: Harvard Press.

Minuchin, S., Fishman, C. (1981). *Family therapy techniques.* Cambridge: Harvard University Press.

Minuchin, S., Rosman, B., Baker, L. (1978). *Psychosomatic families: Anorexia nervosa in context.* Cambridge: Harvard University Press.

Minuchin, S. (1974). *Families and family therapy.* Cambridge: Harvard University Press.

Minuchin, S., Montalvo, B., et al. (1974). *Families of the slums: An exploration of their structure.* New York: Basic Books.

Napier, A. & Whitaker, C. (1978). *The family crucible.* New York: Bantam Books.

Phillips, C. & Corsini, R. (1982). *Give in—or give up.* Chicago: Nelson-Hall.

Sager, C. (1976). *Marriage contracts and couple therapy.* New York: Brunner-Mazel.

Satir, V. (1972). *Peoplemaking.* Palo Alto, CA: Science and Behavior Books, Inc.

Sholevar, G. (1981). *The handbook of marriage and marital therapy.* Jamaica, NY: SP Medical and Scientific Books.

CHAPTER NINE

WHEN THE FAMILY IS EXTREME

EXTREMES cause problems for children. This is evident when we observe the various ways in which power is distributed in families and the variety of boundaries that are established to separate families from the outside world. Extremes in the organization of power within a family can run the gamut from a rigid dictatorship to a loose permissiveness. Boundaries surrounding a family can vary from being so thick that there is almost no communication with the outside world to being so thin, or permeable, that no real sense of family identity and pride develops.

Dr. Ray Bardill has combined the ideas of many family therapists in creating the Bardill Grid. This grid displays the ways in which families differ in their establishment of organization and boundaries. Although Bardill uses the grid for a variety of purposes, it will be used here to discuss the four extreme combinations of organization and power which tend to elicit uncommon misbehavior in children. The four extremes described by Bardill include:

Quadrant A Families: Rigid Organization – Solid Boundaries
Quadrant B Families: Rigid Organization – Amorphous Boundaries
Quadrant C Families: Loose Organization – Amorphous Boundaries
Quadrant D Families: Loose Organization – Solid Boundaries

Most people do not live in families which represent these four extreme situations. Instead, most are situated toward the middle of the grid. Some may even change in nature from year to year, while others can have a different atmosphere, depending on whether the mother or father is present and in charge. The terms Quadrant A, B, C, or D families are used in this section only to represent the extreme possibilities. These are families that lack the flexibility to change, despite the individual needs of children or the family as a whole. They are rigid, whether it be in their authoritarian use of power or their inability to control a family because of permissiveness.

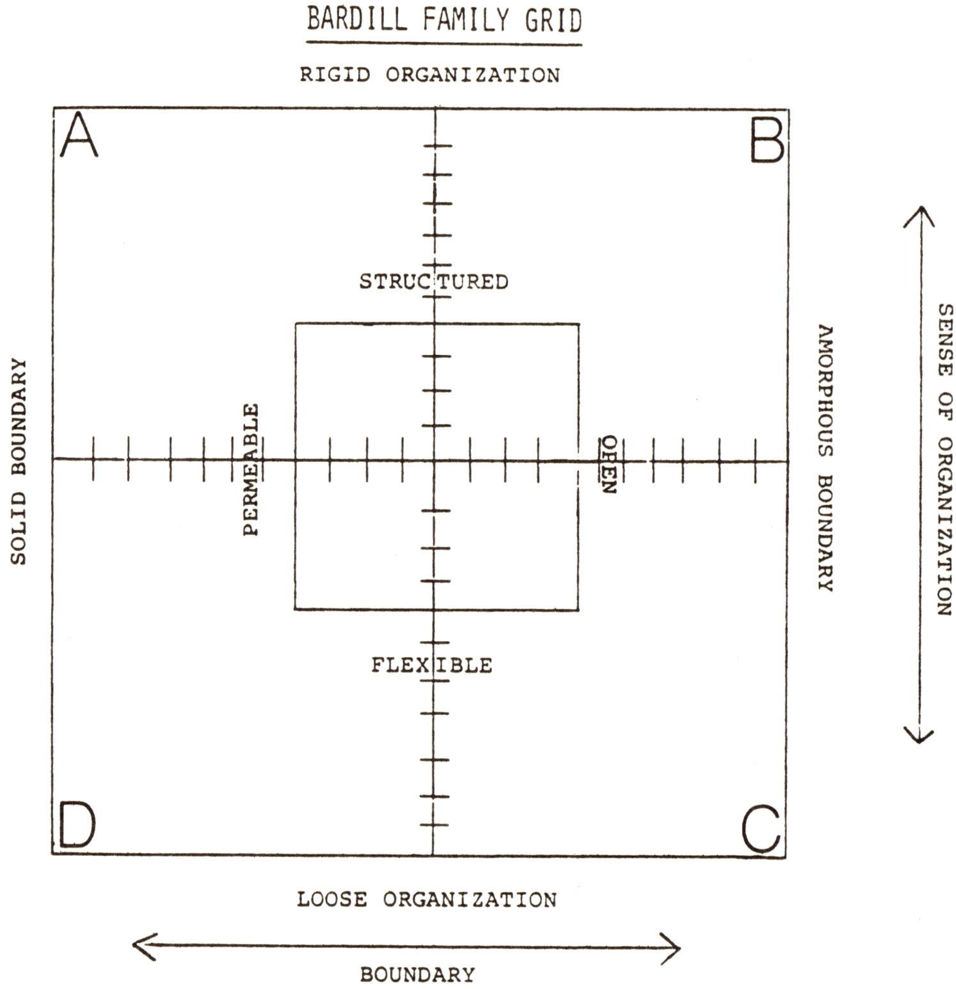
BARDILL FAMILY GRID
RIGID ORGANIZATION
A
B
STRUCTURED
SOLID BOUNDARY
PERMEABLE
OPEN
AMORPHOUS BOUNDARY
SENSE OF ORGANIZATION
FLEXIBLE
D
C
LOOSE ORGANIZATION
BOUNDARY

Following a discussion of Bardill's four extreme quadrants, a model based upon the ideas explained in this book will be presented. It is a paradigm which offers the flexibility needed for families to change from extremes by making small steps, rather than attempting gigantic leaps. The democratic-authoritative model features the use of family councils and consequences. Although homes can vary greatly in their use of such techniques, they still stand in stark contrast to the four rigid atmospheres represented by the extreme quadrants.

Finally, a discussion of the challenges that will stress the organization and boundaries of all families as children grow older is provided. No matter what the age of one's children, family therapists urge parents to prepare for the future. By thinking ahead, parents can prevent the multitude of complications which arise if families move through life blindly.

QUADRANT A FAMILIES: RIGID ORGANIZATION—SOLID BOUNDARIES

In the past, through necessity, families were often organized in inflexible ways. The family itself, particularly in rural communities, was often a self-contained unit for work, play, and social life. Because the work of families usually required clocklike precision, it was practical to have one person in charge who was experienced and powerful. In that era, rigidly organized families were very effective. But as society has grown more complex and demanding, most families have changed. Fewer families exist in the extreme represented by Quadrant A. Yet, still many exist, particularly in communities in our nation which still share the values, traditions, and customs of their forefathers. Although many remain patriarchal in form, some are dominated by a strong woman.

In Quadrant A, a rigid family organization generally revolves around a strong leader whose authority is rarely questioned. Rules are made by the leaders and delivered clearly to the children. Rules are not made to be broken. Discipline is immediate and usually overt. Exceptions are rare for children who miss the mark for whatever reason. Communications about responsibilities and expectations are explicit. However, communications do not usually include emotional content. Quadrant A people are usually rigid in their emotions, expressing few variations. Neither laughter nor tears are common in these homes.

Roles in this family are often stereotypical. For example, adult males generally act as head of the family, bread winner, outside worker, and fix-it man. Women's roles revolve around domestic responsibilities. The children are trained early in these stereotypes, as jobs assigned in and out of the home reflect. Females help in the kitchen. Males take out the trash and cut the grass. Everything generally runs by a family clock. Supper is always at 6 o'clock, as it has been for generations. No one is allowed to miss supper or be late for bedtimes. It just is not done. The family clock rules. Schedules will be the same each day throughout the family's life together.

Even the organization of space is a testimony to the rigidity of organization. Everything in the home is clearly divided. Dad has a certain chair at the dinner table and in the television room. He may have a study or workroom which is also his alone. No one would dare violate his space. If he is not home, his chair remains empty. Children rarely sneak into his workroom, and if they do summon the courage to enter, they never touch anything in it. The same is true of mother's space. The kitchen is her domain, and all tread lightly around it. Children also have certain parts of the house which are theirs, although parents maintain the right to enter those areas when necessary.

Solid boundaries separate the family from any unwanted influences from the outside world. Time is predominantly spent with the family. Bardill calls this the "wad effect." Individual family members are rarely seen in the community. Instead they are seen enmeshed in a family unit which always seems to share the same recreation and interests. An observer might often comment: "There goes the McGregor Clan," rather than "There goes Tom, Marcia, Sally, and Benjamin." Individuals are lost in the "wad."

Only the right kind of child with the right kind of parents can become a friend of Quadrant A children. Those who come from families with different values are certainly not allowed into the child's world. Friends can enter the home through invitation only. Such encounters are arranged by the parents of the children. Also, television, movies, and schools are screened. Parents carefully teach their own values to their children. This teaching is direct. Children are always aware of their family's beliefs, which are generally the same values held by past generations. Media that reflect different values are not allowed. Public schools are often abandoned because the values taught are inconsistent with those of the family. What teachers say in the classroom is reviewed by parents. Action is often taken against teachers who defy the family's value system.

The solid boundaries which separate this family from society give outsiders an impression that the family lives in a guarded castle. Occasionally, the drawbridge is lowered to allow a group out or individual in. But the particulars of what happens inside remain private. Fortunately, the strong value system of the family is generally well known. Therefore, society as a rule does not worry about possible misconduct within the walls.

Extremes lead to difficulties in families. For children of Quadrant A families, individuality is discouraged. Conformity to rules, values, schedules, and togetherness is expected. The normal misbehavior necessary to develop autonomy and initiative is suppressed. A two-year-old, for example, is not allowed to say "NO!" to the leader of the family. Many children give up and conform. They become miniature adults who sacrifice individuality in exchange for acceptance by their loved ones.

But others rebel. Since open rebellion is often met with severe discipline, many children rebel covertly. They play it safe. Many underfunction in order not to conform. Some develop school problems. This allows a little control over their lives, even if it is negative. Others develop eating disorders, such as anorexia nervosa or bulimia. At least they have control over what enters their body. Major difficulties can occur if normal emotions such as hate, anger, or grief are repressed. Such emotions are quite normally directed against all parents because they, by necessity, provide limits for children. But if the family organization allows no criticism, then the emotions must find other outlets. Some children may be cruel to weaker children or to an "outgroup." Others may take the hostility inward and become self-punishing. Depression, accident proneness and, in extreme cases, suicide may result. At the worst, the Quadrant A world can be so confining that a child will neither conform to it nor have the courage to resist it. These children may enter their own world of "psychosis" which is free of all restraints.

The following example displays how even the most elementary misbehavior in a Quadrant A family can have enormous ramifications:

The Reverend J. Martin Jackson and his wife, Grace, were the heart of their congregation. He was the minister and she was the secretary and choir director. Their three sons were constantly reminded that on Sunday morning they were to be an example of propriety to the entire congregation. One day, the congregation was shocked to hear the second son, Timothy, (age eight) curse at another child. Timothy created the scene in full view of the congregation.

Although Dad spanked Timothy and confined him to his room for the rest of the day, Timothy continued to curse and drive his parents to distraction. Punishment did not solve the problem. The cursing seemed to grow with every spanking. After much public humiliation, Reverend Jackson brought his son to counseling to be "fixed up." Grace protested: "How can Timothy hurt us so badly, when all we want is for him to be a good boy?"

Timothy was a strong person. His zest for life and individuality was greater than that found in his brothers. When faced with a system which allowed no individual freedom, Timothy brought the system down with a single word. He displayed his autonomy for all of his parents' world to see and hear. Although the words were curse words, they might be translated: "Help! I want to be myself."

Ray Bardill suggests that families need to add what is missing. In this family, what is needed is individual freedom. Children should be allowed to participate more in creating the family rules. They need to be allowed to leave the family to enjoy sports or clubs of their own choosing. Creativity, which formerly was viewed as an enemy, needs to be encouraged. And most of all, emotions should be shared. But all of this is difficult. Freedom is antithetical to the system. Movement needs to be in very small steps.

One must look to the family's leader to change the family, or nothing will change. Since the leader may consider sharing power and emotions to be a sign of weakness, it takes a gifted teacher or therapist to reinterpret the world for the leader. The leader must learn what courage, strength, and faith it requires for a person to allow children age-appropriate responsibility. It must be emphasized to the parent that permissiveness is far from the goal of the parenting group or therapist. Instead, responsible decision making and closer emotional relationships should be sought.

Prognosis for this family's change is better than is generally believed. Many in this quadrant change through traditional educational programs. These parents have several marvelous characteristics. The greatest of these is their unquestionable love for their children. When convinced their children will profit through changes in the family, the leader will seek such changes. Additionally, these parents do have the courage to act in the face of their children's misbehavior. Therefore, logical and natural consequences, once understood, are easily implemented. Whenever intelligent parents have the courage to act, combined with a love for their children, progress will be made.

QUADRANT B FAMILIES: RIGID ORGANIZATION—LOOSE BOUNDARIES

While the number of Quadrant A families may be decreasing, Quadrant B families are becoming more common. This may be due to the increase in single parent homes, which occasionally lean toward this particular structure. Therefore, many families may find themselves in Quadrant B for a few years, although the remarriage of a parent may bring a different structure to the family. Certainly not all or even a majority of single parent families utilize this structure. Indeed, more intact nuclear families may well belong to this extreme. But it is likely the increase of Quadrant B families in our society is linked to the high divorce rate.

As in the extreme Quadrant A family, a rigid organization characterizes Quadrant B life, but often the reasons for the enforcement of strict rules and regulations is different. While the Quadrant A's rigidity might be reflective of tradition and values, Quadrant B's tight organization often exists to benefit the parents. For example, single parents are so often overburdened that it seems strict home rules and expectations are necessary to avoid total chaos. Everyone must conform to the leader's demanding schedule. The less social support or help from relatives that is available, the less flexibility is likely. Necessity seems to require rigid organization.

Rules for the home are arbitrarily made by the parents. Flexibility is rare, as the parents closely oversee the children's conformity to rules in the home. Rules are often strict. But they may be based more on how much a person can be expected to help the home run smoothly than on sexual stereotypes. Because of the rigidity of the atmosphere, few emotions of joy are expressed. Life is not relaxed and free. At the extreme, this home is not one that is enjoyable to live within.

Children often look outside of the home for enjoyment in life. Amorphous boundaries allow the child freedom to leave the home whenever the child is not needed. Outside of the home, children do largely as they wish. Their freedom includes little supervision and few enforced rules. Children choose any friends they wish. There is no screening of friends, and often the parents are not familiar with their children's friends. Soon the children's friends begin to have more influence than the parents over their beliefs, values, and behaviors.

Because there is little supervision of children outside of the home, parents often are unaware of what problems they may experience or cause in either school or the community. As long as the child conforms to the expectations and rules of the parents inside the home, parents are generally satisfied. Reports by teachers or neighbors of behavior problems are often met with shock and disbelief. A common response may be: "I find it hard to believe my child is doing that (misbehavior). At home, she is perfect." And, indeed, she may well be, because at home the rules and regulations are explicit and enforced. Outside of the home, there are neither serious regulations nor real attempts at supervision.

Problems of Quadrant B children are predictable. With little joy to be found inside the home, children escape through the loose boundaries. They become overly influenced by peers and may easily fall prey to experimentation with alcohol, chemicals, or other risky, group-influenced behavior.

Should the atmosphere in the home become too negative, children may attempt to be free of obligations and restrictions. Some children may run away from home. Others may seek their freedom through pregnancy or early marriage. The loose boundaries appear to them to be the ticket to a happier life. Unfortunately, it is often the passport to further and more serious problems.

Sarah was the mother of two children, Nancy, age 13, and Jack, age 9. Two years after her divorce, Sarah began to recreate her life by returning to full-time graduate work. To help meet expenses, she also worked part-time between classes. When she returned home in the late afternoon, her voice thundered through the graduate housing complex. Everything had to run smoothly so she could return to her nightly studies. Her children jumped at her commands and accomplished everything required of them.

But between the time the children arrived home from school and their mother's arrival, the son had a field day. He hung out with a group of similarly free children, playing pool and video games. When their money was exhausted, the gang of kids would walk through the neighborhood, intimidating smaller children and causing minor disturbances. Jack took a can of gas and set fire to the rough in the adjoining college golf course. Fire trucks were summoned and angry neighbors identified the culprits.

When the fire chief disturbed the mother's studies later that evening with a personal visit, Sarah was shocked, and she vehemently denied her son's involvement: "If only you knew him. He is a perfect gentlemen. He helps me constantly. He couldn't possibly be involved." This mother was out of touch with her child's life. Inside the home, life ran precisely by her direction. Outside of the home, her children wandered without direction.

The prognosis for such families is excellent. Most of the parents are already good at making and enforcing rules. Their regulations and supervision must simply stretch outside of the home. Care must be taken to make arrangements to keep in contact with their children when they are outside the family's domain. Parents must develop "with-it-ness," or the ability to know what is happening to their children in all areas of their lives. Additionally, the family will profit by developing joint interests, recreation, and projects outside of the daily routine. Anything which extends a parent's influence outside of the family's home will help.

Inside the home, family councils work well for this quadrant. Children need to be given more responsibility to make decisions and think for themselves. Consequences (see Chapter Six) should be arrived at mutually. Activities which make home life more enjoyable should be developed. Shared times inside the home for discussions and enjoyable recreation will be helpful. All of these movements by parents can be accomplished easily, because these parents truly love their children and they can act in a crisis. It is true that time management may be an obstacle. But through parenting groups or family therapy, the changes needed to construct firmer boundaries and to make life inside the home more enjoyable are attainable and likely to occur.

QUADRANT C FAMILIES: LOOSE ORGANIZATION—AMORPHOUS BOUNDARIES

Members of Quadrant C families often come into opposition with society more frequently than do other families. Because of this friction with the establishment, these families pay a high price in terms of restrictions imposed on them from outside. Since their structure promotes unlimited individual freedom, Quadrant C members often are initially restrained by the rules and regulations of society itself.

In contrast to the first two families discussed, Quadrant C families are unable to provide structure within the home; although many rules may exist, few are enforced. Since this kind of discipline is permissive, there is a tendency for individuals to "do their own thing." No family leadership dictates recreation or interests to be enjoyed. No family clock runs the family. Instead, times for supper, bedtime, and other activities can vary from day to day. Children are often left on their own authority. They may wake themselves up in the morning, prepare their own meals, and put themselves to bed. Children are often left alone while parents conduct personal affairs, or young children may be seen accompanying their parents long past the appropriate bedtime for children.

Parents do not practice consistent roles. Therefore, children may lack a model for self-discipline. Little time is spent together as a family, making communications haphazard, at best. Emotions often replace reason as the basis for making decisions and are loudly expressed.

Boundaries are amorphous. Children and adults travel in and out of the house at will. Much of a child's time is spent with friends from whom they learn most of their values, attitudes, and beliefs. Individual privacy within the home is rarely found. People are unlikely to have a desk or quiet place to work, but whether a child completes her homework or not is a personal choice which receives little active parental encouragement. Adults are usually out of contact with the academic progress of a child or the problems the child may experience in society.

Many difficulties exist for children and adults in these families. Lack of practice in following rules, combined with a consistent display of emotions, makes discipline in school difficult for both the child and teacher. Lack of encouragement and modeling make success in school too infrequent. Because these children are often allowed so much time outside of the home without direction, juvenile delinquency is a strong possibility. Social interest and sensitivity to others may be lost to an unrestrained individualism.

A federal grant allowed our parenting program the opportunity to work with parents of first-time offenders. Many of the parents came from Quadrant C homes. Although court ordered, their attendance was irregular, even though transportation was provided. Mrs. Jackson was the single parent of three sons, all of whom had court records. Her youngest, Alfred, was arrested for possession of marijuana at age 11.

As she discussed her home life, it became apparent that no firm rules and the consequences for breaking them existed. For example, she begged and pleaded with her sons to come home before midnight, but her pleas went unanswered. She had no control of the home. Mrs. Jackson repeatedly told the other parents: "They are really good boys. They are just sowing their wild oats. You can't blame them for that."

All of our efforts to influence her to make contracts with her children or to act to enforce suggested consequences were unsuccessful. She would agree to implement a plan, but then she failed to follow through. "I feel so mean when I have to discipline them," she would say. Her permissiveness, along with the lack of family boundaries, led to a tragic conclusion. The police caught her youngest child selling drugs and chased him to a nearby river. The child dove in but did not make it across. He was dead on arrival at the hospital. Finally, life set a limitation the son could not avoid. But the consequences were severe and final.

The prognosis for these families is not always optimistic. Often such families are required by court systems to seek help; yet because of their lack of organization, it is difficult for them to regularly attend either parenting classes or therapy. Parents may, for a short time, try to be effective with children, but without the self-organization and self-discipline necessary to be consistent and to follow through on discipline, progress is often short-lived.

Nevertheless, progress in Quadrant C families can be of great benefit to our society, as well as to them. Parents need to be encouraged to take charge of the home. Contracts defining explicit consequences for misbehavior can be helpful. Any activities that bring the family together or that develop pride in the family are tremendously helpful. Loyalty, which is often underdeveloped, needs to be fostered.

These families do have many strengths to build upon. Because their lives take more unpredictable turns than most, flexibility is developed. Resiliency is a trademark of Quadrant C members. Additionally, the emotionality, which may create problems in some situations, also gives spontaneity, enthusiasm, and energy to life. Grandparents and extended family who have little opportunity to contribute in some families may become the key to stability and guidance of this family. Finally, parents really love their children. Many will seek ways to be more effective. With encouragement and patience, new skills and ideas can add to the quality of family life.

QUADRANT D FAMILIES: LOOSE ORGANIZATION—SOLID BOUNDARIES

If you remember the old Hatfields and McCoys legend, you have a sense for what a Quadrant D family is like. Inside the home, almost anything goes. But outside, each member remains faithful to the family. Like the Quadrant C family, this family has loose internal organization. There is no strong leader and no set of rules which govern behavior within the home. Little recreation or time spent together is shared. Productive communication is poor and emotions run high. Destructive behavior by both adults and children runs rampant and meets only inconsistent resistance.

However, solid boundaries are strictly enforced. There is little contact between these individuals and the outside world. When there is contact, there is an unofficial but strict rule "When you leave this home, you must never criticize the family." An absolute allegiance to the family exists, regardless of the difficulties or problems present within the home.

Family members do not often participate in activities outside the family boundaries. Few outsiders really grow close to them. In some ways, this family remains a mystery to society. Rarely do they come to counseling or parenting classes because of the thick boundaries that surround the home. Generally, counseling is required for misbehavior within the family which society finds offensive. This may include such things as wife and child abuse, incest, neglect, or psychosomatic illnesses.

A colleague of mine told me of a case involving a young teenage girl who was paralyzed from the hips down. Medical experts could find no reason for the paralysis. Eventually, her family was sent, against their will, to a therapist for another matter. After hours of counseling, it became evident to the therapist that the father had sexually abused the young girl. Even though everyone in the family was aware of it, the secret was held tightly within the family. The paralysis of the young girl was developed unconsciously as her way of protecting herself without violating family rules for secrecy. Fortunately, the therapist was able to work indirectly to loosen up the boundaries of the family and to create family discipline which relieved the child. Once the daughter felt safe, she no longer needed to rely on her symptoms. Incest was eliminated, although it was never openly discussed.

Whenever boundaries are high between a family and the outside world, it is difficult for therapists or educators to "join" the family, as Minuchin says. The family may view enforced help as "tampering" by outsiders which, of course, it is. But if an expert in the field can win over the family, then success is possible. Structure can be added to the family by encouraging family councils or by teaching a parent how to assume a role of authority in dispensing discipline. Boundaries may also be opened enough to allow both adults and children to participate in life outside of the family. Part-time jobs, sports, scouts, church groups, or other activities which increase interaction between a child or adults and the world outside of the family can be helpful.

A MODEL FOR GROWTH: THE DEMOCRATIC-AUTHORITATIVE FAMILY

While no perfect formula comfortably fits all families, a general model, based on the skills presented earlier in this book, is offered below. The model represents a flexible approach that allows parents to step away from extremes in organization and boundaries. Making small steps in a comfortable direction is important. Parents using this model should attempt changes which comfortably fit their family. With practice, small moves can be made. Afterwards, additional challenges can be added. This paradigm utilizes the ideas of Rudolf Dreikurs's democratic family, communication theorists, and active approaches to family therapy. The goal is to encourage individual freedom with responsibility, while maintaining a strong sense of family.

In the democratic-authoritative home, the use of the family council and establishing natural and logical consequences to handle misbehaviors are the tools of the family's organization. Suggested principles for operating family councils and for applying consequences are found in earlier chapters. The emphasis in this section is on the flexible application of these tools, which will allow a family to change comfortably in the directions indicated.

Families who prefer to be more structured in their organization give more authority to the parents. There is a tendency to create more rules and allow fewer exceptions. Consequences may frequently be determined by parents alone, although family discussion of the consequences is encouraged. Structured families may use the family council to discuss major challenges to the family and to set a schedule for the week. Duties will be divided and consequences may be created in advance, before actual difficulties arise. A tendency exists to retain the council's plan for the entire week, rather than to make exceptions for individual members. Particular emphasis in the family meeting will be on the needs of the family, although individual concerns are discussed. Parents will carefully limit the number of topics that they are willing to have decided by the family. Parents will wish to make many decisions alone. Nevertheless, the entire family will take part in those decisions that seem appropriate for them to do so.

For families that emphasize flexibility, more power is shared with the children, but lesser issues may be reserved for parental decisions alone. Although duties and schedules may be set during the council, it is understood that changes may have to be made during the week if unforeseen needs arise. Similarly, should a decision of the council not be working well, changes can be made between meetings, rather than held over for the next council. Discussions may be emotional at times, although emotions eventually will be directed toward solving problems.

Discussions may bridge a wide range of ideas and plans. Children will be encouraged more than in structured families to create consequences for problem behaviors. The quality of leadership for each meeting may change, because leadership is rotated weekly to give each person an opportunity to be in charge. Individual needs and goals will be emphasized during the meeting, although family needs will be discussed. Parents generally lean over backwards to support their children's initiatives.

Although both structured and flexible families differ in their use of family meetings, both do use the councils as an opportunity to organize the family and discuss problems. Parents in both of these families will use natural and logical consequences during the week when unforeseen situations and problems present themselves. Structured parents often may choose stricter consequences. These consequences may be set before any anticipated misbehavior can occur. Flexible parents have a tendency to allow the child more input in a consequence, even in a time of crisis. Often the consequences are set only after the first offense has been made.

Individual responsibility is stressed in both structured and flexible families. For example, both will generally grant allowances to children, allow the child some freedom to take care of her bedroom, and allow time for personal recreation. More structured families may have tougher consequences for each of these areas. They both have an "enough is enough" rule and specific consequences tied to cleaning rooms. While the flexible parent may simply close the door of an intolerably messy room, the structured parent may give the child a deadline to clean it. If work is not completed, the parent may enter with a snow shovel and finish the job. Structured parents may set some general guidelines for what children can spend their allowances on, while flexible parents may leave such decisions entirely up the children. Structured parents may allow a certain amount of time for play or to watch TV, but that time is usually organized around designated homework periods. More flexible parents may leave such scheduling entirely up to the preference of the child.

Boundaries in democratic-authoritative homes may be either permeable or open. Families with permeable boundaries expect children to spend as much time with the family as is reasonably possible for a child, depending on his/her age. Parents who prefer open boundaries will allow the child to follow personal inclinations more often; although at least some family time together is required each day.

Families that are more structured usually plan family activities during the week that will require the presence of the child. At other times, children may play with friends who are generally well known by the family. The parents will always know where their children are. Often a child's play at another child's home is preceded by a phone call to the friend's parents. Permission needs to be obtained before friends are brought into their own home. Family plans come first, but on occasion, if the child has an unusually important event planned, the family will schedule around it. The child is aware that the parents are making an exception on her behalf.

Families with a larger degree of flexibility have less family time scheduled during the week than structured families. Children are allowed to do what interests them, except on those infrequent occasions when family times are planned. Friends of children are generally known, at least by name. Children are free to play at another child's home or to bring children home with them. They check in with parents but do not ask formal permission to visit or bring children home. Individual pursuits of children are extremely important to these parents. Family plans are carefully arranged around the children's schedule. On occasion, a trip or important family activity demands that the family schedule outweigh the child's planned activity. The parents usually are somewhat uncomfortable about making the child miss her planned engagement.

By using family councils and defined consequences, structured and flexible families avoid the extremes of the four quadrants. Although very different in how they apply techniques, both families use family councils to solve problems and to discuss challenges as a family.

Communications in both families are facilitated by consistent meeting times. Rules are made, and consequences are set and enforced. Both families emphasize a balance between individual development and family interaction, although the balance is different in each family. Additionally, both families allow children to enter the outside world with varying amounts of supervision.

Structured and flexible parents need to be aware of potential weaknesses. Structured parents may take charge too much and move toward rigidity. They need to monitor themselves at family meetings to insure that everyone feels free to talk. There may be a tendency to be arbitrary in setting consequences; if so, the children will rebel and force power struggles. Structured families need to concentrate on promoting individual autonomy.

Flexible parents may find themselves surrounded by small lawyers who use the flexible nature of the organization to try to impose their own will through argument. These parents must prevent their authority from becoming weakened by looseness. Children can, in such instances, become parent-deaf. Particular monitoring needs to be done to make sure parents consistently enforce consequences. Overtalking to parent-deaf children is a sign of problems. Flexible parents need to concentrate on promoting individual responsibility and consideration for others in the family.

LOOKING DOWN THE ROAD: DEVELOPMENTAL STRESSES ON FAMILIES

Time will present each family with a series of predictable challenges. many families are flexible enough to be successful during each of these periods. Others are more successful in one developmental stage than another. Family therapists can forecast what challenges are likely to demand change in a family. These periods occur most often when members are added or removed from the home. Preparing for such inevitable situations can help families meet the challenge to change with a larger degree of success.

MARRIAGE

The importance of a strong marriage was discussed in the last chapter. The challenge for a person to move from primary gratification to cooperation in meeting life's normal developments is considerable. As Minuchin points out, there are people who have held marriage contracts for many years but have never really married. Instead, their behavior and thought remains similar to those of a single person. During my postdoctoral work, I had the experience of living next to a young couple with two preschool aged children. The father never really became married. Although the couple drew welfare payments, the 26-year-old father joined a fraternity at the university. At night he would return past midnight in a loud, drunken state, awakening his wife and children. When the family decided to buy a car, the father came home with a Trans Am.® The children and luggage could barely be squeezed in for trips. This male never married. He lived for his own gratification. The challenge of adding a wife and children to his life was never adequately met.

BIRTH OF THE FIRST CHILD

What a difference this addition makes. Life will never be the same! Parents need to rework their relationship in order to prepare for the changes demanded by the arrival of the first child. Even those with an excellent husband and wife relationship need to prepare. Some individuals are excellent couples when childless, but they do not adjust well to living with a third person. After a period in which they enjoyed the carefree life of spontaneity and freedom, many couples are not prepared to be tied down by the necessary demands made by a growing child. Others resent the sacrifices required in time that children take from careers, interests, and hobbies. The addition of a child requires more cooperation, social interest, and concern for others. In recent years this stage may have become a stumbling block for greater numbers. Those of the fabled "me generation" who have learned to champion their own pleasures may find that the needs of children constitute a devastating blow. Instead of adding to life, their children may be viewed as detractors.

Mark and Sally were both successful professionals. Both enjoyed traveling at will with their many friends. They were able to share marvelous adventures. Neither Mark or Sally particularly wanted children, but both felt that they should have a family. As Sally approached her early 30s, she decided to have a baby before her age began to increase the risks of childbirth.

Once the child was born, these parents were miserable. Because they lost the freedom to travel, they began to lose contact with their carefree friends. Also, time was lost from work in order for them to care for the child's needs. Employers indicated minor dissatisfactions with the work of an often tired mother. With personal pressure building at home and on the job, Sally began to be less tolerant and supportive of Mark. Soon the once maverick couple was considering divorce. Clearly, this couple was not prepared to add a dependent member to the family! The child was born for all of the wrong reasons. A marvelous couple do not always marvelous parents make!

FIRST CHILD ENTERING SCHOOL

When the first child enters school, many sense a passage in their own life. Their children are growing up. For some parents, surrendering total influence on the child by sharing it with teachers is difficult. For other parents, the child's hours in school will leave free time, which requires the creation of new goals. However, it may be that this traditional stage is difficult for fewer families because of the increased number of working mothers, as well as the renewed emphasis on adult self-exploration and growth.

Nevertheless, it is always painful to see parents and children paralyzed with fear and grief on the first day of school. When parents view school as an alien place, they pass their fear on to the child. Neither can adjust to a world which requires the ability to cooperate with forces outside of the home.

FIRST CHILD IN ADOLESCENCE

Parenting adolescents requires a particular set of skills and relationships. Parents need to shift from having considerable control over children to having a modified and limited influence. Should frustrated parents not be flexible enough to change their parenting techniques and goals, warfare may result. When children are approaching teenage years, it is a marvelous time for their parents to take a course on how to best parent adolescents. Some personalities are suited for parenting either older or younger children, but not both. Study helps bolster the weaker area, whichever it may be. The techniques and problems are so different that our parent-study program is separated into two distinct fields: one for parents of adolescents and the other for parents of younger children. Different teachers and resources are used in each of the courses.

CHILDREN LEAVING HOME

When the first child leaves home, parents must again begin to reorganize. They must avoid the temptation to overdirect the children remaining in the home. Likewise, parents may attempt to overcontrol and influence the child who has left home. Again, a change in the parenting role is faced. Parental influence weakens.

Additionally, primary gratification through family relationships begins to shift back to the couple. As parents let go of their children, they need to increase the quality of their own relationship and their enjoyment of each other. Many couples find it exciting to be able to enjoy adventures that were limited in their childraising days. Spontaneity can return. Trips can be taken. Movies can be attended without any communication with or arrangements for a sitter! The "empty nest" does not have to be a negative milestone in life. Instead it can be an opportunity to be "young and free" again.

As a professor, I often see families trying to hang onto the past by overdirecting a child's college life. Because they are unable to adjust to the challenge of their children's growing independence and the family's dwindling numbers, many try to keep in daily contact. I can remember one father who called from New Jersey to ask for his child's assignment in my class. She had been absent with a cold and was, he reported, too shy to ask for it. It is to be hoped that these children will rebel and thus enable their parents to grow up.

MARRIAGE OF CHILDREN

As children marry, their parents should make another major shift. Minuchin suggests parents should treat children as equals. No longer should they be treated as sons and daughters of the old family, but as husbands and wives of a new family. What a difficult challenge! Should families continue to treat their children primarily as members of the old family, resentment and anger will grow. New in-laws will resist the pull to remain in the past. Conflict will occur. Minuchin observes that it is equally a mistake for sons-in-law and daughters-in-law to attempt to become a son or daughter to their in-laws. Instead, they should conduct themselves as equals.

So many external reasons may contribute to a divorce. In one instance, a young woman's parents put such intense pressure on her to remain in the old family that she never had the opportunity to bond with her new husband. This only daughter's parents never took a sincere interest in her husband. They rarely spoke to him and never asked him questions about his business or interests. He, unfortunately, responded in kind.

The parents most often talked of the good times their family had had in the past. Their conversations never ventured into the new life of the couple. Although not actively disruptive of the marriage, her parents made constant requests for the daughter to visit home for a variety of reasons, which extended from family birthdays, to anniversaries, to special events, and even to minor illnesses of various family members. The daughter wanted to be loved by them, but also, she wanted her new life. Although she tried to compromise (by not meeting all of her family's demands), the influence was too strong. She was between "a rock and a hard place," and her marrige was the victim of the crushing process. Her husband used the conflict as a reason to abandon the marriage. The daughter returned to her parents and angrily accused them of tampering with her marriage. Of course, their reply was one of hurt: "What did we do? You can't blame us for just loving you. You could have said 'No' anytime you wished." And, of course, she could have.

Life requires many adjustments if healthy relationships are to continue. For people to grow, each must respond positively to the conflict inherent in new challenges. Whenever a person refuses to change, growth will stop. And, unfortunately, that person will no longer make a positive contribution to family members.

RAY BARDILL

Dr. Ray Bardill is the Dean of the School of Social Work at the Florida State University. Bardill was educated in his home state of Tennessee and received both his BA and MSSW at the University of Tennessee. After working as a clinical social worker in Oklahoma and at the Walter Reed Army Medical Center in Washington, D.C., Bardill earned his Ph.D. at the Smith College School of Social Work in 1967. Bardill continued his work at Walter Reed as the Chief Social Worker from 1968 to 1970 and as a Social Work Researcher for the Walter Reed Army Institute of Research until 1975. His final work at Walter Reed was as Director of Education and Training Social Work Service. In 1979, Bardill joined the faculty of Florida State University. Dr. Bardill's awards include the National Defense Medal, the **Certificate of Achievement** from the Department of the Army, and the Meritorious Service Medal. He is a Fellow in the American Association of Marriage and Family Therapists. Dr. Bardill is the author of numerous publications and is widely known for his workshops in family therapy.

RELATED READINGS

Ackerman, N. (1966). *Treating the troubled family.* New York: Basic Books.

Becvar, R. (1982). *Systems theory and field therapy: A primer.* Washington, D.C.: University Press of America.

Boszormenyi-Nagy, I. & Spark, G. (1973). *Invisible loyalties.* Hagerstown, MD: Harper and Row.

Carter, E. (1980). *The family life cycle: A framework for family therapy.* New York: Gardner Press.

Dinkmeyer, D. & McKay, G. (1983). *Systematic training for effective parenting.* Circle Pines, MN: American Guidance Service

Dreikurs, R., Corsini, R., Lowe, R. & Sonstegard, M. (1959). *Adlerian family counseling—A manual for counseling centers.* Eugene, OR: University of Oregon Press.

Erickson, G. (1981). *Family therapy: An introduction to theory and technique.* Monterey, CA: Brooks/Cole Pub. Co.

Framo, J. (1982). *Explorations in marital and family therapy: Selected papers of James L. Framo.* New York: Springer Publishing.

Framo, J. & Green, R. (1980). *Bibliography of books related to family and marital systems theory and therapy.* Upland, CA: American Association for Marriage and Family Therapy.

Gurman, A. & Kniskern, D. (1981). *Handbook of family therapy.* New York: Brunner/Mazel.

Gurman, A. (1981). *Questions and answers in the practice of family therapy.* New York: Brunner/Mazel.

Haley, J. (1976). *Problem solving therapy.* New York: Harper and Row.

Haley, J. (1971). *Changing families.* New York: Grune and Stratton.

Hansen, J. (1984). *Family therapy with school related problems.* Rockville, MD: Aspen.

Hansen, J. & L'Abate, L. (1982). *Approaches to family therapy.* New York: Macmillan.

Levant, R. (1984). *Family therapy: A comprehensive overview.* New York: Prentice-Hall.

Madanes, C. (1981). *Strategic family therapy.* San Francisco: Jossey-Bass.

Papp, P. (1977). *Family therapy: Full length case studies.* New York: Gardner Press.

Satir, V. (1969). *Conjoint family therapy.* Palo Alto, CA: Science and Behavior Books, Inc.

CHAPTER TEN

SINGLE PARENT HOMES

THE MOST BASIC need of children is to love and be loved. So many challenges seem to confront a child as she creates a significant place in the family. Some challenges present themselves as the family changes and sibling rivalries abound; others are ushered in with each new stage of development. Throughout this book, the reader has discovered the many common misbehaviors that are shared by children of similar ages throughout the world. As emphasized earlier, these daily misbehaviors are predictable misbehaviors.

There are some obstacles in life, however, which create reactions and misbehaviors that are not shared by all children. In America, three common challenges to children's identity and need for love are divorce, daycare, and the remarriage of parents. Although these experiences are not shared by all children, they are so frequent that this book would not be complete without an investigation of these circumstances. Like all conflicts in life, experiences in these three areas can be positively overcome. But children will find it easier to both receive and give love if parents understand the hurdles such situations create for their children.

While earlier chapters are written with the child's point of view as the focus, Chapters Ten and Eleven are written from the parents' perspective. Parents, as well as their children, may experience periods during which they feel isolated and unloved, particularly during the process of divorce and/or remarriage. The key to working successfully with one's children is to realize that such reactions are indeed experienced by the majority of adults who share these particularly trying life events. Parenting without guilt requires parents to understand and accept both their own and their children's reactions to special challenges faced in life.

SINGLE PARENT FAMILIES IN TODAY'S SOCIETY

Although one-half of the infants born today may spend several years with a single parent, our society still looks askance at divorced and unwed, single parents because they are at variance with the American ideal of nuclear family perfection. These single parents survive and nurture children in an atmosphere of anxiety, under misapprehensions and conditions that largely are not understood by those who live in traditional nuclear families.

Despite daily attempts to prosper against difficult odds, single parents are often considered to be failures; this is largely because of decisions made and relationships formed in their past. Indeed, on some scales that measure stress, divorce is considered a more difficult experience to overcome than the death of one's own child. Possibly this is due to the traditional reactions of a society that offers support for the survivors of a dying child but prefers, with the death of a marriage, to bury the survivors.

Single parents too often accept this judgment based on society's prejudices against them. To liberate themselves, they must no longer accept the outdated notion that only intact families are healthy and acceptable. Single parent families are neither superior nor inferior to intact families. They are simply different.

These differences can become sources of strength, rather than symbols of failure. To compare single family life to nuclear family life is like comparing the magnificence of the night sky with that of a clear morning. Both enjoy unique beauty; nevertheless, advocates of the night can make the morning seem dull and routine, while daytime enthusiasts can make the night seem cold and chaotic. Yet each of us knows that both can be beautiful.

THE SHADOWS — TRIALS OF SINGLE PARENT FAMILIES

PERSONAL TRAITS

Despite the widely varying circumstances in single parent families, there are recurring themes shared by many. The majority of single parents have experienced a major change in life, either through death, divorce, or desertion by a spouse.

The personal trials for the single parent begin with this major loss of a spouse and parent from the home. With this change, a grief process begins which may endure for months, or even years. Generally, the more difficult it is for a parent or child to release grief, the longer it takes to regain emotional stability. For the widow and widower, grief can usually be shared with relatives and friends, and this sharing facilitates the healing process.

For the divorced parent, the loss is more abstract. It is a death of early hopes and dreams. This feeling of loss is complicated, for many, by the relief of being free of a stressful relationship; despite these conflicting emotions, the feeling of grief is usually strong. For children, the loss of a parent from their daily lives can be doubly difficult. For them, seeing other families still intact is a constant reminder of loss.

No longer following the path of a nuclear family, single parents often are forced into a radically different existence. Divorced women, particularly, may experience economic crisis because the available money is now divided between two households. Financial strain may cause as much change as the end of the marriage. In the United States, over 50 percent of those living below the poverty line are single mothers. Even for those who do not face stark poverty, a change in life plans is generally necessary for families if they are to maintain their goals.

Particularly, the change may be drastic for women who planned to stay home with their children, or who worked only to supplement their family income rather than to develop careers. These single parents may lack the training necessary for a career. Without further training, many women are eligible for only the lowest paying jobs. Therefore, many single parents must work full-time and study to be retrained at the very time they feel most needed by their children.

An associate of mine with three children under ten years of age returned to graduate school to complete his doctorate. As part of the parents' agreement, the wife returned to the full-time secretarial work she had left after the birth of their first child. As soon as he finished his work, she planned to return to work at home. After four years of graduate study, the husband completed his doctorate and ended their marriage. The father moved with his new wife to a different state.

Although court systems are beginning to award more reasonable settlements to spouses whose work helps to educate and improve the careers of mates, the amount in this case was too small to allow the new single parent family to sustain their standard of living. Instead of celebrating the completion of her husband's degree with a return to the home life she loved, this mother entered the rigors of college to prepare for a higher-paying profession. Only with an increased income could she help her children reach their goals. The dream of life on easy street was replaced by a daily struggle to keep the family's goals alive.

As many single parents with young children return to full-time work, some form of daycare becomes necessary. The challenges of choosing adequate daycare are discussed in the next chapter. For parents with older children, proper provisions must be made for their safety and supervision between the hours when school ends and the parent returns from work. School vacations and summer months pose monumental difficulties for many single working parents with school-age children.

The end of school means the beginning of baseball games, swimming and tennis lessons, and a host of exciting adventures for children. I met one single mother who tried to insure that her three children could experience everything. Despite working forty hours per week, she encouraged her children to register for all of the activities enjoyed by their peers. Two of her sons were on my son's little league team.

At first, all went well. Then games were routinely missed. Only eleven players were on the team, and when her two sons were absent, games were usually forfeited. Coaches and parents were angered by what appeared to be irresponsibility. Only after hearing her story, did we realize that she suffered from overresponsibility. Her job ended at 5:00, and games began at 5:30. To arrive on time, she had to travel across town, depend on her sons to be dressed, pick up her daughter, and journey back to the other side of town where the games were played. At first, the plan worked. But then, her daughter's swimming lessons began at precisely 5:30. The children were forced to alternate their attendance at events because their mother was too proud to ask for help. She tried to do everything for everyone and was unsuccessful.

Quickly, the days become too short. If time is left over after work, it is lost to the new explosion of responsibilities. A single parent is responsible for all of the shopping, homework, errands, yard work, cooking, bookkeeping, household repairs, car maintenance, taxes, and planning. In addition, single parents must react to all emergencies, begin or continue a career, and remain a nurturing parent. As one mother said, "I did 90 percent of the work anyway, but the 10 percent extra took all of my free moments."

Possibly, the most difficult times for single parents are when unexpected events interrupt the intricacies of daily scheduling. Illness of either the parent or the child presents a crisis. Some parents report having bosses who do not tolerate absences; thus, when a child is sick, the mother faces a difficult situation. It is not unusual for single parents to rely on older children, who must remain home from school to care for sick toddlers.

A striking situation, relayed to me by a single parent, was described in this way: "One day I had intestinal flu, and the same day one child fell and knocked out both front teeth. A year earlier, his father could have taken him to the hospital and comforted him. I was so ill that I had to try to find a friend who would come and take him to the hospital. When my son returned, crying over his toothless appearance, I couldn't stay in the room long enough to comfort him. I was as sick emotionally as physically in those moments. We all felt so alone."

School emergencies can also complicate the lives of working single parents. Often, phone calls or conferences with teachers are difficult during working hours. Children who become sick during school hours may, through necessity, force parents to leave, or at least interrupt, the work day. Obviously, frustration builds when much is demanded and little flexibility is possible. For the single parent, tight schedules and unforeseen emergencies are a daily reality. It is no wonder that one single parent reacted so negatively to a married friend who announced: "I can't take my turn driving us to class tonight because my husband is out of town and I just can't teach school, cook supper, get dressed to go out, get the kids fed, the dishes washed, drive for the babysitter myself, and still leave early enough to pick you up."

When life becomes hectic, there is less time for an individual to care for herself. As one mother said, "I have developed a great capacity for crisis, but I have lost my capacity for joy."

Under pressured conditions, animosity often builds toward the absent parent. One mother complained: "It does not seem fair that Bob can be off doing his own thing and basically only seeing the kids at his convenience. Why is it o.k. for him to leave and be so free of major responsibilities?"

Stress and exhaustion may make it difficult to continue giving to others. "It seems all I do is give, give, give. Yet there is so little time for me to receive—even from myself. There are some days when I simply feel I have given everything I have to give. I need a vacation, a rest, or just something. . .but there is none available. . .just tomorrow, and with it, another day of obligations."

Although the descriptions above may fit the personal situations of single mothers more often than dads, fathers have their unique difficulties also. Many single dads were active caretakers before divorce, yet many are not accustomed to spending long segments of time with demanding young children. Being solely responsible for the shopping and cooking, as well as clothing, bathing, and caring for children can be an overwhelming challenge. Limited knowledge of what normal misbehaviors can be expected and how to deal with misbehavior can particularly handicap single fathers. Nevertheless, single fathers often have some advantages. Many enjoy established careers and can be aggressive in finding social opportunities and in meeting new people. However, the pressure of increased responsibilities at home can be very taxing after the loss suffered from a terminated marriage.

As one father shared, "People always assume men are strong and can take almost anything. Well, I guess I thought so, too. But even though my wife walked out on us, I had to fight for my children in court. It was a nasty ordeal. Until the end of the proceeding, it looked as if I might lose my children to her, solely because she was the mother. Although that battle was won, I didn't feel like celebrating. I had to learn to cook. And people laugh at this: But I didn't know things became dirty so quickly. The work at home overwhelmed me. Also, I tried to keep up with my job, but because I travelled, the job became impossible. Finally, I resigned to enter a manageable profession. I like my work but it threw my career plans out of line. The saddest part of all of this change is that I am not the one who left, and I am not the one who wanted a new spouse. I liked everything the way it was. I'm ashamed to admit it, but I would return to my old way of life immediately if I could erase this past year. I never knew life could crumble in such a short period of time."

SOCIAL TRIALS

Loneliness often follows divorce. As parents begin to work longer hours, either in the home or in a career, or both, there may be more of a feeling that time left over should be concentrated on children. Children do require much time during this period. Many single parents are thrown into the dilemma of choosing between spending time with their children and developing a new social life. To choose a personal life generally leads to increased guilt and anxiety over the quality of one's parenting. Consistently choosing time with one's children contributes to a world dulled by the lack of stimulation that comes from association with other adults. A feeling of losing out on one's youth and a craving for adult companionship and interaction is often experienced. It is difficult to find a middle road.

A mother in a singles' parenting class explained: "It's like the old story of the speaker at the banquet table who took a mouthful of scalding coffee as he stood up to speak into the microphone. No matter what he chose to do next, it would be wrong. I begin feeling trapped and hopeless when I stay home, but I feel anxious and guilty when I date. My most irrational thought is 'I had my chance and blew it. Now I should give my children a better chance in life.' But I know that this is a simplistic and self-punishing belief. Potentially, I have many good years to enjoy personal happiness, and it hurts to leave my children when I know they want me to be with them. If I found someone I felt a true interest in, it would seem more reasonable to leave frequently, but I am going out simply to enjoy the adult company which I need. It seems no perfect solution exists."

Single parents with young children are young enough to create an entirely new life with another person. They need to attempt to find a person with whom to share life; yet many are uncomfortable with the new role of being single. Society itself is not supportive, as the negative connotation often associated with the term divorce indicates. Feelings of rejection and failure left over from their former relationships may undercut social confidence. Such social uneasiness reverberates through the household. As one parent said, "I had my most difficult time handling rejection by my spouse, feeling like **nothing** and still being **something** for my kids. I felt o.k. as a married lady; I am very uncomfortable as a single."

Although family members can be a salvation to a single parent, they also can join society in being a guilt dispenser to divorced parents. Particularly if the split was the first in the family, parents and siblings may regard the situation to be a family failure or an embarrassment. As is true of young siblings, many adult siblings with intact marriages may take advantage of a sister or brother's divorce in order to highlight their own place in the family. At worst, divorced individuals may find themselves looked upon as the family's black sheep or scapegoat.

A divorced woman shared these observations: "My sister and I have a history of fighting for our parents' attention and approval. For her, my divorce promised to be a great victory. She bragged about her successful marriage at every family gathering and always gave her own analysis of why my marriage ended. When I returned to work, my mother took care of Sammy, my preschool child. Of course, Mother became very close to him because of the time they shared together. My sister became irate. She claimed it was unfair for a grandmother to spend such a disproportionate amount of time with one grandchild. She accused me of using my situation to dominate my parents' time. My divorce opened up old wounds and exasperated the problems which existed in my own family of origin."

TRIALS OF PARENTING

The needs of children from single parent homes may differ significantly from those of other children. After they have experienced the major loss of a loved one, children often are confused and angry. In addition, they have lost an important role model and may become less sure of how to handle their own personal and sexual roles.

If divorce or death has left a single parent with complicated feelings, the emotions of their children may be particularly difficult to handle. In the case of divorce, it may be uncomfortable for a parent to allow a child to freely express the deep love for, and longing to be with, the absent parent. The temptation to influence the child to share the parent's negative feelings toward the absent parent may be hard to avoid.

A divorced friend of ours explained: "It is so hard for me to see the children worshipping their father when they return from a weekend with him. Because he rarely sees them, he can always show them his good side. In fact, I fear they see my bad side too often. Sometimes I want to balance their opinions of the two of us by telling them about some of his many weaknesses. But so far, I have controlled my temptation. To attack him would lead to more problems."

Children need to express their feelings. Whether they are shared through private discussions, artistic performances, or family councils, children's emotions and thoughts should be attended to by parents. Parents need to use their best reflective listening skills. Preschool children, particularly, have difficulty at times expressing their emotions. Remember that it is not unusual for children to fear that the remaining parent will also leave. Additionally, it is common for a child to blame herself for the divorce of parents. Emotions arise and setbacks occur frequently for children. There are constant reminders in our society that children of single parents are not equal: "Kenneth always wanted to be in Indian Guides. One day he came home from school with a picture of a brave and his son and a form for kids to fill in and sign up with their fathers for this Father and Son Y program. Kenneth was excitedly filling in the form and talking about joining up. He was dismayed when I told him he could not join because his father was in Chicago. "You mean you can't join with your mother instead?" I looked into it. No way. I would have to find a male sponsor. I knew no one to ask. The commitment involved weekly meetings, weekend camp-outs, and projects to be done together as father and son through the week. It was a very bad time for the family."

Along with their other challenges, children living with a divorced adult must handle the emotions of that single parent. Children are not equipped to counsel adults or to be sounding boards for complex problems. Often, children can be therapeutic in their love and in their daily actions, but they should not be expected to shoulder the burden of parental emotions. As in other cases, parents must decide that, despite their pain, it is best to act as an adult when with a child. Children need mature behavior as a model. Parental strength becomes the anchor that gives stability to the young in changing times.

It is not surprising that behavior problems may arise in the midst of this kind of emotional climate. As we have seen, some acts of misbehavior are part of normal development for young children. Also, some forms of misbehavior may be normal for children raised in single parent homes. This does not mean that such misbehavior should be ignored. Parents, however, should not become overly concerned by minor disturbances.

A major challenge for single parents is to insure that acceptable behavior occurs when the parent is not at home. In addition, the parent's absence from home may prevent a discussion of the behavior problems with the child when the crisis occurs. As one working mother explains: "When I'm not home, my kids have much unstructured time. I have no way of knowing what has gone on. There is no backup, and it is hard to keep my firmest resolve and best intention to follow through and hold my ground. If I arrive home from a late meeting, grab a quick supper, and have another required meeting to attend at 7:00 or so, I may only see the kids a half hour in a given day. When they were old enough to no longer need a sitter, I had no assurance they would go to bed. If I have another commitment on the following evening, it can create a situation in which I go two or three days and never see a kid more than a half hour or so a day, and that is on the run."

Family structure can also be unsettled by almost any pattern of visitation. For example: With joint custody, a child often returns from visits overtired, overstimulated, and emotionally confused. Often, it is the parent with whom the child lives who seems to pay the price for the child's visit with his other parent in an unstructured environment.

A single parent shared her problems with visitation: "Because Jack lives three hours away, he only wanted to see his children one weekend per month. On those days, he would take them on wild tours of the city. They would attend late-night movies, eat anything they wanted, and go to bed late. Although he was required to have the children home by 8:30 on Sunday night, they usually arrived, excited and exhausted, after 10:00. The next morning, it was my responsibility to wake them at 7:00 to attend school. When they returned home after school, they were always tired, bored, and mean. Their father works on their emotions, trying to make them believe that living with him would be marvelous. Sometimes they seem to believe that staying with him would be better. It takes a week to recover from one of their visits. But I imagine their father's life returns to normal immediately after the children are brought home."

Additionally, visitation often occurs on special holidays, when the single parent has time to give full attention to the child. For many, it seems that the absent parent has a disproportionate amount of vacation time to celebrate with the child and has very little of the daily routine, when friction and difficulties most often arise. Visitation also takes many children out of the routine required by neighborhood groups—organizations and peers—to develop a sense of belonging. Limited interaction among peers can prevent the growth of strong social support and camaraderie.

After Judy and Jason divorced, both remarried, and Judy moved from Virginia to Oklahoma. Both parents loved their children. To try to be fair to each, the judge ordered the children to visit their father's home during Thanksgiving, Christmas, spring break, and the first two months of summer. Although the arrangement may or may not have been fair for the family, the children were placed in a difficult situation with peers. During vacations, when friends were forming neighborhood clubs and playing together, these children were packing to leave town. One foot was always in the neighborhood door, and one was outside. Children are flexible, but they prefer constancy when making "best" friends. A child who always disappears during holidays does not offer, or enjoy, consistency in friendships.

Sharing children with a former mate's new spouse may also present difficulties. As one women explained: "It is so hard to share my precious little girls with another woman. My ex-husband had a vasectomy, so she will never have any children. And she just loves playing Mommy and Daddy with mine on these visits where there are no responsibilities. I am tired and grouchy often. I didn't want this broken home in the first place. And I resent sharing my girls. No wonder they like to go there, where they are spoiled..."

In addition to these problems, children can experience an increased number of school-related problems. Occasionally, teachers are prepared through training, experience, or natural ability to handle the emotions and behaviors of children from single parent homes. Just as often, their understanding of single parent families is limited to a short section covered by a human development course in college. Such courses often unwittingly support the attitude that children from single parent homes are destined to regress academically and increase in delinquency. Such does not have to be the case, but if teachers expect children to misbehave and to perform poorly, children will.

During a class break, I overheard two graduate students, who were teachers, discuss a child both were instructing. The first said, "That Johnny Roberts is driving me crazy. He seems to always demand attention, and his work is poor. If he doesn't improve on tests, he may fail." The second teacher replied, "Are you aware that he has problems at home? His parents are divorced." The first acknowledged the information in a tone which indicated that the entire situation made sense and that Johnny's performance could never change: "Oh, that explains it," she said.

That does not explain it. Yes, children who encounter unique situations in life may display a variety of reactions. But all children can behave, and each can enjoy academic success. Children must experience both success and encouragement. Teachers properly trained in the art of encouragement and discipline will be able to lead children experiencing situational stress in life to success in school. But those who expect children to misbehave or to decline academically will allow misbehavior and school failure to occur. As with all individuals in society, teachers vary in their ability to work well with children who are experiencing situational problems. Parents must support good teachers and insist that poor teaching policies and techniques be eliminated.

In addition, some teachers put pressure on parents to make their children behave in the classroom. It is not the parents' job to provide classroom discipline. At best, parents can give support to the teacher for reasonable classroom plans for discipline. Never accept the guilt for a teacher's lack of ability to properly motivate a class.

Many shadows fall on the lives of single parents. Yet single parents make it. And many prosper, as do their children. Successful single parents are a blessing and encouragement to all parents. No matter what odds must be faced, the single parent usually seeks the light beyond the shadows.

THE LIGHT: OVERCOMING THE TRIALS

Anticipating and admitting the challenges facing them is the biggest step that single parents must make to create a strong family system. By utilizing strengths and organizing resources, the single parent moves the family away from difficulties and toward fulfillment.

Before the business of creating a new family life can be successful, ghosts must be exorcised, and losses of the past must be buried and mourned. Single parents must accept the death of old hopes and dreams, just as children must mourn the loss of an absent parent from daily life. As noted earlier, a child's mourning may be more difficult to handle than one's own. A child's expression of grief is often mixed with anger and longing for the return of the lost parent. Such emotions may elicit a sense of guilt. Parents may blame themselves for failing a child.

Parents must remain calm, assured that the dissolution of a destructive marriage is better for a child than its continuation would have been. That self-assurance, plus one's best listening skills, minus the need to justify previous actions, will allow the healing process to begin.

Some parents do not divorce but remain separated for years, despite the fact that no move toward reconciliation is intended. Such arrangements can impede the normal mourning process. Children may cling to the hope that the marriage will rekindle. Without the ceremony of divorce, there is no symbolic end to the relationship. Like families who refuse to surrender hope for a son missing in military action and presumed dead, children—and maybe parents—find it difficult to accept the end of a marriage, also missing in action and presumed dead. Not experiencing the finality that divorce brings, family members find readjustment more complex. In such cases, divorce may be a healthy release.

An early task of a single parent is to build a cooperative relationship with the parent who will share custody of the children. Most divorced couples who failed to establish cooperative custodial relationships will testify that nothing would have contributed more to the mental health of the entire family than peaceful relations with ex-spouses. Sometimes, mediation counselors or family counselors can be helpful in establishing healthy lines of communications and mutually agreeable rules. It is not unusual for couples who could not tolerate intimacy to be able to work cooperatively at a distance.

Unfortunately, many divorced couples continue fighting, at the emotional expense of their children. Because their feelings are unresolved, the parents use custody and visitation issues to express anger, or as tools for revenge. The best interests of the children are ignored because of the parents' attempts to win battles with their former spouse. Whatever adult victories may be won, the children are automatic losers. Mature adults should be able to judge when their personal disagreements are hurting their children. Sometimes, aid from a third party is necessary to create healthy interactions.

For the new single family to exist smoothly, support from outside its boundaries is often helpful. Many old relationships may lend support to new single families. Such relationships should be nurtured and cherished. Grandparents can come to the support of their children and grandchildren in a variety of ways. For some single families, it can be helpful for the children if the family can live with grandparents who are able to give emotional, economic, or child care support until the single parent is reestablished.

Some grandparents are able to provide role models for children during a period when proper models are difficult to find. As one single mother of two sons reported: "Ours was a grandfather who delighted in his grandchildren's very being. He was devoted to them, always dependable and creative in his relationship with them. He captured their imaginations in many areas and did much for them that he wished he had done for his own kids when they were little. He got them interested in various sports, encouraged the development of honesty, integrity, etc. Best of all, he loved them, and they knew it. They liked how they felt about themselves when they were with him. For them, he was a light in the shadows. He was the man for our family."

Other members of the extended family can be a positive influence on children and a supportive network of friends for single parents. These valuable friendships must be carefully courted. Every adult has problems, feelings, and goals. Each needs a turn in the limelight.

Too often, when people experience long periods of stress, they fail to be considerate of their friends and families. Occasionally, they forget that others may not be prepared to discuss complicated problems. For example, family get-togethers often provide vacations from the stresses of life and an opportunity for people to relax. Such occasions are not always the most appropriate time to discuss personal challenges and difficulties.

As one family member commented, "Each vacation, I visited my parents' home in a state of mental exhaustion. I wanted to relax, have fun, and play with my kids. I knew my brother wanted to talk about his divorce. When we talked, I actually listened for hours. The first time, it was all right. I wanted to share his difficulties. But each succeeding visit, it seemed I was expected to listen to the same problems told in the same exhausting way. Emotionally, it was difficult for me to handle his stress at a time when I needed to relax and enjoy life. Soon I began to spend my vacations elsewhere. I no longer looked forward to spending time with him. At first, I felt guilty. But now I enjoy my vacations more and return to work in a better frame of mind. Although I am aware of his problems, I am also aware that we have forgotten how to have fun together."

Since family members or friends may have differing plans for gatherings, it may be best to schedule special meeting times or to make visits specifically for the purpose of discussing life situations. This respect for the goals of each may strengthen the bonds of the relationship. On the other hand, being overenthusiastic in sharing one's pain with those who are unprepared may cause family and friends to avoid those who most need support.

Even when care is taken to nourish old relationships, some married friends may drift away from single parents. This movement should rarely be interpreted as an offense. In fact, some married couples remain marvelous friends with single parents, but for others, the awkwardness of being with one member of a former couple is difficult to overcome. Individual interests begin to differ. A newly single person often develops a new set of interests and, of necessity, tasks. The married friend may continue to be concerned with maintaining a strong husband-wife relationship, continuing a career, and basically maintaining or improving the status quo, while the single parent is creating both a new career and social life and, at the same time, working through complex feelings and difficulties. Since two different sets of developmental tasks are present, common groups of interest are reduced.

For newly single parents, it is difficult to give up the dreams and friends from the past, but many do experience this double-edged sword. Forming new relationships is a difficult challenge, yet new friendships can greatly reduce the loneliness of transition.

So many people have shared the experiences of single parents. Their empathy, support, and love can be helpful. New careers and jobs may allow single parents to meet empathetic people. Organizations such as

Parents Without Partners are also helpful, as are special church groups, resource centers, and support groups. For children, such organizations as Big Brothers, Big Sisters, Boy Scouts, Girl Scouts, Foster Grandparents, and various youth and church groups can provide modeling and support. Being a member of an athletic team is helpful to the child of a single parent home. However, one should be cautious not to overestimate what such organizations can provide. The challenges facing single parents and their children will endure for quite some time. Organizations offer support, not relief from difficulties. Still, a few new friends can go a long way in soothing pain and easing isolation.

When friends and family are not available or do not fulfill one's needs, counseling is a marvelous option. Trained counselors will provide an atmosphere of acceptance where discussions are possible without risk. Well-trained counselors may also provide insights and give information helpful to those trying to cope with important relationships, both inside and outside the family. Trained family therapists are particularly helpful in working with the entire family to establish new roles and regulations. Few individuals can contribute more to a family than a well-trained family therapist. Before selecting a therapist, be sure to check her credentials with past clients and with the licensing board of your state. Counselors usually vary in training, experience, and ability. Once in counseling, follow your feelings. If the therapist or her ideas do not fit your family, find another.

A newly divorced friend of mine entered family counseling. The first counselor chosen was one who possessed marvelous credentials and enjoyed an excellent reputation. However, this therapist had recently experienced a divorce of his own. He was bitter. His personal feelings began to interfere with his objectivity. Observations and suggestions he made seemed more appropriate for the therapist's situation than for my friend's. The counselor still provided outstanding help to individuals experiencing life challenges other than divorce, but he was no longer effective with divorced individuals. By changing counselors, my friend found a therapist who was stable in the area of love and marriage. Then, counseling proved to be beneficial.

Career counselors can give invaluable help to parents reentering the work force. A variety of professional options may be suggested. Specialists in career planning may be contacted at universities, clinics, or in private practice.

One of the major responsibilities of a new single parent is to become an adroit handler of emergency child care. After the major arrangements are made for child care (see Chapter Eleven), parents must develop a complex system of backup for the inevitable emergencies that ensue. A list of sitters, emergency drivers, and general trouble shooters must be developed. Friends, neighbors, family members, single parents, and other associates should be contacted. Establish, to your satisfaction, their willingness and general availability to help in an emergency.

Groups of single and married parents often join together in babysitting co-ops or in emergency child care support groups. Although it requires your energy to institute these groups, they can literally save both lives and careers. Often, separate lists must be made for nighttime and vacation emergencies. The key is to anticipate potential difficulties and then plan for them before a crisis occurs.

CHILDREN AND THE LIGHT

Volumes of research have been gathered on the effects of divorce on children. Much of it is contradictory. None of it will determine the quality of your child's life. Instead, you and your family are free to create a family atmosphere and order that can produce strong, sensitive, and healthy members. Children in single families can experience unique opportunities to be significant and needed. Their contributions to the family are essential for the welfare of the whole. Without their work in the home and their support of fellow members, the entire family will suffer. In the process of becoming significant to the family, children may develop what Dreikurs believed was the most essential ingredient to mental health—"social interest"—or, the desire to contribute to the welfare of others.

Parents must avoid feeling sorry for their children. To be empathetic with their pain is necessary, but pity is harmful. A parent in a singles' parenting class told the group of her determination not to allow her divorce to change life for her children. For example, she attempted to complete all of the chores that she and her husband had shared prior to their divorce. Eventually, she became exhausted and depressed. Additionally, she robbed her children of the opportunity to feel significant through their contributions. Divorce does change life, and with the changes comes a need for renegotiation of the responsibilities for work, as well as play. Children can benefit from assuming responsibilities that make them feel needed.

Another advantage of living in a single parent home is the possibility of learning dual roles. The single parent, by necessity, does the work usually done by both the male and female. For children, this blended role can lead to learning skills and attitudes that transcend stereotypical thinking. Modeling after an integrated role model can lead children to be more self-confident and self-sufficient.

Sharing critical life events of such an emotional nature may allow single parents and children to create a special bond. A lifetime of closeness can come from the conquering of challenges together as a family. Living at times within the shadows allows a family to explore the meaning of human life in ways that are not always available to traditional families.

While sensitivity to the feelings of children in single parent homes is essential, equal attention must be focused on behavior. Good behavior should be expected. Logical and natural consequences must consistently follow poor choices of behavior.

Children need structure. They especially need structure at the times when everything around them is changing. Family councils are required more often and on a regular basis in single parent homes. In family councils, rules for living can be established, chores divided, problems discussed. Additionally, meetings provide opportunities for sharing feelings. Such exchanges are tremendously important to children living in challenging times. Nothing can save more time in the long run than the time given to developing family meetings.

In response to a suggestion to hold family meetings, one single mother who worked full-time exclaimed, "I don't have time for meetings." I challenged her to keep accurate records on how much time she used to complete various home activities. She was surprised to find that almost an hour per day was required to organize children, force them to do their chores, and discipline them for offenses. When family councils are used consistently, these problems can be solved routinely and in a reasonable amount of time. Consistent communications save, rather than waste, time.

Rules and consequences must be established for times when parents are away from their children. It should be clear to children that they will be held accountable for their behavior at all times. Due to the hectic schedules of single parents, it is difficult to keep up with children's actions while the parent is not home. If efforts are not made by the parent to keep informed about possible difficulties, their children develop two sets of behavior: good self-discipline when the parent is present and lack of self-control in their absence. Today, this situation is becoming more common in our society. For further information, reread the section on Quadrant C families in Chapter Nine.

For single parents, time may become the most valuable and rarest resource. No investment of time will be more precious than that spent listening to and interacting with children. They have so much they need to share. In discussion, be liberal in your encouragement of positive contributions and achievements. Take care to build upon the positive, when possible.

Particularly, encouragement may be needed for children's schoolwork. If a family has lost a parent, schoolwork may become less important to a child. Good students usually have one person who supports and encourages their work. Be that person. Become involved and supportive.

Two single parents, neither of whom were employed outside of the home, enrolled their children in a Suzuki violin class where parental attendance was expected. I observed that one parent faithfully supported her child by participating. The other used the time to complete chores and didn't attend class. As one might expect, the child whose parent chose not to attend soon fell behind, became embarrassed, and eventually quit. The other child became one of the most talented members of the class. Encouragement is important to a child's success. Sometimes adults forget how much a school age child benefits from parental support and interest. When schedules prevent parents from actively participating in school functions, time should be taken at night to discuss the child's daily activities. Discussion can become part of a nightly supper or bedtime ritual. If nighttime discussions are missed, use breakfast as a setting to explore your child's interests, progress, and problems.

Also, be aggressive in demanding that your school meet the individual needs of your child. Schools need to establish discussion groups for children of single families, flexible hours to accommodate working parents, and parent-education classes for all parents. In addition, school systems should provide in-service workshops which help teachers learn to work with the special challenges of children from single parent homes. Good teachers, as always, need to provide structure and encouragement for each child. With children from single parent homes, teachers must be firm but also understanding of the variables in the behavior of a child experiencing long-term stress.

Society has not changed adequately to meet the needs of all of its families. Single parent families occupy a large segment of American homes, yet schools still revolve around the schedules and needs of intact nuclear families. The final chapter will investigate some of the changes needed in our society. But here some primary guidelines need to be highlighted. First, single parents must be militant for their children's rights, because no one else will be. Also, a lone parent must be assertive in building a personal life, because no one else will carry the banner. Learn to say "NO!" to friends, organizations, employers, and your children in order to provide time for yourself. If a parent burns out, she will have difficulty contributing positively to anyone. Learn what it takes to keep your spirit ignited. And make it happen! Your lives and the lives of others depend on your flame.

THE VICTORY

Victory for single parent familes will come as members actively encourage each other for contributions, achievements, and strengths displayed in the course of living. Encouragement grows as single parent families are willing to think outside the limits of the ordinary. Only when the narrow norms and judgments of society are no longer accepted will it be possible to establish pride in a family that is different and unique from any other.

Nuclear families are not necessarily the finest system for all children. Yes, many are successful. Many are not. Single parent families who overcome the challenges facing them and produce highly successful individuals are equally, if not more, impressive in their contributions to society.

For example, along with the courage to be different, members of single parent families develop the courage to be imperfect. No longer intimidated into doing things in conventional ways, risks are taken to allow for new experiments. Some may pool money with other single parents to buy mutually-owned homes, appliances, or cars. Others may take part-time jobs, resign from jobs, or take "unusual" jobs if any of these steps will benefit the entire family. Sometimes, risks will not pay off; but that is the cost of serious attempts to improve the quality of life. It is a risk taken by those who display courage.

As single parents become more assertive and successful in their ability to cope with and conquer life for themselves and their children, our society will be liberated of the conventionalism which can plague it. Just as many women have liberated men to become true parenting partners, single parents may force society to support and celebrate the lives of the single family. Until that day, single parent families must become bilingual. They must talk and think in ways that are representative of their world, while they live in a society still patterned for nuclear families.

This is ironic because the successful single family is a family of courage in America today. They are the victorious ones. They are the ones who never lost sight of the light beyond the shadows.

RELATED READINGS

Allers, R. (1982). *Divorce, children, and the school.* Princeton, NJ: Princeton Book Company.

Anderson, H. & Anderson, G. (1981). *Mom and dad are divorced, but I'm not: Parenting after divorce.* Chicago: Nelson-Hall.

Anderson-Khlief, S. (1982). *Divorced but not disastrous: How to improve the ties between single-parent mothers, divorced fathers and the children.* New York: Prentice-Hall.

Atkin, E. & Rubin, E. (1977). *Part-time father.* New York: Signet Edition.

Buchanan, N. & Chamberlain, E. (1982). *Helping children of divorce.* Nashville, TN: Broadman.

Duncan, T. R. & Duncan, D. (1979). *You're divorced, but your children aren't.* New York: Prentice-Hall.

Francke, L. (1984). *Growing up divorced.* New York: Fawcett.

Gardner, R. (1971). *The boys and girls book about divorce: With an introduction for parents.* New York: Bantam Edition.

Goldstein, S. (1984). *Divorced parenting: How to make it work.* New York: Dutton.

Goldstein, S. & Salnit, A. (1984). *Divorce and your child: Practical suggestions for parents.* New Haven: Yale University Press.

Krantzler, M. (1975). *Creative divorce: A new opportunity for personal growth.* New York: M. Evans.

Krementz, J. (1984). *How it feels when parents divorce.* New York: Alfred A. Knopf.

Krementz, J. (1983). *How it feels when a parent dies.* New York: Alfred A. Knopf.

Morgenbesser, M. & Mehls, N. (1981). *Joint custody: An alternative for divorcing families.* Chicago: Nelson-Hall.

Ricci, I. (1980). *Mom's house, dad's house: Making shared custody work.* New York: Macmillan.

Stuart, I. & Abt, L., eds. (1981). *Children of separation and divorce.* New York: VanNostrand Reinhold, Co., Inc.

Walczae, Y. & Burns, S. (1984). *Divorce: The child's point of view.* New York: Harper and Row.

Wallerstein, J. & Kelly, J. (1980). *Surviving the breakup: How children and parents cope with divorce.* New York: Basic.

Ware, C. (1984). *Sharing parenthood after divorce.* New York: Bantam.

CHAPTER ELEVEN

NEW CARETAKERS: DAYCARE AND STEPFAMILIES

AMONG THE MOST emotional decisions made by parents are those that involve daycare. Social and economic changes in society have brought young mothers into the work force in record numbers. Estimates of the percentage of mothers who use daycare facilities for preschool children range from 42 percent to 60 percent. Certainly each, if not all, are vitally interested in the potential effects of daycare on their young children.

Researchers have been unable to agree on the long range effects of daycare. In fact, findings are often totally contradictory. Studies can be selected to show any result. If one wishes to read that daycare, under even mildly acceptable conditions, will positively contribute to a child's well-being, such studies exist. If one wishes to show that daycare, even under exceptional conditions, may have a negative effect on children, such studies exist. In my experience, I have not found researchers so divided in their findings as they are in this area.

This academic disagreement may reflect a growing uneasiness, if not tension, between two groups of parents—those who use daycare and those who do not. Both sides are emotional. Both have sacrificed for their beliefs. Both wish to believe that theirs is the better choice.

Each side presents arguments to support the belief that children should, or should not, be raised in daycare situations. Working mothers often point to the benefits a woman enjoys pursuing a career, which allows for the development of her talents and abilities. Personal development, it is maintained, yields a self-confidence which is reflected in one's children. Whatever small losses may accompany the use of daycare, they seem outweighed by the benefits of modeling competency and of being content with one's self-expression and self-actualization.

Mothers not using daycare maintain that no one can take a mother's place. They want to ensure that the values and beliefs learned in the early years are those of the parents. They wish to be present for the first step and the first words of their children. Some claim that there are critical periods in a child's early years when adequate love and support simply cannot be purchased.

Anger often disrupts relationships between mothers working full-time in the home and mothers using full-time daycare. Disagreements may sound polite on the surface, but below, there exists enough passion to justify major life decisions. A script common to the debate is seen in the following exchange:

Daycare Mother: "Joan, when are you going back to work?"
Home Mother: "I am at work. My work is to raise my children. It's a full-time job."
Daycare Mother: "I just couldn't do that. To me it is so boring to stay home every day. And the bickering drives me frantic. If I stayed home every day, I'd become a mental vegetable. I think I am a better, more patient mother because I work during the day."
Home Mother: "I'm just not willing to allow someone else to raise my children. They are only young once, and I can work outside of the home for years when they are older. It is the little things my children do and say each day that I love. I couldn't bear to miss their development during these critical years. They need me."

Unfortunately, such exchanges are becoming more common. Always, they are destructive. The discussions represent a society that has not addressed sufficiently the challenges of daycare or family life.

Although many parents are adamant about using or not using daycare, the majority are caught in between these two opposing factions. Such parents are neither enthusiastic about developing careers nor excited about staying home full-time. Some work to supplement the family income, while others find the daily routine of staying home and working with children incompatible with their life goals and/or personalities. These parents are often caught in the cross fire between two different systems of belief and styles of living.

Whatever decision a family makes, it should be one that seems best for their particular family. Whether one decides to use daycare or to stay home, reactions from society and extended family will be mixed. Parents must decide what is best in their situation and realize that both support and criticism will follow. For those who decide to use daycare, additional considerations need to be made.

DAYCARE—A RATHER MEANINGLESS TERM

To say "I support" or "I do not support" the use of daycare is a senseless comment, because so many critical variables influence the use of daycare that rarely are two situations alike. For example, some parents use daycare for two or three hours per day, while others may use daycare for forty or more hours a week. Some time away from the rigors of childraising will benefit most parents. For example, Burton White (1985) suggests that almost any family could profit from using daycare for two hours or so a day. Both parents and children may benefit from the time spent away from each other. But current research gives no definitive answers concerning the effect of full-time daycare on children. Too many variables exist within each family for a single answer to be meaningful.

Another major variable involves the quality and qualifications of the person or people who will care for a child. For example, frequently, children are cared for by grandparents. This situation is usually so ideal that many in the field do not refer to it as daycare. At the opposite extreme, many children are cared for in large, commercial daycare centers where the ratio of children to caregivers may climb as high as fifteen to one.

Other variables influencing the effects of daycare include the sex of the child, the number of siblings in the family, the socioeconomic situation of the family, the stability of the child's family, the quality of the daycare setting, and the training of its workers. Little good is done in citing research that shows differential effects of daycare on any single variable mentioned above. Each family's situation includes a unique combination of variables. It is a situation similar to but not exactly like any other family's. What matters most is that parents find the best possible daycare situation for their child. Positive results can happen when decisions are made with care and, occasionally, some sacrifice. Negative results can happen if decisions are handled poorly.

SELECTING DAYCARE

In his book **The First Three Years of Life,** Burton White (1985) encouraged parents to agonize over the specific choice of daycare situations. His suggestions are listed in the following order of preference.

The statistics noted are from the Bureau of the Census for the year 1982, not from Dr. White's work.

1. Individual care in your home by a trained person. Twenty-six percent of Americans use this option.
2. Individual care in the home of another person who is satisfactorily trained in child care.
3. Family daycare—this should involve a trained person with no more than three children in her or his care. Forty-four percent use an option similar to 2 or 3, although the ratio may vary from White's suggestion.
4. Nonprofit daycare centers run by universities or other organizations that provide a ratio of no more than 4 to 1.
5. Daycare centers which are profit-oriented and carefully selected. Nineteen percent use options 4 or 5, although the ratio again may vary.

Finding a caretaker who is well trained can be a challenging task. Parents need to find an adult caretaker who is demonstratively warm, caring, and totally trustworthy. Parents should ensure that discipline techniques and communications skills are compatible with their own. References should be requested and investigated. Parents need to feel that their child is basically being cared for as well as if the parents themselves were the caretakers. In fact, many parents prefer having an outstanding caregiver who keeps eight or nine children to having a less qualified caretaker who keeps fewer children. Parents often cannot find a perfect situation and, therefore, must use their best judgment in choosing the best setting.

Parents who feel uncomfortable with potential daycare workers, for any reason, should probably follow their intuition and look elsewhere. Ample time should be taken in the selection process. After the choice is made, parents should continue to make certain that the child's reports about personal treatment are closely considered. Any reported or potential difficulties should be investigated. Although reports of abuse in some daycare centers have arisen in past years, abuse seems to be a rarity and should only serve to suggest that continual supervision of the daycare setting is advisable. In other words, parents must be careful never to lose contact with the sitter's conduct. Daycare operators are paid to be at their best for children all of the time.

Choosing a quality daycare center that employs multiple staff members is complicated. Some centers are nonprofit organizations. They often have the advantage of providing supervision from college faculty or trained administrators. In some cases, due to their nonprofit status, more money can be spent on needed supplies and supervision. If parents are interested in nonprofit centers, they should contact local colleges, universities, community colleges, churches, or social organizations that may offer such information.

Commercial daycare centers must be scrutinized thoroughly. Some reports estimate that as few as 25 percent of the employees in childcare operations have been trained to work with children. There are few, if any, national or state laws to regulate who works at such centers. Care must be taken to insure that workers are well trained and are emotionally supportive of children.

Certainly, many profit-oriented daycare centers carry high standards. At best, their staff ratio should be in the range of one teacher to each three to five children. In good centers, the teachers should be screened and well-supervised. Quality centers must be located by parents. Paying extra fees to insure increased excellence is money necessarily spent. It should be helpful for the parent to observe for a day at the center to gain insight into the quality of the care.

Once you have chosen the setting for daycare, then relax and enjoy the fruit of your decisions. Many books and articles are available that discuss quality-time and enrichment ideas for parents. Use your creativity and enjoy the hours you are able to spend with your children. At the same time, continue to ensure that the quality of care remains high.

Parents should have confidence in the fact that the use of daycare offers positive potential for the family. Working parents need help. This needed help allows children the opportunity to feel important to the family. Family councils can clearly point out the value of each child's contributions. Mothers must help by deciding what is most important to them. One cannot work a long week and accomplish all that mothers who work in the home do. Priorities must be set. Expect the rest of the family to help tie up loose ends. As Brooks (1981) suggests, at its best, daycare may encourage children to be more responsive, father to be more nurturing, and mothers to become more independent and self-confident.

To allow these developments to occur, mothers must not place the pleasing of family members too high on the priority list. Mothers should insist that everyone in the family contribute a fair share. Failure to do so may transform mothers into over-burdened servants.

When the Johnstones' family goals were challenged by economic difficulties, Margaret Johnstone accepted a fulltime position as a receptionist. But the work load of the family did not change to accommodate her new lifestyle. Margaret continued to be responsible for meals, dishes, clothes, cleaning, and transporting children. Her days held no time for personal relaxation or for individual growth. Because she wished to keep family members happy, she never complained. Although nothing is wrong with such a system if everyone is content, too often women who feel an excessive need to please others are not happy. However, they allow family life to remain unchanged because they are reluctant to rock the boat.

THE FUTURE OF DAYCARE

Soon, our nation must move from professing concern for the future of America's children to action that will ensure that future. It appears that young mothers will remain, and may increase, as an important part of our labor force. If they contribute to our country in such a significant way, then the gift should be returned with active concern for children's welfare.

Money should be provided to support quality daycare. Centers should not be forced to cut corners by hiring fewer teachers and buying fewer supplies. Additionally, state regulations should protect citizens from underqualified daycare workers, as well as from inadequate centers. In particular, low-income parents who lack political power and economic flexibility should be protected from poor daycare conditions. Many studies are showing very positive outcomes for lower-income children involved in full-time daycare. For many poor children, daycare offers increased stimulation and a positive atmosphere for learning.

The government is not the only institution with the moral responsibility of guarding the future of our children. Industry also should look toward improving the morale and quality of life of its workers by providing quality daycare. Some industries are already providing quality daycare. Others are delinquent in doing so. Historically, the business world has looked to women to supplement sagging economies, without consideration given to the cost of such sacrifices involving the children of these women. Industry is beginning to and should intensify its efforts to return interest on the riches they have received.

The future must be a time of expanded imagination and initiative. Mothers can combine to form cooperatives. The sharing of time, money, and responsibilities is possible. Also, noncareer mothers might help in the care of working mothers' children, if the tension between the two sides can be ended. Schools can take more responsibility for helping.

There are some estimates that suggest that as many as 30 percent of children between the ages of six and thirteen are latchkey children. Care for the children of working parents could be provided after school. For younger children, daycare centers could schedule opening times in conjunction with public school schedules in order to help children and parents, as well as possibly to give future student teachers the opportunity to work and learn on the job.

Another change that would benefit our nation's families is increased respect for those who carry the responsibility of childraising. Fathers, in particular, need to become more involved in caring for children. To an extent, this is beginning to happen. Parenting is an art, as this book declares. When our nation begins to regard good parents with high esteem, then more opportunities will open that support parents. Businesses may allow fathers and mothers to share jobs or split hours. Fathers will feel more comfortable staying home with children while the wife may support the family. Raising children should become the most cherished occupation in our nation. If children are indeed our nation's most valuable resource, then it is time for all of us to actively contribute to its development.

NORMAL CHALLENGES OF STEPFAMILIES

Seventy-five percent of women and a higher percentage of males who divorce eventually remarry, and 60 percent of those will become stepparents (Cherlin, 1981). A child born today has about a 20 percent chance of experiencing the divorce of her parents before her eighteenth birthday (Bogue, 1985). A stepfamily is defined by Visher (1979) as a family system in which at least one of the partners has a child by a previous marriage. Over 13 percent of America's families are stepfamilies, and one of every six children under eighteen is a stepchild. Many terms are now used to describe the stepfamily experience, including blended, merged, or reconstituted families.

Blended families experience major emotional challenges and differences in family structure which distinguish them from nuclear families. Although all families may experience feelings of loyalty and guilt, anger, mourning, fear, and grief, these emotions are intensified in stepfamilies. Also, roles tend to be more complicated and less defined. As with single parent families, differences do not necessarily handicap children. Many prosper under such unique conditions. Yet the challenges of living in a stepfamily does create stress, much of which is largely unknown in most nuclear families. The extremely high divorce rate of 44 percent of remarried couples is evidence of the complications of blending families.

Blended families that realistically anticipate the challenges facing them can be more successful in establishing a feeling of family belonging, despite their complex circumstances. Flexibility and courage to be different from most nuclear families in both structure and roles is necessary. Ironically, many adjustments needed, if the blended family is to be successful, are the same movements nuclear families are encouraged **not** to make. All of these adjustments occur within a society that often complicates the lives of stepfamilies through lack of understanding and limited adjustment to the needs of this large minority.

NORMAL EMOTIONAL CHALLENGES

Overambition for the stepfamily to establish instant intimacy often causes early disappointments for blended families. Acceptance of and love for new family members usually come slowly. Time is required for each person to learn to cope with both old and newly emerging feelings.

One stepfather reviewed the high and low points of his first four years in a blended family. His lows, he explained, came because of his own unrealistic expectations. "I am a sports enthusiast, and so are my three sons. Jo Ann has two sons whose ages are the same as my children's. Before we were married, I had fantasies of having a family basketball team. I was certain we would all be close, just like a team. But I didn't know Jo Ann's sons. Neither of them enjoys sports. Still, I tried to push my interests on them. Of course, they resisted me, tooth and nail. I really did not know how to relate to them. But when I began to discover and share their interests, our lives improved. My own dream was unrealistic, maybe even silly. But it was difficult for me to let go of it."

Children carry many emotions from the past. As the Vishers explain in their excellent work **Stepfamilies** (1979, p. 254), "A stepfamily is born of loss." Rarely does a child wish for the break-up of his original family. As discussed in Chapter Ten, whether a parent left the family through death or divorce, the loss is mourned. Mourning lasts, often for several years.

Although adults often assume children will look forward to the remarriage of a parent, this is not always the case. In fact, remarriage can double the sense of loss for a child. Particularly this is true if the single custodial parent was very close to the child before plans to remarry were formed. After remarriage, a new couple, by necessity, spend much of their leisure time together. Therefore, many children feel deserted by their parent and angry with the stepparent who entered their life.

Following her divorce, a friend of ours did not resume dating or involve herself in significant social interactions for two years. Instead she became involved heavily with her children. Particularly, she became close to her fifth grade son. They developed a relationship characteristic of best friends. After two years, the mother met a man she enjoyed and began dating regularly. Soon she was spending less time at home. Her son was demoted from a full-time friend to a seldom-seen child. Possibly as a reaction to his loss of position, the son developed symptoms for which no physical basis could be found. In a sense, his psychosomatic problems may have been a protest against the demotion, as well as a plea to be returned to significant status. In this situation, it was unrealistic to expect the son to accept his mother's new friend with enthusiasm.

In addition, children are usually faithful to the absent parent. Sons and daughters want to be loyal to both natural parents. For most, this is true, even when their feelings are ambivalent toward one parent. Therefore, the marriage of a parent poses a problem for the child: "How can I be loyal to my natural parent and love a stepparent?" For many, the answer initially is, "I can't." To love a stepparent appears to be an act of treason. Thus, some children resist becoming close to the stepparent because of a false loyalty to their biological parent.

Many authors point out that, as strange as it may seem, loyalty conflicts escalate if a new stepparent is kind and caring. For them, there exists a tendency to like the new adult, but some children are guided by the mistaken notion that to be close to a stepparent is to be disloyal. This attraction creates guilt. Unfortunately, many young people handle this guilt by becoming angry with the stepparent or by avoiding the adult totally.

Adults must help children realize that being close to a stepparent is not betrayal: Love is not a competition which eliminates an adult. Instead of losing an adult figure, because of love, one is added. Children can be close to three or four adults—as many parents are close to their three, four, or more children.

Parents also need to be realistic. Children should not be expected to love a stepparent automatically. Ironically, children may hold a stepparent responsible for the breakup of the nuclear family, as well as for the loss of time spent with the custodial parent. If this is the case, barriers will be present. Affection builds slowly. Stepparents need to court children. Common interests should be developed and special times spent together. Adults need to travel at the child's pace. Don't be overanxious. Time is your ally.

How children respond to both divorce and remarriage may largely depend on their ages and corresponding Piagetian stages. (See Chapter Four for Piaget's stages.) Children, two and under, should have little difficulty in adjusting to the loss of one parent or to living in a blended family. In later childhood or in teen years, these children may take an active interest in knowing more about their natural parents; yet during these first years, few problems should occur.

Children in the imaginative preoperational world may have more trouble. Young people from age two to seven may frighten themselves by imagining that they will be abandoned by the custodial parent or the remarried couple. After all, they have lost at least one loved person from daily life. It is not unusual for the fears of a child this age to cause regression to more dependent, immature behavior. They need security and consistency. Such normal behaviors should be handled as suggested in Chapters Six and Seven.

At age six, Allison, an only child, was highly in need of control. The divorce of her parents was a great blow to her. Following the divorce, Allison became frantic every time her mother left home. The mother, Mrs. Smythe, attributed the anxiety to Allison's immaturity and assumed she would soon grow out of it. Instead, the anxiety increased. Allison insisted on knowing where her mother was going and exactly when she would return. Particularly, this was true when she was dating. While away, Mrs. Smythe was often called on the phone by her anxious daughter. Finally, Mrs. Smythe discovered that Allison actually feared that her mother would desert her, as she believed her father had done following the divorce. Allison's fears were not caused by immaturity but by an active imagination spurred on by an actual event. In time, Mrs. Smythe was able to help Allison regain trust in the predictability and faithfulness of "Mom." Only then could Allison, whose thinking was limited to the preoperational world, surrender the painful fantasy.

Concrete operational children (age seven to eleven) often feel omnipotent. Therefore, many may feel that they caused the parents' divorce. Don't forget, this is an age when a child may believe she has the power to influence the outcome of football games by simply wearing certain clothes or by saying magic words. So it is not difficult to imagine this same egocentricity leading a child to believe she is responsible for the family's present status. This guilt can be unbearable. In addition, children may add to their own guilty feelings by believing they are causing problems now between their parent and stepparent. Unfortunately, this guilt often can be well-founded in blended families; nevertheless, it is unproductive and destructive.

Children in this difficult world can be stubborn. When they believe they are right, it is difficult to change their opinions. Since, for them, thought is limited to a black and white simplicity, the complexity of divorce is rarely understood. Feelings are intense but often may seem unreasonable to adults, who live in the world of formal operations.

STRUCTURAL AND ROLE CHALLENGES TO STEPFAMILIES

Traditional families have a power structure and informal boundaries that protect the family's integrity. In healthy nuclear families, such boundaries and family structure are clear. People not living in the home are permitted to move in and out, but only at the will of the parents or the family itself. Those not living in the home do not, as a rule, play a role in the power structure. Roles and identities of family members are developed through the years and become very clear. A consistency develops as the family becomes a smooth, functioning system.

A major change in the boundaries of stepfamilies born of divorce and remarriage is obvious: One natural parent lives outside the territory of the new stepfamily. Yet this person possesses both influence and power. Boundaries are consistently crossed because of visitation arrangements, as children freely join and leave families for varying lengths of times. Such looseness in family boundaries is rarely tolerated in healthy nuclear families. In blended families, they become a way of life.

For those who have not experienced the potentially negative side of shared custody, imagine that a former roommate with whom you began to fight—and whose companionship was terminated because of irreconcilable differences—continued to have power over your life. Imagine that this individual held the freedom to periodically remove your children from your home, train them in ways you might not prefer, and share values you may find objectionable. Imagine that you were required to consult with your ex-roommate before lengthy family trips could be planned or job opportunities in other states considered. Not only must you continuously interact with a person with whom you were dissatisfied and uncomfortable, but also, you must allow your ex-roommate to have considerable power over your family and the major decisions that affect it.

In addition to stepchildren becoming members of two different households, numerous extended family members exist outside of the family unit. For example, there may be four sets of grandparents. Many grandparents wish to spend time with their natural grandchildren and step-grandchildren. Such grandparents can add greatly to the enrichment of children's lives. But, for various reasons, some discriminate against step-grandchildren by not inviting them to their homes, or by refusing to give them presents, or even by failing to acknowledge their existence in the family. Such inappropriate behavior complicates the lives of young children.

With a natural parent living outside the home, with children joining and leaving the home, and with an expanded extended family, the boundaries of a stepfamily must be more permeable than those of nuclear families. Boundaries, however, are not all that change.

If two sets of children are involved, each child may find herself in a new ordinal position. An oldest child may become a second child, or a youngest may be replaced by a still younger child. Old ways of finding a significant place are lost, and a crisis in identity often follows. Occasionally, children will handle the crisis by remaining close to their family of origin. Here, each identity is secure.

Christy, age seven, was an oldest child until her mother remarried. Suddenly, Christy lived with a stepsister, Marcia, who was one year older. The two were typical of the traditional oldest children described in Chapter Two. Both of these girls chose to excel in school, in helping around the house, and enforcing family rules. But Marcia was better in each area. Instead of enjoying a secured identity based on superior accomplishments as she had in the past, Christy felt overshadowed by Marcia's abilities. At age seven, Christy felt she had been dethroned. Until she could create a new, positive position of significance, Christy became discouraged and angry. She disliked her rival and felt insecure. It takes time for children like Christy to create a new identity. When children are blended into a single unit, parents need to appreciate the profound changes that ordinal position cause in identity and the difficulties children have when that position is threatened.

Walter Toman (1976) suggests that when one set of children is older, it is more difficult for them to blend smoothly with other stepchildren.

Older children tend to unite to keep their family bonds and history alive. Particularly, Toman believes this may be true if one constellation of stepchildren is smaller. No matter what parents do to try to create intimacy between stepchildren, strong bonds will not always develop. This should be considered neither surprising nor negative.

Because of visitation between families and difficulties in unifying stepchildren, it may be inevitable that stepfamilies will be less "together oriented" than families in nuclear homes. Particularly, this is true when visitation requires children to join and leave homes where other children live. This situation is difficult for both the permanent siblings and the more transient ones. Such movement compounds the challenges of creating a consistent identity within a family unit. Parents need to help such children by giving them their own personal space—including physical space such as drawers and closets. Also, any distinct and consistent roles and duties that can be assumed will be helpful to a child.

When Tommy visited his father's new family, he shared a room with his stepbrother, Marvin. Because of limited space, other options seemed impractical. But Tommy and Marvin hated the arrangement. Before each visit, Marvin was required to remove personal belongings from his drawers and keep his clothes in one end of the closet only. Fighting raged over keeping the room clean. Marvin was impeccably neat, while Tommy seemed to enjoy filth. Even during the rare moments when Tommy tried to clean the room, his efforts never met his stepbrother's standards. Although they chose to fight over the cleanliness of the room, their real fight was over territorial ownership. Marvin was saying, "This is my room and you are a guest." Tommy was replying, "No, this is **our** room. I am not a guest." Parents need to help children by giving each a private space, even when some areas must be shared. No child wants to feel like an intruder.

Since children may be members of two families and are preoccupied with handling difficult emotions and in establishing new identities, the strength of blended families usually rests upon the marital bond. As mentioned above, the difficulty of forming this bond is reflected in the extremely high divorce rate among remarried couples. The bond is threatened by intrusions from inside and outside the home; challenges that are not present in first marriages.

Intrusions on the new marriage come from both the past and the present. If there are children from a previous marriage, a continued relationship with a former spouse is necessary. Transactions must be made with ex-spouses over money matters, visitation schedules, discipline, and future plans for the children. Emergencies involving children will require unexpected communications.

It is best for all involved if the relationships between ex-spouses is cooperative and cordial. Children adjust more quickly without continuing warfare between adults, which puts stress on their loyalties and peace of mind. Meetings with ex-spouses should be pragmatic, solving only those problems involving children. As a rule, it is not beneficial to discuss past relationships or problems that existed between the divorced persons.

One stepmother analyzed her relationship with her first husband this way: "Frank and I work well together now that our marriage is over. In a real sense we are like business partners who do not approve of each other's personal lives. But approval is not necessary. All that is important is that our business be conducted in a way that benefits each member of our family as much as is possible. No, keeping emotions and personal opinions under control is not always easy. But I can do it, because everyone benefits from peaceful transactions."

Another reality from the past is that at least one relationship between a parent and child began before the new marriage. Occasionally, such relationships complicate the process of bonding. Particularly, this is true if loyalty or guilt leads the natural parent to allow a child a special position or unwarranted privileges. For example, a parent may overprotect a child from the stepparent or may spend so much time with a child that the new spouse feels alienated.

If too much power can be realized, children may become manipulative. A child can endanger a couple by encouraging disharmony. Such a situation leads to the destructive triangles discussed in Chapter Eight. Although children often cause friction between parents, triangles occur when any two people oppose a third in predictable ways. For example, parents may join forces against a child, or two siblings may attempt to create misery for a third child. In stepfamilies the opportunities for triangles to form are greatly increased because there are more people involved and emotions are often intense.

Additional stress can come to a new marriage from relatives who oppose either or both the divorce and the remarriage. Opposition from a few relatives to a marriage involving children from another relationship is not uncommon. It would be better if newly formed couples could count on the support of an extended family, but this is not always possible. To prevent or anticipate as many problems as possible, couples would be wise to spend time **before the marriage** discussing new roles, expectations, discipline, boundaries, relatives, and the flexibility needed to solve potential areas of conflict. When stepparents marry, they inherit a family that is in full swing. Little time will be available to anticipate difficulties.

The average couple expecting a child will have several months to plan for her arrival. As discussed in Chapter One, Lamaze and parenting courses offer marvelous opportunities for parents to create ideal conditions for adding a new relationship. The majority of problems with infants remain predictable, as do the misbehaviors common to early childhood. With training, parents can anticipate and then meet the challenges children create. But stepparents do not have nine months to prepare. Instantly, children exhibit not only predictable misbehaviors but also the more complicated situational misbehaviors which arise in blended families. Instead of looking forward to life shared with an infant, couples may find that they immediately are thrown into a cauldron of boiling emotions and complicated interactions for which no person can be totally prepared.

It is upon the strength of the new marriage that stepfamilies rest. Time is required to build and maintain bonds. The routine communications necessary for any relationship are essential even more frequently for couples facing such complexity. In families where change and motion continuously rock the emotions of family members, the stability of the marriage becomes a common anchor for all.

THE NORMAL CHALLENGE OF FINDING ONE'S ROLE IN A BLENDED FAMILY

What is this new family? What traditions from the original families should persist, and what new ones should begin? What new roles should each member assume? Blending the histories and roles of two families is a formidable challenge. As mentioned above, children who are members of two households often feel uncomfortable with identities in both homes. Are they guests or family members? How can each be unique and significant?

Children are not the only ones who seek new roles. Stepparents must find new identities. Are they parents or friends? Do they have authority, or will they be resented for disciplining stepchildren? Visher believes that many stepparents wander from role to role, trying to discover who they are. Complications exist. For example, stepparents have few legal rights. Often they can't even authorize emergency medical treatment for stepchildren. So who are they?

As one stepfather, Harold, related, "I always try to be sensitive to my stepchildren. In fact, they often come to me first to talk over problems. I love our intimate moments. Usually, I feel so close to them that I begin to believe I am the most significant adult in their lives. But on several occasions I overheard my stepchildren explain to their friends who I am. Their explanation goes something like this, 'Oh, he's not my real father. My real father lives in Appomattox. My real Dad is the greatest. Harold's only my stepfather.' Then I fear I am not as significant to them as I hoped I would be, and I'm no longer sure how my stepchildren really feel about me. It hurts to be thought of as second best, despite all of the time we spend together and all of the talks we share. I know I should be satisfied with being helpful, no matter what my status is. But my feelings don't always agree with my insights."

Both stepmothers and stepfathers have unique challenges. For example, stepfathers often suffer ambivalence over spending more time with their stepchildren than they are allowed or are able to spend with their natural children. Some stepfathers are overanxious to become good parents. In their enthusiasm, they may begin to apply discipline for their stepchildren too soon. If they do, they risk open rebellion from the children. In addition, they may place mothers in a position of feeling forced to come to the aid of her children. Particularly, this is true if it appears that the stepfather is too severe in his discipline. Stepfathers often feel that no matter what they do, it is wrong. But as time passes and relationships grow, stepfathers find roles which are comfortable and unique to the particular needs of their families. There are no blueprints for success, since each family is different, unique in its own way.

Many psychologists believe that an initial step in helping stepfamilies find new identities is for the family to move to a new residence when the families are joined. A new home cuts down on potential territorial battles and eliminates many sentimental attachments which could create obstacles for togetherness. Psychologists also suggest that stepchildren be included in future planning. For example, Jane Brooks (1981) points to the benefit of allowing children to join in planning for the wedding and in deciding what to call the new stepparents.

Parents and stepparents should begin to treat children as an equal part of two families. Most stepchildren live between two homes. Trying to influence a child to give up or de-emphasize membership in one home will create a rivalry which can be highly detrimental. Competing for the loyalty of a child is a mistake. In fact, Vishers (1979) suggests that stepparents should consciously avoid developing roles already assumed by the absent, natural parent. For example, if the natural father stresses taking a child to football games, the stepparent needs to find a different interest to share with the child.

Time is the primary ally of stepparents. So many mistakes are made when relationships are being rushed to meet unrealistic expectations. For example, as suggested above, disciplining a stepchild requires a firmly established relationship. The Vishers (1979) estimate that such a bond may take from 18 to 24 months to create. Until the new relationship is stable, the natural parent must take greater responsibility for discipline.

Natural parents who are passive disciplinarians often set up the stepparents for defeat. If the natural parent fails to intervene when children misbehave, the task of disciplining children may fall to the stepparent. If this system of discipline works well, then few problems will occur. Too often, however, following a stepparent's discipline, a child will complain about her treatment to her natural parent. In turn, the natural parent criticizes the partner's efforts. In other words, the natural parent's original passivity in discipline says to the stepparent, "It's OK. **You** discipline my child." But after discipline has occurred, the natural parent says, "But not in this way!" The stepparent is put in a double bind. She feels she must discipline the child, but whatever she does will probably be wrong! Couples need to agree on whose task discipline is. Also, it is preferable to agree on acceptable techniques of discipline for all family members. Parenting classes can offer stepparents an invaluable forum in which to make such decisions.

Family meetings are of absolute benefit to stepfamilies. Mutually made plans and rules can create an optimistic view that all family members will have importance. In a period when complicated feelings arise, family meetings insure that an opportunity will be available at which all can express their thoughts. Family councils may be chaotic at first, but in the long run, they will allow each member to find a positive place within the family in a shorter period of time. Parents should be careful to express their feelings, as well as to listen. If a parent is feeling unloved, left out, or betrayed, it is helpful to share these emotions in a positive manner. Such sharing goes a long way in tearing down walls.

Family councils provide a consistent opportunity for members to discuss feelings. Many individuals in our society are reluctant to discuss sensitive emotions. Some are shy, others avoid potential conflict. Family meetings can become a forum for open discussion. When regular discussions become a family tradition, then it is easier to share feelings which would otherwise be awkward to discuss.

For example, in one family, a father coached a community swimming team and was hurt that his stepson showed no interest in the team. The stepfather hid his feelings for almost a year. When the family began meetings, the father was able to bring up his disappointment. He was shocked to find that his stepson had also harbored pain over the stepfather's interest in the team. The stepson believed that the time his stepfather spent coaching the team indicated a preference for the company of other children. For both the stepfather and stepson, the swimming team represented what they had interpreted as a lack of love. Until feelings were openly discussed, the problems could not reach a productive conclusion.

Additionally, if reasonable consequences are jointly decided upon during family meetings, it would be easier for stepparents to manage disciplinary problems. Rules become family rules, rather than parental restrictions. Also, chores and responsibilities can be selected each week to allow family members to feel that they are a contributing part of the family.

Stepchildren who come to live with a family for short periods of time should become part of the family meetings. As family members, they are allowed to join in creating the rules that they will be expected to follow. Problems that arise between children who live in the home for varying periods of time need to be solved in family meetings. Feelings, attitudes, and complaints should be aired openly, rather than hidden. The brief turmoil caused by this honesty is well worth the benefits to be reaped in cooperation, fair play, and positive feelings.

The need for, and the techniques of, discipline and communication are not unique for stepfamilies, but they occur in a more complex set of circumstances. As in any complex organization, stepfamilies need to be constantly involved in communications. Once rules and regulations are made in family meetings, adults need to allow consequences to occur with the same consistency that is required in traditional families. Allowing exceptions and feeling sorry for children does not encourage them to make good decisions or to be responsible.

Never forget that half of discipline is encouragement! It is easy to focus so intently on handling problems and putting out fires that one forgets to consistently encourage children for their contributions and personal successes. Encouragement should be given daily. By circumstance, stepchildren are exposed to conflicts other children may never face. With encouragement and support, stepchildren can, through these experiences, grow into exceptionally strong and flexible people.

To be effective in handling communication and discipline, adults should know their own personality traits. Individuals with an excessive need to be in control are particularly vulnerable in stepfamilies. Flexibility, not structure, is the key to happiness in blended families because very little can be controlled absolutely. Boundaries cannot be closed. Therefore, ex-spouses, in-laws, and children will come and go as the law or agreements will allow. Love and attachment come slowly and not at the will of any individual. Adults are wise to work on what they can control rather than to feel humiliated by what they cannot.

Adults considering remarriage occasionally join our parent study classes. Sometimes it is easy to spot a personality which may not be suited for the complexity of blended family living. It should be added that such personalities are more likely to encounter problems in situations that require flexibility. For example, Tom Givens was a successful accountant who was engaged to a woman with three preteenaged children. Tom liked everything to be clear and simple. He seemed unable to live with uncertainty. Therefore, Tom constantly demanded specific solutions for a host of imagined problems. What he actually wanted was a blueprint and a guarantee of success. None exists. Tom's need to control situations and people may serve him well in some areas of life, but it led to frustration in a stepfamily. Tom knew all of the principles and techniques our courses offered, but we could not give him flexibility, nor could we save him from the stress inherent in living with children.

There is no substitute for flexibility when we live with children, especially in blended families. Principles and techniques of family living give parents guidelines and strategies. But changing emotions, behaviors, and situations require special application.

Parents with a strong need to please others also encounter problems. In stepfamilies it is difficult, if not impossible, to make everyone happy. Children may not blend together well, ex-spouses may be upset over visitation rights or money, and in-laws may fail to be supportive. Children may react negatively to some forms of discipline, and many regress temporarily in their behavior. All of these possibilities will cause trouble for the person who needs to feel that everyone is happy. Pleasers may often feel rejected by others, despite the fact that they try to be everything to everyone. To survive, pleasers need to become more realistic in their expectations and less critical of their own performance.

Jason realized his stepmother, June, would do anything to keep him happy. To avoid his disapproval, she gave in to each demand. Once he discovered her need to please him, Jason became a master at controlling her. Whenever he did not get his way, Jason accused June of favoring her own children. When pushed into a corner, he would demand to be returned to his "real mother." June would respond by granting Jason whatever appeased him. Her need to please a stepchild resulted in her becoming a living puppet. Jason, in a sense, was a five-year-old puppet-master.

Blended families should not wait for problems to arise before seeking support from professionals. Parenting courses for blended families can be beneficial. Family counselors can give invaluable support by helping families set up routine family meetings, develop new rules, and establish roles. Like more complex organizations which benefit from consultants, families can benefit from the work of a family therapist.

Schools should be of significant help to children in blended families, but they seldom are. Often they add to the frustration and anxiety of children. Simple class projects can turn into headaches. For example, which father should receive a single father's day card made in class, and which mother should be presented the valentine entitled "to Mom"? Even school forms can present room for addresses of only one set of parents. Notices for PTAs and school performances often are not received by both sets of parents. Such situations show society's slow reaction to changing times.

Nevertheless, there is movement in the right direction. Some schools are forming discussion groups and support groups for children of both single parent homes and blended homes. Teachers are often provided in-service workshops on how to create stable, structured classrooms which will benefit stepchildren. Many teachers lead discussion groups in their classrooms that are geared toward helping children of blended families. These discussions enable each member of a class to grow in appreciation of the special challenges that face stepchildren. Continuing education in many schools provide classes and programs for parents of single families and blended families. Education is the key ingredient for preventing difficulties in the future lives of stepfamilies.

Blended families form a large and vital portion of the United States' population. In blended families, children experience situational misbehaviors, and parents experience challenges unknown to most nuclear families. Although new stepfamilies can benefit from knowing the difficulties common to similar families, each new blended family must find its own way. Stepfamilies each possess a unique history, unique boundaries, and a unique structure. The complexity of each individual stepfamily requires parents to be flexible in their efforts to handle the variety of both predictable and situational misbehaviors experienced by each family member.

REFERENCES

Bogue, D. (1985). *The population of the United States: Historical trends and future projects.* New York: The Free Press.

Brooks, J. (1981). *The process of parenting.* Palo Alto: Mayfield Publishing Company.

Cherlin, A. (1981). *Marriage, divorce, and remarriage.* Cambridge: Harvard University Press.

Toman, W. (1976). *Family constellation: It's effect on personality and social behavior.* New York: Springer Publishing Company.

Visher, E. & Visher, J. (1980). *Stepfamilies: A guide to working with stepparents and stepchildren.* New York: Bruner/Mazel.

Visher, E. & Visher, J. (1983). *How to win as a stepfamily.* Chicago: Contemporary Books.

Visher, E. & Visher, J. (1980). *Stepfamilies: Myths and realities.* Secaucus, N.J.: Citadel Press.

Visher, E. & Visher, J. (1979). *Stepfamilies: A guide to working with stepparents and stepchildren.* New York: Bruner/Mazel.

White, B. (1985). *The first three years of life:* The revised edition. Englewood Cliffs, N.J.: Prentice-Hall.

RELATED READINGS

Ainslie, R. (1984). *The child and the day care setting: Qualitative variations and development.* New York: Praeger.

Auerbach, S. (1981). *Choosing childcare: A guide for parents.* New York: Dutton.

Bradley, B. (1982). *Where do I belong? A kids guide to stepfamilies.* Reading, MA: Addison Wesley.

Burt, M. & Burt, R. (1983). *What's special about our stepfamily? A participation book for children.* New York: Doubleday.

Berman, C. (1982). *What am I doing in a stepfamily?* Secaucus, NJ: Lyle Stuart.

Bustanoby, A. (1982). *The readymade family: How to be a stepparent and survive.* Grand Rapids, MI: Zondervan.

Clarke-Steward, A. (1982). *Stepfamilies: New patterns of harmony.* New York: Messner.

Dreskin, W. & Dreskin, W. (1983). *The day care decision: What's best for you and your child.* New York: M. Evans.

Endsley, R. & Bradbard, M. (1981). *Quality day care: A handbook of choices for parents and caregivers.* New York: Spectrum.

Filstrup, J. (1982). *Monday through Friday: Daycare alternatives.* New York: Teachers College Press.

Glickman, B. (1978). *Who cares for baby.* New York: Schoeken Books.
Jensen, L. & Jensen, J. (1981). *Stepping into stepparenting. A practical guide.* Saratoga, CA: R & E Research Assoc.
Jolin, P. (1983). *How to succeed as a stepparent.* New York: New American Library.
Juroe, D. & Juroe, B. (1983). *Successful stepparenting.* Old Tappan, NJ: Revell.
Krementz, J. (1983). *How it feels to be adopted.* New York: Alfred A. Knopf.
Lewis-Steere, C. (1981). *Stepping lightly: An a to z guide for stepparents.* Minneapolis, MN: CompCare.
Maddox, B. (1975). *The half parent.* New York: Evans.
Mitchell, G. (1984). *The day care book.* New York: Fawcett.
Noble, J. & Noble, W. (1977). *How to live with other people's children.* New York: Hawthorne Books.
Ross, K. (1984). *A parent's guide to day care.* Blue Ridge Summit, PA: TAB Books, Inc.
Scarr, S. (1984). *Mother care, other care.* New York: Basic Books.
Visher, E. & Visher, J. (1983). *How to win as a stepfamily.* Chicago: Contemporary Books.
Visher, E. & Visher, J. (1980). *Stepfamilies: Myths and realities.* Secaucus, N.J.: Citadel Press.
Visher, E. & Visher, J. (1979). *Stepfamilies: A guide to working with stepparents and stepchildren.* New York: Bruner/Mazel.
Reingold, C. (1976). *Remarriage.* New York: Harper and Row.
Rosenbaum, J. & Rosenbaum, V. (1977). *Stepparenting.* Corte Madera, CA: Chandler and Sharp Publishers, Inc.

CHAPTER TWELVE

PARENTS AND REVOLUTION

HAVE YOU EVER thought of yourself as a revolutionary? Most parents have not. Yet parents, by definition, are vitally concerned about the future world their children will inherit. Although parents may vary in individual beliefs about religion, politics, or economics most agree that institutions should continue to adopt changes that will allow our future generations to seek better opportunities for self-fulfillment and happiness.

To raise children without regard for the values and institutions maintained by society is as irresponsible as freeing domesticated animals in an unfriendly jungle. There are more parents, as a group, in our nation than any other group that shares a common concern. If the majority of parents united to bring change to society, the world would become a better place for new generations to enjoy. There are directions in which change needs to continue, and there are new directions for change that should be initiated. If parents accept the challenge to continue the improvement of our society, then they may become the most influential revolutionaries since the country's founders.

NEW DIRECTIONS: "TO BE RATHER THAN TO SEEM"

Our society professes to value the nurturing of children. But does it? Or, does it only seem to value children, while in actuality its resources are channeled in other directions? For example, if nurturing children is of value to society, then shouldn't parents be held in high esteem? Shouldn't the work of parents be celebrated? Shouldn't the task of parents be supported in every practical way?

Prestige is high in many deserving professions in the United States. Pediatricians, who care for the health of the young, are highly respected.

Child psychologists, special educators, professors of child development, and family therapists enjoy respected careers. In other words, professionals who care for sick children, help families understand and meet challenges, or work with troubled families are admired. But it is ironic that equal esteem is not shared by primary caretakers whose major task is to nurture children.

Our society's future success depends upon whether parents will raise autonomous, confident children who will contribute generously to society, or will produce weak, dependent, even hostile children who will experience a string of difficulties that will be expensive to themselves as well as society. The nation's future, in a very real sense, depends upon parental successes or failures. Yet parents increasingly feel isolated from support and generally unappreciated for their daily work.

This lack of esteem may be felt most by those parents who choose to make raising children their full-time occupation. Questions often asked of full-time parents that display the contemporary lack of appreciation for parenting include, "Do you have a job, or do you stay home?" Or, "Do you have a **real** job?" Or, "When do you plan to go back to work?" Mothers returning to the work force often meet employers who consider them unqualified for jobs because of "lack of previous work experience." To the contrary, most full-time parents practice a variety of skills and display daily responsibility in the demanding profession of child-rearing.

For example, many full-time parents maintain a strict budget, conduct major purchasing, develop nurturing skills, handle interpersonal conflict, and establish cooperation within a complex organization. These are the skills required in a person who must work seven days per week and be constantly on 24-hour emergency "call." Responsibility is frequently taken to make major decisions, often of a medical nature, that will irreversibly impact on human life. Yet because a nine to five time-clock is not punched, or because a specific job involving limited skills is not held, full-time parents planning to return to the work force are considered inexperienced. Unfortunately, unlike those for veterans of military service, no laws facilitate a parent's reentry into the job market, and no organization exists with the specific goal of expanding the opportunities of parents on whose work the country's future depends.

Parents working outside of the home to support the family or to pursue careers face additional difficulties. Daycare too often can be unsatisfactory due to poor quality control. Most public daycare centers are understaffed. Many daycare workers are not qualified to teach and are sometimes negligent in providing basic warmth needed by children. Inexplicably, daycare continues to be considered a family problem rather than a national challenge. Yet it is the nation that needs more adults in the work force. It is the nation that is experiencing economic conditions which force many parents into the work force. It is the nation that will feel the impact of the increased use of daycare. Daycare is a vital, national concern for which the government should take responsibility.

The private sector also should become more responsive to parental needs. It is regrettable that major companies enjoy the full-time work of both mothers and fathers, yet feel a limited responsibility to the families of employees. Neither the nation nor private industry, as a whole, is investing its energy in our greatest resource: Children.

When it comes to helping children, the motto of our society might well be "to seem rather than to be." Many influential people talk about the importance of nurturing children, but when it comes to financial commitments, money goes elsewhere. Establishing quality daycare should become a national priority. The nation benefits from the large work force which requires the increased use of daycare, but if daycare is weak, the cost in both human and financial terms may be astronomical in the future. Nationally, money for social programs generally support only the programs required when parents or schools fail. These funds are needed. In addition, funds are needed for programs that stress success and will help prevent failure. As our forefathers suggested, "an ounce of prevention is worth a pound of cure."

Where should the money come from? Obviously, this is complicated; no simple answer exists. Major changes in national priorities—and maybe values—must be made. Change will require a national struggle of conscience and a growth in wisdom. But for starters, why not develop a supertax on those products which are the enemies of childhood, such as tobacco products, alcohol, gambling, and pornography? As a symbolic first step, our government could use these taxes to benefit children directly. When our nation establishes a goal, whether it be in space or in defense, progress is certain. An initial step toward enriching the lives of children by supporting the goals of responsible parents will be a "giant step" toward our national security.

Our nation often looks for enemies outside of its own borders. It is assumed that enemies always take the form of foreign nations or movements, but it could be that our greatest enemy lurks within. The greatest threat to our survival may be the neglect of our children. The times call for change. Business needs competent workers. Women need freedom of choice in careers. The poor cannot afford quality daycare. The middle class can no longer afford to support a full-time parent. Never before has the nation faced such a crossroads. Competent parents need assistance. Change is required.

Many fathers are stirring conventional waters. Males are beginning to see their role change from financial provider and vacation dads to nurturing fathers. This change of philosophy allows women an opportunity to develop their potential and gives children two parents on whom to depend. But there is a cost to such fathers. For every male spending more of his time nurturing children, there is a traditional male exploiting weekend and nights to advance in a competitive career. Individual advancement for a father may well be the cost paid for the emotional progress of his family.

Fathering is a career in itself. That few fathers are impressed with the prestige associated with fathering is sometimes evident when fathers introduce themselves to strangers. Usually the introduction goes like this, "I am Ed Jacobson; I am a computer programmer for IBM. I've worked at IBM for ten years and am presently the director of computer services." After a cocktail party for businessmen, an observer might assume from the introductions that each participant is a bachelor. As values change, males may boast equally to strangers about being a father, "I am Ed Jacobson. I am married and have three children. Also, I am a computer programmer for IBM."

Loss of parental prestige is a rather recent phenomenon. It is a trend that needs to be reversed. Industries and businesses can help restore prestige to parents by actively acknowledging the importance of parenting in the lives of employees. Flexible jobs can be created that will allow men and women to work part-time or that can accommodate the requirements of family schedules. Some success already has been achieved by job-sharing opportunities being offered to couples or individuals. Also companies can sponsor on-site daycare for parents. It is true that all of these changes will require a revolution in current thinking. Such a revolution may be necessary to insure that the strength of our country continues. The times require change.

Single parent families now constitute a significant portion of our population. They, too, need to insist on societal change. As suggested earlier, single parents no longer should accept the role of being examples of the failure of the nuclear family. Instead, single parent families should develop their roles as alternatives to nuclear families. Like any alternative system, single parent families will prosper when society accepts them and provides services needed to allow each family member to prosper.

Often, attitudes change only after behaviors change. When society makes changes that help single parent families, then single parent families can experience more success. Consequently, single parent families will grow in self-confidence and enjoy a respected position in society. Success breeds success.

Not only do single parents need affordable, high quality daycare, but they also need supervised after-school programs. Such programs will keep children from being alone and unsupervised and will build skills and self-confidence in each child. Churches and schools could assume a major role in after-school care. Both institutions own facilities which often are unused in the late afternoons. Again, funding for these programs will require a change of thinking by those in national, state, and local governments, as well as in businesses in the private sector.

Support groups for children and adults in single parent families are needed. Schools could provide discussion groups for children facing the special challenges of single parent homes. Children need to discover that their experiences are not "odd" and that they are not alone — others share similar situations. In addition, suggestions for handling problems in a single parent home, stepfamily, or other shared family experience can enable a child to achieve a larger degree of success in life. In addition to the possibility of schools providing support groups, churches and local agencies could be of service.

It is difficult to change the attitudes of members of society, but attitudes toward parents and families will inevitably change as behaviors in society do. Behavior changes will occur after a true commitment is made by society to the welfare of its children. At that point, the United States' motto may truly become "TO BE RATHER THAN TO SEEM."

PARENT EDUCATION

Good parents are a national treasure. Few adults are naturally skillful as parents. Parenting techniques are often passed imperfectly from generation to generation. Rarely are adults confident in their abilities, even though most are competent. Although most adults spend the major portion of their mature years raising children, there is no formal education for how to be good parents in our society.

Public schools teach skills such as typing, masonry, and woodworking. They teach sports to be enjoyed for a lifetime, such as golf and tennis, yet little or nothing exists to help develop the complex skills parents will need.

Since parenting is the most important profession in life, the public schools should develop curriculum that teach basic child development and parenting skills. Students should be prepared for the real challenges in living. Adults rarely, or never, are called upon to use the theorems and equations memorized in schools, but understanding and responding to a child's misbehavior is often a daily task. What curriculum could be more relevant to living and more beneficial to our society than that of parenting?

Obviously, the content included in parenting programs will be debated. Citizens need to ensure that positive techniques are taught. It seems practical that those programs should be emphasized which teach children to live in a democracy, to take responsibility, and to think logically. Such programs would do well to follow the democratic principles established by Adler and Dreikurs and presented in this book, as well as a host of others that are contemporary.

Particular care should be taken to avoid "pop psychology" in parenting. Such programs tend to serve a limited population experiencing a specific need and are, therefore, not broad enough to meet the needs of the majority of parents. An example is the new fad called "Toughlove." While "Toughlove" may be a positive philosophical change for permissive parents, it is not helpful for parents or children in the majority of homes where parents are not permissive.

Parenting programs must teach the skills and values needed to live successfully in a democracy. As well, parenting techniques should be based on commonsense ideas that have stood the test of time and that will endure through generations to come. Establishing broad parenting skills, rather than emergency techniques for patching up problems, should be the primary emphasis of these programs. The time is right for making parenting skills available to everyone. In the 1950s, the nation made the space race a priority. The schools reflected this in the curriculum, and now astronauts travel routinely in space. Similar success will be enjoyed by parents when our government agrees that raising children properly and lovingly is a national priority.

Opportunities for learning to become better parents should not end in school. Hospitals can begin to offer parenting courses along with Lamaze or other birthing courses. Videotapes that teach parenting and discipline skills should be available to mothers in the hospital with their newborn children. Cable television can routinely show parenting courses on their service channels. Colleges and community colleges can offer parenting courses for traditional or continuing education credit, while local newspapers can present columns with advice for parents. Skills needed by parents will be used for a lifetime. Teaching basic parenting techniques needs to become a national priority, for the good of the nation.

THE SCHOOLS

Schools, next to parents, offer the greatest influence on children's lives. As Erikson suggests, children will either gain a sense of competency and industry in the primary years, or they will suffer from a feeling of inferiority. William Glasser calls this inferiority a "failure identity." Both theorists agree that a pessimistic view of one's abilities and one's chances for success in life is established by the age of ten and may endure a lifetime.

Nowhere does the public tend to level more criticism than at the present school system. For many critics, what students are learning in the schools seems irrelevant. Bright children complain of boredom. Unprepared students experience failure. Teachers and parents report that poor discipline is a major concern. A 1983 national report, "A Nation at Risk," stated that:

> "If an unfriendly power had attempted to impose on America the mediocre educational performance that exists today, we might well have viewed it as an act of war."

Alternatives to existing school systems have appeared from time to time and enjoyed various degrees of success. An alternative developed by Dr. Raymond Corsini is the Corsini Four-R School System (C4R). C4R is stated to be cost effective, preferred over traditional schools by participating students and teachers, and has increased the academic success of students. The C4R system is discussed below as a paradigm for positive change in education.

Corsini developed his system by means of inductive logic. Over a period of three and one half years, on the basis of his experience as a student and teacher, educational counselor, and editor of books in education, Corsini established some 450 propositions relative to his conception of an ideal school. These propositions were based on a number of "critical incidents," real and imagined. For example, he considered the common situation of a child being placed in a particular classroom because of age. Suppose three children, each ten years old, who entered the same school at the same time and who have had the same teachers are each put in the fifth grade in a traditional school. But let us say that

Albert on English tests 5.1 grade, Benjamin tests grade 9.7, and Carl tests 2.3 grade. As a result, only Albert is properly placed: Benjamin is placed too low for his abilities, and Carl too high.

This common practice generates problems for bright children who become bored by being taught what they already know, for dull children who are not able to learn what is taught, and for teachers who face disciplinary problems due to the boredom and the frustration of students.

Corsini came to these two theoretical propositions on the basis of considering such problems:

> In an ideal school, a child would not be forced to study something that he already knew.
>
> In an ideal school, a child would not be forced to study something that he could not learn.

As a consequence of these two assertions about an ideal school, in his schools, formerly called **Individual Education** schools and now **Corsini Four-R** (C4R) schools, the C4R system calls for children to be pretested to see how much they actually know of subjects taught and then advised at what level to study, and then are monitored weekly relative to academic gains in terms of passing tests that measure the weekly units of instructions.

While developing his system Corsini tested the acceptability of 450 propositions on a number of teachers and principals, and he found that they accepted the logic of his ideas. Later, Peake (1985) found substantial agreement by teachers that (a) the various C4R propositions made sense, and (b) that teachers preferred the C4R system to their traditional system.

Many members of **Individual Education International,** the organization of psychologists and educators that support the C4R system, believe that, in the future, C4R will become the educational system of choice in that it has demonstrated its general superiority of children learning more in less time; parents, faculty, and children approving the system; and considerable reductions in disciplinary problems.

The basic reason for all these advantages? Simply that the C4R system is psychologically sound. Although developed by a logical process, the system is completely in accord with the principles of Alfred Adler's Individual Psychology, as well as the various humanistic systems discussed in this book. However, the C4R system—and indeed any innovations in education—suffer from almost automatic rejections on the part of people who control schools, since they depend strongly on the dead hand of tradition. It is a very interesting situation: Everyone complains about the schools as they are now, and when a new and better solution is suggested, it is usually not considered.

Educational specialists, according to Pratt (1985), agree upon three major tenets which should govern the operation of schools:

  a. Every child should have an opportunity to build a special relationship with at least one teacher.
  b. Children should not be made to learn what they already know or are unprepared to learn.
  c. A student who disrupts instruction should leave the classroom.

Three programs exist in the C4R schools: **Academic, Creative,** and **Socialization.** Each program is individualized. For example, the academic program allows each child to work where she wants to begin and at her own pace. Dividing the curriculum into small pieces allows a student, on the average, to complete one academic unit of instruction each week. Students are advised to begin work on the specific unit that matches individual ability. For example, pretesting may show that a student should be in unit 42 in math (3rd grade) and unit 17 in English (1st grade). The student's teacher-advisor will discuss the tests results with the child, then advise her where to begin. The student may take this advice or may decide to select a more, or less, difficult challenge. Thus, as the majority of educational psychologists suggest as ideal practice, the C4R school starts where the student is. Students can learn the various units in any one or any combination of five methods.

1. **Classroom Instruction** (as in any traditional school).
2. **Peer Instruction** (in the study hall with small student groups working together).
3. **Self Study** (in the library).
4. **Tutoring** (Every teacher is to have at least one weekly "free" period for tutoring.
5. **Home Study.** Studying—parents, siblings, and including self-study.

Academic progress charts, updated weekly, display the students' accomplishments. A student's academic progress can be seen in visual graphs which display what skills have been mastered. National tests and exams are taken, just as they are in the public schools. The national test scores allow a more precise estimate of a child's achievement, since traditional grades vary greatly from teacher to teacher and from locality to locality.

An important center for learning in C4R schools is the library. Here, absolute silence is the rule. In the library, children may read novels, look at pictures in books, daydream, meditate—and study their lessons from textbooks and reference books. Study halls are available for help with specific academic problems and for peer studying. Whenever a student becomes bored in class or already understands the work being done, she may go either to the library or to the hall. Both rooms have a teacher in charge. Any child who behaves in a manner to disturb other children is sent out of the room by means of a nonverbal hand signal—the **Go Signal**.

Preliminary results from C4R schools show that students progress better academically than those in traditional schools (Froeme, 1980; Krebb, 1982; Pratt, 1985; Whittington, 1977). Many students who experience failure in traditional schools flourish in the 4R system (Madden, 1977; Whittington, 1977). Other areas where students show marked gains over students from traditional schools are in interpersonal skills (socialization) and creativity.

The key to the socialization program is the nomination by the student of a homeroom teacher called the teacher/advisor. The TA may accept the student's request to become the child's advisor. The TA becomes the child's "school parent" and can remain the child's TA each year. A close relationship usually is established between the student and her TA.

Homeroom periods, which take place the first period of every school day, usually last a full period of 45-50 minutes, all for socialization. They allow the students in a democratic relationship to the teacher/advisors to discuss problems, plan trips, teach interrelationship skills, and prepare children to meet problems in life. The day begins and ends with the homeroom. A special feature of the homerooms is a Class Council, which serves the same purpose in the school as the family council does in the home. The class council and the homeroom activities teach children to discuss and solve problems in a reasonable way. Because their feelings and ideas are heard and understood, students are less likely to engage in destructive misbehavior. Instead, improved interpersonal skills and problem-solving techniques help children gain the ability and self-confidence needed to face personal problems successfully.

The creative program, which occurs every afternoon, capitalizes on the interests of students and teachers by allowing a variety of traditional and nontraditional studies. Students are encouraged to suggest activities or courses which interest them. Instructors can teach personal interests, which may include a variety of activities, like chess, basketball, or computer programming; the possibilities are endless. If students have an interest that the teachers cannot meet, a specialist may be invited to the school to teach a creative course, such as computers in science or the utilization of business principles in a large corporation. Because teachers and students enjoy pursuing areas of personal interest, learning becomes more enjoyable.

No special requirements beyond certification exist for teachers who are given freedom to teach by using their own methods. Not surprisingly, teacher satisfaction is very high in the C4R schools (Armstrong, 1985; Pratt, 1985). Also, parental satisfaction is high (Paresa, 1977; Richardson, 1985). Since C4R schools are an alternative to public schools, parents may enroll their children in the schools only after understanding and accepting the system's philosophy. Parents are to attend free parenting classes which emphasize principles and techniques similar to those emphasized in the school. Home atmospheres often improve, because parents are freed from the obligations of forcing children to do homework and "making children behave" in school. Teachers and students take responsibility for these areas of concern. Any conferences between parents and teachers are attended by the student. Students are always aware of their academic and disciplinary status in the school. By sharing open relationships, teachers, parents, and students develop a mutual respect for each other.

As might be expected, some discipline problems do occur. They are dealt with by the C4R's unique disciplinary program. The school has three rules: "1) do nothing that could harm yourself, others, or school property; 2) always be in a supervised area, or enroute from one supervised area to another, and 3) if, during a class, the teacher should point at you, leave the classroom immediately and in silence. . ." (Pratt, 1985). Teachers are not allowed to berate or yell at students, and students are not allowed to disrupt classrooms. Students who choose to misbehave are given the GO signal, where one must leave the classroom and, once out of the room, she can (a) decide to return, (b) try to enter another classroom (but it is up to any teacher whether to allow the student to enter), (c) go to the library, or (d) go to the study hall.

However, in each case, the teacher or librarian or study hall monitor, by using the "stop sign," can indicate to the child that she does not want the child to enter. Consequently, a tight system of consequences is established in the school. The logical consequences for misbehavior are known in advance by all students; therefore, students are aware of what each misbehavior will mean to them. Each violation of a rule must be recorded. After a predetermined number of violations, parent-student-TA conferences are required. After twelve violations, expulsion is considered.

Through its various programs, involvement with parents, outlets for creativity, and discipline principles, the Corsini schools hope to build the 4R's which are:

1. **Responsibility** — to be built by involving children in decisions about their own education, under close, realistic guidance.
2. **Respect** — to be nurtured by treating the student with respect and by requiring respect for others.
3. **Resourcefulness** — encouraged by opportunities to prepare for the three main tasks in life: occupation and leisure, family life, and membership in society.
4. **Responsiveness** — encouraged by striving for a school environment in which people demonstrate trust in others and caring for others. (Pratt, 1985).

The C4R schools represent an innovative system for educating the "entire child." Positive gains made by students in academics, creativity, and self-confidence are encouraging.

Despite criticism directed toward them, public schools are slow to change. Parents need to unite to demand innovation in their school system. Whether or not schools will eventually move toward a system similar to Corsini's 4R system is unknown. But schools must change in order to eliminate boredom, failure, and gross misbehavior. Parental involvement will be the key to the rate and direction of progress in the schools. Insist on change!

CHANGES IN SOCIETY

How curious are the economic values in the United States! Pretend you were from another planet and were asked to determine the worth of various earthly occupations. Suppose the work of a full-time parent, a teacher, an actor, and an athlete were described to you. Would you be shocked to find that a mother or father who is involved 24 hours a day in order to raise the future citizens of our nation is paid nothing, while a grown man who runs down a field with a football while others try to knock him to the ground is paid millions of dollars? Would you be surprised to find that those who are hired by schools to teach skills to children and nurture growing self-concepts are paid less for five years' work than many television actors make in a single week? How could a rational being possibly understand such values?

Inequities in pay are only a sideshow for the real problems that engulf much of our population: poverty and ignorance. Families of poverty level often remain captive in a cycle that they are powerless to break. Unemployment increases tension and emotional problems in families that often are already troubled. Parents may be employed around the clock to make ends meet. But their efforts take them away from their children who need them. Poor parents often feel such low self-esteem they must fight for their own self-enhancement, rather than have the luxury of putting their energy into the development of their children's self-confidence. Poverty breeds a never-ending cycle of problems for a nation.

How to end poverty in the world's wealthiest nation remains a national mystery. It is a challenge which has been tackled for years by our political leaders without success. Parents need to play a role by insisting on change. More of the same will not work. New vision is needed. Our country must move from a wealthy nation where successs is **possible** for all to a nation where success is **probable** for all.

An epidemic of unplanned pregnancies and the continuation of unwanted births in our nation constitute another challenge to our society. As with the poverty cycle, it is mysterious that unwanted pregnancies abound in a nation which has the resources to end the problem. A variety of birth control methods and an extensive system of public education exists in this nation, but the most recent data from the Statistical Abstracts of the United States shows that for every 1,000 live births there are 426 abortions in the United States (Statistical Abstract, 1985). Still 7.7 percent, or more than one of fourteen children born, is unwanted. Some unwanted children may be adopted by deserving stepparents. Others struggle through a lifetime of feeling unloved. Once an unwanted pregnancy occurs, for most, some trauma is inevitable despite personal stances on abortion. Parents owe it to future generations to take charge of sex education in the home and to back sound programs intended to prevent unwanted pregnancies.

Do individuals have the moral right to mother or father children beyond their capacity to care for them? Indeed, this is a delicate question. Direct sterilization of parents who are judged "undesirable" has led to great abuse in the past, particularly for retarded citizens and minorities. Dr. J. David Smith, in his book **Minds Made Feeble,** warns of the dangers inherent in eugenics programs. Solutions to problems often are worse for a nation than the original problem, as Smith suggests. Yet our social policies may financially encourage individuals to have children past their ability to care properly for them. In a land of individual freedom, restraints on family size are ill-advised. Perhaps financial policies should be considered that do not reward parents for having children solely for financial reasons. Children do have a right to be born to parents who truly want to nourish and raise them. But how do we insure that a child's right to positive treatment is balanced with an adult's right to bear children? This is a problem yet to be solved.

Parents must be revolutionaries if our society is to keep up with the needs of its people. In some cases, fundamental values need to change in the direction of supporting families that are functioning well, while continuing to support families doing poorly. Mothers and fathers must demand services that will allow them to make professional and life choices that help, rather than hinder, children. Schools need to educate the whole child and cut down on the all too frequent incidents of failure and boredom.

There are many fronts on which to fight battles. Many parents will ignore all challenges, but if enough parents unite in demanding change, our society will be greatly enriched. Families need to become our nation's number one priority, not only in rhetoric but in actuality. Parents, take courage, give your children a better world.

REFERENCES

Peake, E. R. (1985). Teachers develop their own school system. *Individual Psychology, 41,* 63-68.

Krebs, L. (1982). Summary of research on Individual Education schools. *Journal of Individual Psychology, 38,* 245-252.

Pratt, A. B. (1985). Summary of research on Individual Education to 1984. *Individual Psychology, 41,* 39-54.

Armstrong, R. B. (1985). Individual Education: Principals' evaluations. *Individual Psychology, 41,* 8-21.

Elkins, P. H. (1985). Individual Education: A critical review. *Individual Psychology, 41,* 30-38.

Dubrovich, M. (1985). Individual Education from the point of view of a principal. *Individual Psychology, 41,* 30-38.

Jones (1977). From the viewpoint of a teacher. *Journal of Individual Psychology, 33,* 353-355.

Madden, J. (1977). Staff training for Individual Education. *Journal of Individual Psychology, 33,* 359-365.

Muirhead, M. & Fong, J. (1977). An analysis of visitor's responses. *Journal of Individual Psychology, 33,* 366-370.

Pratt, A. B. & Mastroianni, M. (1984). Summary of research on Individual Education. *Journal of Individual Psychology, 37,* 232-246.

Richardson, G. (1985). Individual Education from the point of view of a parent. *Individual Psychology, 41,* 88-89.

Smith, J. D. (1985). *Minds made feeble: The myth and legacy of the Kallikaks.* Rockville, Maryland: Aspen.

Whittington, E. R. (1977). Individual education at an alternative school. *Journal of Individual Psychology, 33,* 356-370.

CONCLUSION

PARENTING WITHOUT GUILT

IN THE ANNALS of folklore, there is an old story about a king who believed he was so powerful that he could prevent the tide from moving onto the shore. First, he ordered his throne to be placed on the shoreline. Then the king commanded the waves to stay out at sea! Of course, the sea overwhelmed him. How foolish he was to defy nature.

Likewise, many parents try to defy the nature of children, believing that misbehavior can be eliminated by the use of kingly authority or that it can be avoided if they act as powerless as beggars in the king's court. Others resemble a king one moment and a beggar the next. Neither extreme works. Both leave parents feeling incompetent and guilty.

Like the rise and fall of the tides, most misbehavior in children is predictable. Much is even positive, leading to growth in autonomy, initiative, morality, and creativity. Other challenges, like tropical storms, are spawned under specific, well-known conditions. Situational misbehaviors emerge in many families where marital disharmony, divorce, or remarriage is experienced.

Wise parents neither attempt to command the currents back into the sea nor remain powerless before the force of an incoming tide. Instead, adults confidently prepare for and respond to the energy of the tides. Communications allow families to plan how to use energy in positive ways. Encouragement is used to support cooperative behaviors. When the waters of childhood do storm past acceptable boundaries, logical and natural consequences discipline the child to become more self-controlled and self-directed.

Love is not a one-night stand. It requires patience, understanding, and most of all, work. Even the most skilled parents have children who experience predictable and situational misbehaviors; but the parents who understand the tides of misbehavior and who know the proper techniques for handling the force of storms will escape drowning in the sea of inevitability. The ups and downs of family life are inescapable, but with understanding and competence, such parents will parent without guilt.

INDEX

A

Accomplishment vs. inferiority, 59-63, 85, 141-146
Accordian family, 181
Adler, Alfred, 21, 32-42, 161, 258, 260
Alfred Adler Institute, 42
Allowances, 137, 140, 202
Anderson, Hans Christian, 44
Anorexia nervosa, 177
Assumed disability, 17-20
Athletics (*see* Sports participation)
Attention addiction, 8-10
Attention getting misbehavior, 7-10
Authoritarian, 15, 117-121
Autonomy, 9, 11, 13, 33-34, 40, 43, 53-55, 176, 192 (*see also* Autonomy vs. shame and doubt)
Autonomy vs. shame and doubt, 53-55, 129-136 (*see also* autonomy)

B

Baby Sitter Plague, 52
Babysitters, 52-53, 129
Bardill, Ray, 189-203, 208-209
Bathtime, 12, 130-131
Bedrooms, 135-136
Bedtime, 12, 54
Begging, 132
Birth, 47
Biting, 12, 127-128
Blended families, (*see* Stepfamilies)
Boundaries, 189-203
Bowen, Murray, 171
"Boys will be boys," 26

C

Child abuse, 57-58, 105, 199
Chores, 145, 160, 161-165, 248
Class council, 262
Classroom misbehavior, 142 (*see also* Schools)
Cognitive conceit, 85-86
Cognitive growth, 62-91
Collective monologue, 79
Communications, 9, 17, 153-165, 180-181, (*see also* Family council)
Comparisons, 29-31, 37-38, 60-61
Competition, 30
Concrete operations, 83-87, 138, 240-241
Controllers, 249
Conventional Moral Thought, 99-103
Cooperation, 15, 17, 20, 36, 40, 47, 160, 161-165, 204-205, 223, 244, 248
Corsini Four-R School System, 259-264
Corsini, Raymond, vii-viii, 259-260
Courage, 10, 32, 34, 38, 56, 110-111, 147-152, 156, 161, 182, 184, 194, 229-230
Criticism, 147-152
Cursing, 12, 77, 140-141
Custody, 219-220, 241-243 (*see also* Single parent families)

D

Dances of misbehavior (*see* Goals of misbehavior)
Daycare, 49-50, 211, 214, 226, 231-237, 254-256
Death, 75-76
Democratic-authoritative model, 190
Dependency, 7-8, 33, 45-58, 109, 119-120, 158, 170-172, 175-176

Destructiveness, 136-137
Dethronement, 27
Developmental family stress, 204-207
Dick-Read, Grantly, 47
Discouragement, 17-20, 26, 30, 38, 59-63, 143, 159 (*see* Encouragement)
Disengagement, 178
Divorce, 82, 204-205, 212, 231, 238, 243 (*see* Single parent homes)
Dreikurs, Rudolph, 5-22, 33, 42, 59, 118, 130, 161, 200, 226, 258
Dressing, 10, 124-125, 130-131
Double messages, 157, 247

E

Eating, 5, 12, 54, 78-79, 122, 127
Education (*see* Accomplishment vs. inferiority, Corsini 4R Schools, encouragement, failure, schools)
Egocentric, 77-80, 82, 97-99, 240-241
Elkind, David, 67, 76, 90
Empathy vs. sympathy, 226
Emotions, 14, 33-34, 40, 59, 69, 75, 81, 87, 105-107, 120, 133, 179, 194, 218-219, 222, 237, 241, 247-248
Empty nest, 206-207
Encouragement, 7, 18, 20, 32, 37-38, 58-63, 143, 147-152, 153, 163, 182-183, 221, 228-229, 248
Enmeshment, 175-176, 177, 178
Erikson, Erik, 43-66, 85, 170, 259

F

Family constellation (*see* Ordinal position)
Family counseling, 19, 42, 57, 169-209, 222-223, 225, 250
Family values, 25, 29, 31, 38
Failure, 46, 59-63 (*see also* Accomplishment vs. inferiority, discouragement, encouragement, schools)
Fairness, 154-155, 218-219
Family councils, 109-110, 145, 161-165, 174, 196, 200-203, 227, 235, 247-249
Fathers in transition, 256
Fears, 55, 138-139
Feelings (*see* Emotion)
Fighting, 15, 23, 37-40

Flexibility, 160-249
Forgetting, 123
Formal operations, 87, 241
Four goals of misbehavior (*see* Goals of misbehavior)
Freud, Sigmund, 41, 65, 90
Friendships, 145-146

G

Gifted, 18
Ginnott, Heim, 62, 158
Glasser, William, 59, 85, 259
Goals of misbehavior, 5-22
Gottman, John, 156, 159
Grades, 143-144 (*see* Discouragement, encouragement, and schools)
Grandmom's despair, 51-52
Grandparents, 36, 50, 223, 233, 242
Gravity, 69-70
Great error, 30
Grief, following divorce, 213, 222
Guilt, ix, x, 52, 105-107, 117, 146, 151, 154-155, 211, 217, 221, 239, 269, 270

H

Hitting, 12, 127-128
Homework, 12, 25, 141-142
Humor, 54, 77, 86

I

"I" messages, 159
Icarus, 55
Identity, 170-171
Ignoring misbehavior, 9
Imagination, 73-82
Incest, 199
Inconsistency, 109, 117-121
Independence, 7, 8
Individual Education International, 260
Industry, 43 (*see also* Accomplishment vs. inferiority)
Inferiority, 59-63
Initiative, 43
Initiative vs. guilt, 55-58, 136-141
Injuries, 128-129
Irresponsibility, 16

J

Jehovah's Gift Child, 24

K

Kicking, 12, 127-128
Kierkegaard, Søren, 103
Kohlberg, Lawrence, 93-113
Kvols-Riedler, 9

L

Labeling, 158
Lamaze, Fernand, 47, 245, 258
Language development, 47, 73, 126
Latch key children, 214, 227, 237, 257
Learning disability, 18, 62, 176
Leboyer, Frederick, 47
Lincoln, Abraham, 43-44, 63
Listening, 153-155, 163, 218
Logical consequences, 15, 109-110, 121, 123-146, 196, 201-202, 227 (*see also* Natural consequences)
Loneliness, 216-218
Lost possessions, 122-123
Lying, 83-84, 97, 138

M

Making up beds, 150
Marital enrichment, 181-185
Marriage, 34, 48, 50, 52, 56-57, 119, 155, 169-188, 204, 243, 244
Mental illness, 22, 193
Merged families (*see* Blended families)
Middle children, 36-37 (*see also* Second child)
Mid-life crisis, 107
Mindreading, 156-157
Minuchin, Salvador, 169, 172-181, 186-187, 200, 204, 207
Modeling, 110-111, 162, 227
Money, 151 (*see also* Allowances)
Montessori, Marie, 80
Moral thought, 93-115
Motivation, 18, 25
Mourning, 238-239
Music, 25

N

Napier, Augustus, 169-172
Natural consequences, 13, 15, 121-123, 201-202, 227
Negative attention addict, 9
Negative misbehaviors, 44, 55, 219 (*see also* Goals of misbehavior)
Nightmares, 76, 138
Nonverbal communications, 156-157

O

Object permanency, 70
Oldest child, 23-24, 158, 204-205
Only child, 23, 35-36
Open-ended questions, 74
Ordinal position, 23-42, 242-243
Organization, 189-203
Outdoor misbehavior, 124
Overambition, 61, 68, 81, 150, 238
Overinvolvement (*see* Enmeshment)
Overloading, 159

P

Parent education, 173-174, 197-198, 199, 206, 228, 247, 249-250, 257-259
Parent's prison syndrome, 52
Parents Without Partners, 225
Peek-a-boo, 72
Perfectionism, 28, 148, 152, 161
Permissiveness, 108, 117-121
Physical closeness (*see* Touching)
Physical punishment, 107-108, 119-120 (*see also* Power struggles, revenge)
Piaget, Jean, 67-91, 113, 173, 240
Play, 58 (*see also* Preoperational period, concrete operations)
Pleasers, 249-250
Positive misbehaviors, 43-44, 52-53, 75
Post-conventional morality, 103-105
Poverty, 264-265
Power struggles, 11-15, 17, 133-146
Preconventional morality, 95-99
Pregnancies, unwanted, 265
Preoperational period, 73-82, 240
Prestige of parents, 253-256
Prevention, 126, 138

Private logic, 32 (*see also* Goals of misbehavior)
Problem solving, 159-165
Pseudomutuality, 182
Psychology of use, 42
Psychosomatic illness, 28, 81, 176, 193, 199, 239
Public misbehavior, 131-132

Q

Quadrant A Families, 191-194
Quadrant B Families, 194-197
Quadrant C Families, 197-199, 227
Quadrant D Families, 199-200
Questions, 76-77

R

Reading, 152
Reason, 14
Reconstituted families (*see* Blended families)
Religion, 12, 13, 29, 33, 74-75, 86, 95, 97-98, 100, 107-108
Restaurant misbehavior, 132-133
Revenge, 11, 15-17
Reversals (*see* Ordinal position)
Robinson, Jackie, 14
Roles (*see* Stepfamilies)
Runaways, 14, 195-196

S

Scapegoat, 179
Schools, 12, 15, 17-20, 29-30, 35, 59-63, 81, 84-87, 141-144, 149, 152, 153-154, 176, 178, 192-193, 197-198, 205, 215, 221, 228, 236-237, 250, 257, 259-264
Seatbelts, 12, 54, 117, 130
Second child, 23-32 (*see also* Middle children)
Self-centered (*see* Egocentric and moral thought)
Sensorimotor period, 68-72
Separation, 222
Separation anxiety, 52, 129
Sex, 25-26, 50-51, 106, 137-138, 184, 196
Sex education, 265
Sharing, 126, 136
Shoe family, 181
Shoulds, 28

Sibling rivalry, 19, 23, 37-49
Single parents, 61, 211-230, 256-257
Sleeping habits, 48-50, 126-127, 202
Smith, J. David, 265
Social interest, 226
Spacing, 25-26
Speaking for others, 157
Speech (*see* Language development)
Sports participation, 144-145, 150
Squeeze child (*see* Middle children)
Stealing, 97-98, 139-140
Stepfamilies, 63, 237-251
Stranger anxiety, 51-52
Stress, 61-62, 67-68
Structural family therapy, 172-187
Stuttering, 140
Success, 17-20 (*see also* Encouragement)
Super baby, 24
Superiority, 27
Switchboard mothers, 180

T

Take time for training, 49, 60, 124, 127-128, 130, 132, 150, 164, 228
Teachers, 142-143 (*see also* Schools)
Television, 12, 133-134, 202
Temper tantrums, 133 (*see also* Power struggles)
Thumb-sucking, 134
Time out, 127-128, 133
Toilet training, 54, 126
Toman, Walter, 23, 25-26, 34, 242-243
Tone of voice, 157
Touching, 155-156
Triangles, 172, 179, 244, 247
Trust, 14, 126-129 (*see also* Trust vs. mistrust)
Trust vs. mistrust, 45-53

V

Visher, Emily and John, 237-239, 245, 247
Visitation, 241-243

W

Wad effect, 192
Waking up, 12
War dance (*see* Power struggles)
Whining, 134

Whitaker, Carl, 169-172
White, Burton, 233-234
Whoops child, 24
Wife abuse, 199
Working parents, 61
Writing, 150